Gardening
on Chalk, Lime
and Clay

GARDENING
ON CHALK, LIME
AND CLAY

JUDITH BERRISFORD

FABER AND FABER
LONDON   BOSTON

*First published in 1963
as* Gardening on Lime
*by Faber and Faber Limited
3 Queen Square London WC1N 3AU
New and revised edition 1978
Printed in Great Britain by
Latimer Trend & Company Ltd Plymouth
All rights reserved*

© *Judith M. Berrisford 1963, 1978*

British Library Cataloguing in Publication Data

Berrisford, Judith Mary
Gardening on chalk, lime and clay. –
New and revised ed.
1. Gardening
I. Title
635.9'55   SB454

ISBN 0–571–10952–7
ISBN 0–571–11129–7   Pbk

For Roma and Alan,
the kindest of friends

Contents

Contents

Illustrations

Acknowledgement is made to the following photographs:
The jacket photographs and plates 2, 3, 4, 5, 6, 8, 9, 10, 11, 12, were supplied by Denis Woodland and plates 1 and 7 by Pat Brindley.

Acknowledgements

I should like to acknowledge my gratitude to Mr. Lawrence Hills for his help in formulating the pattern of this book; to Mr. Richard de la Mare for his interest and encouragement, and to the Librarians and staff of the Llandudno and Conway public libraries for their ready help and courtesy.

J.M.B.
1963

Preface

A number of years has passed since the first edition of this book was published, during the course of which my husband and I have moved on from the garden about which I was originally writing. We have since made two more gardens, one in Cornwall —near Falmouth—on acid soil and another in Deganwy, North Wales—only a mile away from our previous site but on a quite different type of ground. Now we are making yet another garden, this time in the Isle of Man. The original garden referred to, however, remains, and so do many of the plants about which I wrote. When we moved we took with us to Cornwall most of the rhododendrons and camellias because we knew they could not continue to flourish in the existing limy soil without the continuous special care we had been able to give them. The others—the borderline cases—still survive.

Asiatic primulas and some of the Chilean shrubs such as the crinodendron (lantern bush) described in Chapter Fifteen were, moreover, still doing well when we visited the garden before leaving Wales last year; the crinodendron had been propagated by means of cuttings and distributed to other gardens in the district on the same soil. That it will grow well in a moderately alkaline clay is beyond doubt; whether it would succeed in pure chalk may well be another matter. As I say in the following chapters, it is for each individual gardener to experiment—if he so wishes—for himself, to determine what plants he can grow on his own particular soil and to concentrate on these. Special fancies such as the Japanese acers, and perhaps a camellia or a rhododendron may be grown in containers in an individually made-up acid-reacting compost as described in Chapter Fifteen. For the rest, whether one gardens on chalk, lime or even upon clay there is a great variety of bulbs, shrubs, climbers, roses, alpines and perennials, which will succeed. One has only to think of the many beautiful gardens in the Cotswolds, on the Sussex downland, and on Herefordshire clay to realize that such gardens have a far greater continuity of beauty, interest and fragrance than the more limited rhododendron gardens upon very acid soil.

I do not recommend the purchase of expensive calcifuge plants for gardens on lime or chalk. Such expenditure would be foolish. What I do suggest is that those who are interested in the matter or who covet, as so many of us do, plants which are reputed not to do well in our own particular soils should experiment a little, cautiously, to find out whether or not, by taking care, we can expand the range of our garden interest. In this way the boundaries of gardening knowledge are pushed back. We learn more, and other gardeners profit.

Judith Berrisford

Ramsey, Isle of Man
November 1977

ONE

Alkaline and Clay Soils
and their Problems

In the present phase of gardening in this country—a phase which has been described as 'an age of shrubs and ignorance'—half our gardeners grumble about clay and the other half about lime. I gardened upon limy clay myself, so perhaps I am in a position to sympathize and advise. I am a lover of shrubs and trees above all other plants and I have found that with care and understanding one can grow as many delightful shrubs on limy clay as on any other soil.

All soils have their limitations, it is by understanding and either accepting or combating those limitations that good gardens are made. When dealing with limy and chalky soils it is as well for the most part to accept their limitations and choose one's plants from among the many lovely subjects which will do well on lime and chalk instead of sitting back and bewailing one's fate. The present-day cult of rhododendrons, camellias and so many other choice lime-hating shrubs and trees makes the dweller upon lime feel that a connoisseur's delight is for ever denied him. Each man loves what his soil will kill, as Oscar Wilde might have said had he been a gardener.

In plain fact there are as many lovely plants which grow well upon a limy soil as upon an acid one. Autumn colour is said to be better upon lime and chalk than on acid soils. The barberries and cotoneasters, the mountain ashes with their graceful growth and brilliant berries in shades of orange, yellow, coral, pink and white, fruit best upon lime. In fact many of the berberis object to too-acid a medium. The autumn cherry, the winter-blooming viburnums, the winter-sweet, the Japanese quinces—even the winter-blooming heaths; all these are lime tolerant. In spring one can grow the beautiful genera of prunus and malus followed by lilac, mock-orange blossom and snowball viburnums. Many brooms will grow on limy soils. Hydrangeas it is true will not 'blue' satisfactorily except on acid land. Nevertheless, there are many satisfying colour compositions to be built from the various shades of pink, rose, deepest red and purple which occur naturally when lime is present. Lavenders, cistuses, rosemary and many roses grow on the chalkiest soil. Certain of the gentians and asiatic primulas can be easily accommodated. All vegetables can be made to grow well upon lime providing their humus needs are met. There is little real cause, therefore, for those who must garden upon lime to feel discouraged. It is more important that they should understand their soil and know how to get the best from it. Later they can, if they wish, attempt the seeming impossible and by the help of chemistry and care attempt some of the lime-haters—those forbidden fruits after which, with the obstinacy of the human race and that persistence common to gardeners, so many of them will undoubtedly yearn.

A geological map of Britain will show that three main types of alkaline soil occur in this country—chalk, limestone and alkaline clays or marl. Chalk is the purest form of limestone and the softest. It may consist of 100 per cent calcium carbonate. Limestone is harder. It may be almost pure calcium carbonate or it may contain magnesium. Marl is unconsolidated limestone and is usually found mixed with clay and sand or silt and there are also chalky sands, the most difficult soils of all. Chalk predominates in the south-east of England. The downs of Hampshire, Surrey and Sussex will come at once to mind. Many parts of Wiltshire, the Chilterns, Cambridgeshire, Lincoln and Yorkshire have chalky soil.

Limestone is found in the Cotswolds, the Severn hills, Dorset, Somerset, Oxford, Buckinghamshire, Bedford, Northampton,

North Lancashire, Derby, Warwick, Nottingham, Westmorland, parts of Yorkshire, Durham, Northumberland and part of the North Wales coastal area.

Marls and alkaline clays are to be found in East Anglia, Cheshire, Worcestershire, Cumberland, in parts of north-west England and in North Wales. Such clays were formed in bogs, swamps and lakes which have since been drained. My own garden lay in an area of former marshland between the limestone hills of Llandudno and Colwyn Bay and was a true example of one of these limy clays.

Even so, patches of acid soil occur even in these limestone areas. In the limestone regions of the west and north the heavy rainfall tends to leach away the lime, while rotted surface vegetation gives an acid or neutral topsoil above limestone rock. Several examples occur in North Wales, in the Carnforth area of Lancashire and also in the Cotswolds. Patches of acid greensand occur amid the chalky soils of Surrey and limy areas of Dorset and there lime-hating plants will thrive. Some of the most famous rhododendron nurseries in the country are situated in the greensand areas of Surrey.

Not all limestone is hostile to lime-hating plants or calcifuges as they are sometimes called. On magnesian limestone, rhododendrons and azaleas thrive while, as mentioned earlier, in some carboniferous limestone areas one may find deposits of acid soil, formed by layers of decomposed vegetation. Such deposits usually occur in the west where the heavy rainfall leaches away the free lime, preventing its absorption into the topsoil.

Again, in Cornwall, in a district where acid soils prevail, belts of limy soil occur in sandy patches near the shore. The sand here is composed of broken sea-shells, which are almost pure calcium in content and therefore very alkaline.

So one may pinpoint one's garden on a geological map and yet still not be quite sure whether one's soil is limy or not.

Further indications may be found in the native flora. Old man's beard, yew, wayfaring tree, mullein and scabious are usually found growing only upon lime or chalk. Heaths, broom, birch, mare's tail and bracken like acid conditions. Yet bracken and birch are sometimes seen growing upon alkaline soils, and on the Great Orme's Headland in North Wales ling and bell-heather, although stunted, grow widespread in the inch or so of soil above limestone rock. It is clear, therefore, that some more accurate indication is needed.

This is conveniently to be obtained from one of the soil-testing kits on the market: they provide a testing fluid which remains green under neutral conditions but which changes colour when an alkaline or acid substance is tested.

The degree of acidity or alkalinity is measured by the pH (potential hydrogen) scale. In this scale pH7 is taken to be neutral —neither acid nor alkaline. Readings above pH7 indicate increasing degrees of alkalinity (pH7·5, pH8 and so on) while those below 7pH (viz.: pH6·5, pH6, pH5·5 and so on down the scale) indicate increasing degrees of acidity.

To test the soil by means of the tester, some soil should be placed in a shallow dish or other receptacle which has first been tested and found to have a neutral reaction. The liquid is dropped spot by spot on to the soil until the soil is saturated and surplus liquid begins to run off if the saucer is tilted. If the soil is alkaline the surplus liquid will turn blue-green. If slightly acid—pH6·5, the liquid will become yellowish-green. Increasing acidity is shown when the liquid turns yellow at pH6, orange at pH5·5, orange-red at 5 and red at pH4·5, the degree of acidity which is thought to be ideal for rhododendrons and below which few ornamental plants will grow.

Soil pH often varies from part to part of the same garden so to get an accurate picture of conditions in any one garden it is advisable to test the soil at several different points. The soil of our own garden in the limestone area of North Wales varied from pH6·5, where repeated mulchings of rhododendron peat and bracken had lowered the pH, through pH7 to something over pH7·5 where artificial liming of a former vegetable garden raised the pH of the already alkaline soil.

Artificial liming is in fact responsible for a great deal of excess alkalinity encountered in established gardens. Gardeners of the old school were apt to look upon lime as a cure for all soil disorders and lime was added indiscriminately to gardens without the realization of the harm that excess lime might do by locking many chemical elements in the soil so that they could not be absorbed by the plants which needed them, often causing deficiency symptoms to appear.

No soil with a reaction of pH7 or over ever needs added lime and if lime is added at all it should be in the form of superphosphate which does not increase the alkalinity.

Soils of pH7 will grow both lime-lovers and lime-haters although many of the 'bluer-blooded' rhododendrons need to be planted in a more acid medium and kept mulched with rhododendon peat or bracken if they are to thrive. Soils above pH7 are definitely limy and the owners of gardens upon such soils will have to recognize this fact and lay their gardening plans accordingly.

There are three ways of dealing with alkaline soils and each garden owner should make up his mind, in the light of his own circumstances, which line he will follow. Once the gardener knows with what type of land he has to deal he must decide for himself how to tackle his problem. If the garden owner is a busy man with little time to devote to gardening, or elderly and so lacking the strength to tackle the heavy digging necessary to alter the soil structure and enable him to grow the widest range of plants, he may decide to limit himself to what grows well by nature on his land. By so doing, if his land is chalky and well drained, by choosing carefully from the quite wide range of plants available he may still have an attractive garden. I shall show how this may be done in Chapter Fourteen. Limy clays, however, are a different matter. Like all clay lands, they need some drainage before anything can be grown well. Later in this chapter I describe how this can be done.

With more time to spare and the necessary strength and energy, or with skilled help available, the gardener may improve his soil by cultivation so as to grow a wider range of plants better. With additional knowledge and care he may fight to achieve the seeming impossible and even to succeed with some of the lime-hating plants that by nature abhor his soil. Modern chemicals will help him to overcome many of his problems. They will cure fruit trees of the symptoms of malnutrition often found in limy soils. They will help him to grow rhododendrons and azaleas in alkaline conditions—I say 'help' because extra knowledge and trouble on his part is necessary to provide the optimum physical conditions of a moisture-retaining yet well-drained soil together with the surface mulching that will encourage the rhododendron roots to thrust upward and so to derive their nutriment from the acid mulching material, thus avoiding undue contact with the alkaline undersoil.

My husband and I gardened upon limy clay for nine years and —by means of considerable trouble and care—succeeded in growing well a number of the bluer-blooded rhododendron hybrids and species, most sections of the azalea group, a number of camellias, summer-flowering heaths, pieris, hamamelis, meconopses, asiatic gentians, primulas and other treasures generally thought to be near-impossibilities on lime. In Chapter Fifteen I will describe in detail how this was done.

So far as I know, nobody has yet managed to grow rhododendrons in a chalk pit—although the late Sir Frederick Stern in his famous chalk pit garden at Highdown, Sussex, grew camellias in prepared sites quite happily over a number of years. I do know, however, of a thriving garden of rhododendrons and other ericaceous plants on very shallow soil above the limestone hills of Colwyn Bay in North Wales. This, however, is a product of freak conditions. I tested the soil and found it to be $pH7$. Fairly heavy rainfall and sharp drainage have leached away the alkaline content while top-mulching and natural leaf-fall have increased the acidity. An intelligent understanding of these conditions by the owner has led to the success of this particular garden. In certain nearby areas, also, patches of silica have been found, which explains the healthy existence of members of the *Ericaceae* thereon.

When gardening on lime, knowledge is all-important.

Shallow chalk or limestone soils and chalky sandy soils are thin and poor by nature. Gardeners and farmers refer to them as 'hungry' because they seem to absorb all nutriment as quickly as it is added and then to be just as poor as before. Organic matter in such soils is exhausted quickly, disintegrating fast. This process is hastened by the fact that the excess calcium carbonate neutral- izes acids as soon as they are formed, making soluble the plant food material so that it (organic manures and composts) is either taken up by the plants or washed down and drained away. Such soils need a great deal of feeding with organic material if plants and crops are to thrive. Organic manuring and composting is the keystone to fertility on chalk, limestone and alkaline clay soils. Fine grades of peat or compost quickly disintegrate and are lost. Coarse materials last longest. Strawy cow manure, fibrous peat, spent hops, old newspapers, shoddy and leather waste take longer to decompose and so their beneficial effect is seen over a longer period of time.

Calcareous soils vary a great deal in depth and this must be taken into consideration. In some only a few inches of topsoil overlies the rock. Here moisture will be retained better if the subsoil is broken up with a pick-axe when planting is carried out. The hard limestone or chalk, once broken into small particles, seems to act as a sponge, holding the moisture, so it will be found that shrubs or perennials planted in such a site will seldom suffer from drought.

Where possible—that is where there is sufficient depth of soil above the rock—the proposed beds and borders of the flower garden as well as the vegetable garden should be given an old-fashioned double trenching.

This is harder work than the shallower method of cultivation known as 'bastard trenching' which is more commonly employed today. It is, however, well worth while. The benefit will last for ever. Such double trenching, involving as it does the cultivation of three spits, enables humus to be incorporated at each level and is therefore of especial value where permanent and deep-rooted subjects are to be planted. The method is as follows:

(1) At the end of the plot take out the usual initial trench of top spit soil about two and a half feet wide. The soil from the trench

should be wheeled to the end where it is intended to finish and left to fill in the final trench.

(2) Divide the initial trench into two long strips. Dig out the second spit of the front strip and wheel away the soil keeping it separate from the *top* spit soil already carried at the far end of the plot. It is very important to return the top spit soil and second spit soil to their respective depths.

(3) Fork over the third spit incorporating the roughest manure or vegetable matter you have available.

(4) Dig out the second spit of the back strip of the initial trench and throw it forward to replace the second spit of the forward strip incorporating more strawy manure or humus as you do so.

(5) Fork over the third spit of the second strip incorporating rough humus material as before.

(6) Take out a new trench of top spit soil, half the width of the first trench and throw it forward on to the vacant front strip of the first trench incorporating still more humus as you do so.

(7) Dig the second spit of the second trench and, incorporating humus and manure, throw it into the vacant second spit of the back strip of the first trench.

(8) Fork over and add manure and humus to the bottom (*third*) spit of the second trench.

(9) Start the third strip, throwing the top spit forward on to the still vacant top spit of the second strip of the first trench and mixing in humus. The first trench has now been completely rebuilt with humus added and each spit has been kept in its proper place.

(10) Continue in this way until you reach the end of the plot to be double trenched, filling in the last trench with the second spit and top spit soil from the first strip of the first trench.

This sounds, and is, hard labour, but there is no short cut. You cannot be a 'no digger' on chalk unless you want to grow first downland turf and then, after thorn scrub, a beech forest!

Limy clays, however, need very different treatment. Such soils are heavy, sticky, cold and deficient in such elements as iron, manganese, and often magnesium which are essential to healthy plant growth. They present some of the worst problems a gardener may have to face. Yet properly treated they are among the most fertile of soils.

Most clay soils suffer from some degree of waterlogging and alkaline clays are no exception. Few plants will grow well or even live long in waterlogged soil.

Pools of water remaining for some time on the soil after rain show the need for drainage but often the necessity may be less obvious. Tests may be made by digging holes about 1 m (3 ft) deep in various parts of the garden. If water appears in any of the holes and remains nearer than 45 cm (18 in) to the surface then there is a definite need for drainage in that part of the garden.

In the absence of a natural stream, ditch or pond, a soakaway should be constructed at the lowest part of the garden. This should consist of a hole about 2 m (6 ft) across and 2 m (6 ft) deep, filled for the greater part with large clinkers, rock, breeze, broken brick, tin cans, etc. Bulky objects should be chosen as these will leave room for the water to pass through. Nearer the top, small stones and smaller pieces of brick should be laid so as to leave room for the water to drain but close enough to prevent the washing away of earth. The top foot or so should be filled with top spit soil. The turf may then be replaced.

Excess water from the various waterlogged parts of the garden is led into the soakaway by means of drains. Earthenware field drains may be used, embedded all round with clinkers to prevent earth silting into the pipes, but earthenware pipes are expensive, and effective drains may be made without their use.

A satisfactory system of drainage may be built up from a herringbone series of narrow, shallow trenches filled with some drainage agent. The depth of these trenches will depend upon the depth at which the 'pan' or impervious layer of subsoil is preventing the draining away of excess surface water. The pan will usually be found at about 60 cm (2 ft) down. In our garden, it lay at exactly one spade depth, but whatever the level at which the pan is found, it is there that the drain should be laid.

The main drain should fall gradually (a fall of not more than

30 cm in 1500 (1 ft in 50) is recommended) to the soakaway and should be fed by a series of gently sloping tributary drains running into it herringbone fashion. In very heavy soils main drains may be needed at $4\frac{1}{2}$-m (5-yd) intervals over the badly drained area. In lighter soil one main drain to every 9 m (10 yd) should be sufficient.

At the bottom of each trench a 23-cm (9-in) layer of rubble, clinker or even hazel twigs should be planted to act as a drainage agent. These should be covered by turves laid upside down and the trench should then be filled in with topsoil.

After draining, or where no waterlogging is present the land should be double trenched in the way advised for lighter chalk and limestone soils, care being taken not to bring the subsoil to the top. On clay soils, however, clinker and weathered ash may be used to replace the rough manure and coarse humus incorporated with the subsoil of lighter land, while stable manure, peat, shoddy, hop manure and even seaweed if available should be incorporated with the topsoil to help break up the sticky particles of clay and to lighten the texture of the soil. It is often beneficial to leave the top spit of a clay soil rough-dug over the winter, so that the frost and wind may have a chance to break up the particles, before adding more humus in spring.

Painstaking gardeners may go further by picking out the worst lumps of clay and burning these on a smother-fire or slow-burning garden bonfire which is plastered over with the clay to form a kind of kiln. Care should be taken to leave a smoke shaft at the top and air-holes near the bottom of the fire which will burn slowly for weeks, reducing the clay to ash. Such clay-ash is invaluable to improve the texture of a clay soil. Moreover it is highly fertile and will greatly benefit the garden.

Whether alkaline or not, all marl and clay soils respond to the same treatment. The peculiarity of clay lies in the extreme fineness of the soil particles, less than 0·002 mm. This causes clay soil to have greater water holding capacity than others. The minute particles cling together. There is high capillarity coupled to slow rate of water movement up or down, leading to cold relative temperatures, poor aeration and high plasticity. Coupled to this is a great capacity for holding mineral salts and nutriment which renders clay highly fertile once it has been broken down. The various treatments described in this and the next chapter aim to do this by improving drainage, reducing plasticity and raising the temperature and degree of aeration. Certain proprietary compounds are also available which are designed to improve the crumb structure and so make clay soils more workable. Of these I have found *Acta-Bacta* to be the best.

Some clays are completely intractable and cannot be made workable without an impracticable amount of labour and expenditure. Such are the blue marls which unfortunately exist in certain parts of the British Isles and on the Continent. Here the most expeditious method has been proved to be the no-digging practice, building up the surface of the soil with coarse peat such as Alex Peat's *Anti Clay*, *Acta-Bacta,* rotted bracken, hop manure, rotted compost, seaweed etc. Thus with soakaways dug at several of the lowest points of the garden, it should be possible to cultivate most plants with reasonable prospect of success. It would be very expensive, though, to treat whole garden areas in this way, so the methods should be restricted to the actual beds which, as the surface is built up, should be provided with low retaining walls so that the fertile growing medium is not lost or drained away. Such raised beds will be warmer than the surrounding clay and should give equally good results with flowers, vegetables, bulbs, shrubs and roses. (See also p. 197) The remaining area should be given sufficient drainage and shallow cultivation to allow grass to be grown. Elsewhere the areas designated for paths or for sitting should be gravelled rather than paved, as the seasonal drying out of the clay during the summer might cause the paving to become uneven or crack. Gravel also has the advantage of draining better during wet weather. If paving is used, it should be sloped slightly towards a drain so that it will not lie waterlogged.

On such soils carnations, damp-sensitive alpines and other plants which tend to die out through winter damp might be found homes in mixed banks of gravel and loam, mounded at the side of a gravel driveway or sitting area. Their foliage would clothe the gravel, giving a decorative effect, and most would flower extremely freely under such conditions.

TWO

Meeting the Humus Need

As explained in the last chapter the presence of excessive lime in the soil means that organic matter, compost, manure, peat, leaf-mould, etc., is quickly lost, thereby denying the plant life the food that it needs. To make a successful garden on such soils organic matter must be added at every opportunity. The organic or humus content of the soil must be built up and maintained at a high level. Organic manuring is the keystone to successful gardening on all chalky and limestone soils and also on clay and marl. As much animal manure as possible should be used—the coarser and more strawy the better, because coarse material takes longer to decompose. Hops, hop manure, peat, leaf-mould and seaweed all help. In addition every available scrap of vegetable and animal waste— plant-stems, straw, hedge and grass clippings, vegetable peelings, vacuum-sweeper dust, coffee grounds, kitchen scraps, etc.— should be composted and turned into a source of rich humus and plant food ready to be dug into the soil or added as a surface mulch.

In nature, fallen leaves and plant remains, animal manure and other oranic matter constantly accumulate on the surface of the soil. Fungi and bacteria work upon it, helping the process of decomposition and turning it into humus, while earthworms and other creatures incorporate it into the soil. Compost-making is man's way of assisting nature by carrying out this process, and— as limy soils need great quantities of humus and organic matter—

compost-making is of first importance in helping the gardener on such land to make his soil fertile so that his plants will thrive.

Every kind of organic material is suitable for composting. In addition to the household and garden waste mentioned earlier, seaweed, animal manure, poultry and pig manure, and dried blood may be included and will help to hasten the decomposition of the vegetable matter. Guano, bone-meal and fish manure are sometimes recommended, but should not be used when making compost for use on limy soils as they have a high alkaline content. Hoof and horn, however, is safe. All materials added to the compost heap should be moist. Unless the heap is already in a very moist condition dry waste material should be wetted with water or weak liquid manure before being added. On the other hand the heap should not be allowed to become too wet and soggy. Very wet material should be mixed with dry soil or peat before it is added.

Coarse, tough stalks of cabbage and other vegetables, or of perennials such as Canterbury bells should be chopped into small pieces with the spade. Only soft prunings of trees and shrubs should be used. Harder wood should be burnt and the ash either added to the soil direct as soon as cool, or incorporated in the heap. Wood shavings, horse-hair, coal ash, broken crockery or glass, tin cans, cardboard, spent matches, etc., are unsuitable for inclusion.

Plenty of room should be allotted to compost-making and it is well to have two or three heaps—one in the process of being made, perhaps one ripening, and one ready for use and added to the soil as opportunity arises.

Compost may either be built up as free-standing heaps, measuring no less than 2 m (6 ft) square by 1·2 m (4 ft) high when completed, or placed in a brick- or turf-walled enclosure, or made in special 'New Zealand' boxes as described later. Care must be taken when building brick enclosures, however, to have gaps in the walls so that air can circulate to the material being composted.

Compost heaps, whether open or enclosed, should always be

built directly on the soil and not on brick or concrete foundations. On light, chalky soils it is a good idea to dig a shallow pit 15–30 cm (6 in to 1 ft) deep, if possible lining the base with clay, and starting to build up the compost heap in the pit.

Compost-making is a natural process of decomposition which is, in the initial stages, carried out by oxidization and by fungi and bacteria which need air. It is vital, therefore, that there should be sufficient oxygen and moisture within the heap. Do not trample the compost or batter it down with a spade but allow it to settle under its own weight. A too-closely packed heap is likely to putrefy instead of to ferment as desired. Moisture is necessary to help the fungi and bacteria to break down the material and assist fermentation but care must be taken to ensure that the heap does not become too wet. Waterlogging cuts off the supply of oxygen and so encourages undesirable putrefaction.

Compost heaps are built up sandwich fashion. As organic material accumulates so it is added to the heap in 30-cm- (foot-) deep layers. So far as practicable, it is helpful to mix the finer material—such as lawn-mowings, which rot quickly—with the coarse to help the decomposition of the latter. The bottom layer of the heap should consist of such coarse material as stalks, twigs and prunings so as to help air to penetrate upwards.

To accelerate decomposition, an activator such as farmyard manure or dried poultry manure should be laid on top of each layer of vegetable matter. (*N.B.*—lime or proprietary alkaline accelerator should never be used when making compost to add to already alkaline soil.) A safe non-alkaline accelerator is *Garotta* and also *Alginure* which is squeezed on to the layers from a giant tube.

The heap should be built up gradually as compost material accumulates, covering it with sacking until it is complete. It should be built sandwich fashion—vegetable matter, manure or accelerator and soil—to a height of about 1·2 m (4 ft). The whole may then be jacketed by a layer of soil, leaving the top flat with a slight depression in the middle. Added ventilation can be given by inserting a pole through the heap and working it round to make a hole through which air can penetrate.

After six to eight weeks the whole heap may be turned, sides to middle, with the top material becoming the bottom of the newly turned heap. Before turning the heap it is as well to rake off the soil jacket, replacing it afterwards, but the whole of the actual compost material should be well mixed. After nine or ten months the compost will have decomposed to a fine, moist, brownish-black earth that is crumbly and sweet to handle. It is then ready for use.

In addition to compost, bulky organic materials such as sea-weed, coarse peat, hop manure, shoddy, etc., are invaluable in the garden. They should be added to the lower spit soil to feed and improve its texture, saving the compost, leaf-mould and finer grades of animal manure for the top spit.

Much success has been gained through the quick-return method of compost-making based on the use of a herbal activator known as Q.R. This method is particularly to be recommended for small gardens. It obviates the necessity to turn the heap and results in a fine compost, full of healthy, growth-promoting qualities, being ready for use in a much shorter space of time.

Quick-return compost is best made in a simple wooden box, four-sided and with no base, standing directly on the soil if it is light. On heavy soils, the top 15 cm (6 in) should be excavated and filled with rubble with a cover of soil on top. This is to enable surplus moisture to drain away. It is helpful to scatter a little charcoal on the earth floor of the box to sweeten the heap.

There is no need for the compost box to be large. For small gardens, two or three boxes, each 45 cm (18 in) square by 60 cm (2 ft) high will be sufficient. For larger gardens, boxes 1 m (3 ft) square and high would be a convenient size. As with the conventional heap, an essential of quick-return compost-making is to prevent the heap becoming too wet. For this reason a shelter of corrugated asbestos or stretched canvas or tarpaulin should be stretched above the box at a slant, enabling air to enter but allowing the rain to run off.

Inside the box, the compost heap is built in the usual way, keeping seeding weeds to the centre where the heat is greatest to destroy the weed-seeds. Build the heap in 10-cm (4-in) layers, alternating coarse and soft materials and adding a 5-cm (2-in) layer of animal or poultry manure to every 30-cm (foot) depth. If no manure is obtainable add a scattering of soil instead. The special herbal activator is not added until the heap is complete. Add material as often as possible. The compost sinks a lot and needs to be allowed to settle and to be added to again every few days until the box is really full when it should be covered with 10 cm (4 in) of soil and again allowed to settle for two or three days. At the end of this time holes should be made at 30-cm (12-in) intervals right through the heap, from the top to within 10 cm (4 in) of the bottom, and a solution of the Q.R. activator (made as instructed on the packet) poured into each hole. Fill the holes with dry soil and ram the soil well down to prevent air pockets. Cover the heap to protect it from rain.

A spring or early-summer heap made with Q.R. activator in the manner described should be sweet, crumbly and ready for use within a month to six weeks. A summer heap takes six to eight weeks to ripen and an autumn heap eight to twelve weeks. During the winter, the heap seems to lie dormant but with the adding of fresh green growth—the first lawn-mowings are ideal—the process of heating and bacterial activity will quickly start. The fresh greenstuff is best added half-way down the heap and the top layers should be pulled aside for the purpose.

This 'box' method of compost-making may be followed with any of the other non-alkaline activators, such as *Garotta* and *Alginure*, spreading the activator on top of each 20 cm (8 in) of compost instead of adding it afterwards to the completed heap as done with Q.R.

To compost straw as mentioned earlier in this chapter it is advisable to alternate the straw with 5-cm (2-in) layers of fresh green nettles or bracken. Manure, or a scattering of earth, should be added in narrow layers on top of each straw 'sandwich'. Q.R. activator may be used; the straw must be wetted before being added to the heap which will take from four to six months to mature. Turning is not necessary if the heap is made in the recommended way and a splendid rich black compost will result.

Those who want to know more about compost and compost-making by this and other methods would find it helpful to study *Common-Sense Compost Making* by M. E. Bruce (Faber).

The New Zealand box compost-container also is excellent, cutting out the necessity for earthing-up the outside of the heap. Compost made in such a box needs no turning and so the method is labour-saving. Suitable for use with any of the activators mentioned, the New Zealand box contains twin-compartments side by side. Ready-made New Zealand boxes can be bought but they may easily be made at home from rough timber, with removable fronts to make forking easier. A suitable size would be 2·4 m (8 ft) long, by 1·2 m (4 ft) wide and 1 m (3 ft) deep, with a partition in the middle to make twin compartments each 1·2 m (4 ft) square. One compartment will hold a heap rotting down and almost ready for use and the other a heap in the process of being built. Inside the boxes, two double rows of brick ends with a 2½-cm- (inch-) wide space between should reach outside the boxes so that the removable front rests upon them, thus creating an air-space or draught-funnel to help keep up the heat engendered by the rotting compost and the activator.

Heaps made in New Zealand boxes of the size suggested should be ready for use, without turning, in three to four months.

Old garden books speak of 'green manuring' but this is not as often practised as it might be. The easiest method is to sow common mustard bought by the half kilo or pound, 17 g to the sq m (½ oz to the sq yd) on vacant ground in late March ready to dig in during mid-April at the bottom of the trenches where the potatoes are to be set, or in May—to dig in during July before sowing the late French beans. Even better for light chalky soil is crimson clover—*Trifolium incarnatum*—sown in July or early August. Sow 17 g (½ oz) of seed to the sq m (sq yd), covering it thinly with soil. It will be up in September and should stand over the winter, thus preventing the winter rain from leaching all the available humus and plant food from the already poor land. It should be dug in during late February and March and will then rot to provide first-class humus and nitrogen to enrich the ground. Particularly useful in the vegetable garden, a winter-standing crop of crimson clover is worth while also to precede spring-planting of herbaceous plants or roses on thin land.

Light chalk and limestone soils should never be left vacant during the winter. Land trenched ready for shrubs or perennials to be planted in autumn should be filled with plants as soon as the soil has had time to settle. When setting out shrubs, carpeting plants should be planted at the same time to form a protective cover so that the rain may not leach the humus away. Helianthemums, aubretia, yellow alyssum, *Erica carnea* (now *E. herbacea*) the winter-flowering heath, periwinkles and perennial candytuft are all suitable, but I shall go into the question of ground cover more fully in Chapter Thirteen.

On heavy soils—clays and marls—it is helpful to leave the ground rough-dug during the winter so that the frost can break down the clay particles. On such land spring-sown clover may be dug in during August.

Leaf-mould is of especial value for shrubs, and for some bulbs and alpines and many of the ground-covering treasures that are valuable to add charm and interest to the limy garden. It is of use, too, in the vegetable garden both for the heavy and light soils. A frame of wire-netting 1·2 m (4 ft) high and square on strong posts will keep the leaf-mould heap tidy and prevent the leaves from blowing about. The leaves should be stacked in autumn as they fall and left to rot down. By the second spring after stacking it will be ready for use, dark brown and flaky like tobacco. It may be added as a surface mulch for herbaceous borders and shrubberies or dug in to add humus to the soil. It is an excellent top-dressing for lawns on shallow soils. Leaves may also be used, just as they fall, as an immediate mulch and are especially valuable as a weed suppressor or a plant food used as a 5- or 7½-cm (2- or 3-in) layer to mulch shrubs and fruit trees. The mulch may be kept in place by a further layer of grass clippings or soil. If clippings are used, care must be taken to keep them away from the stems of the plants as they may heat up as they rot and so cause damage.

Farmyard manure is of course invaluable but hard to come by. Local pony-owning children may be contacted as a source of supply. Droppings should on no account be left in pony pasture and so pony owners may be glad to sell the contents of their muck heap in order to buy winter hay and pony cube concentrates with the proceeds. Local riding stables also should be approached and here and there one may encounter a farmer or smallholder improvident enough to part with his manure for cash.

Ordinary poultry manure from free-ranging hens may be used as a compost activator but poultry farmers using the deep-litter system have wonderful value to offer in the litter from their poultry houses which they clean out once a year. This is as good as farmyard manure and the straw, wood shavings or peat which have been used as litter are splendid humus to add bulk to the soil although care must be taken to ensure that the shavings and straw are not forked in until they have decomposed to a crumbly black mass. Broiler litter, however, is usually disposed of after three months and when bought in the autumn, as is the custom, needs to stand over the winter. It should be stacked in a heap and jacketed with earth to prevent the winter rains leaching away its goodness. Poultry manure from battery hens should be composted with baled straw, built up in layers—10 cm (4 in) of straw then 5 cm (2 in) of manure and jacketed with soil and allowed to stand for a year before use.

Pig manure also is worth buying and mushroom compost made with gypsum, which has a neutral reaction but not if it is made with chalk.

Tea leaves and cold tea have a slightly acid reaction and are invaluable to add as a tonic to individual plants. The contents of our teapot are emptied in turn around every plant in the garden and everything, from primroses and violets to cherry trees and rhododendrons, seems to respond well to cold 'Earl Grey'! More scientifically, perhaps, tea leaves, either wet or dry, are known to be rich in nitrogen and potash and richer still in phosphorus, which explains the benefits they confer.

THREE

How Chemistry Helps

N.B.—when I wrote the bulk of the present text in 1963, we were using sequestered iron in the product *Sequestrene 138 Fe* which contained neither magnesium nor manganese sulphate. Fortunately, following the early trials, Murphy Chemicals Limited formulated the product *Murphy Sequestrene* in which manganese and magnesium sulphate are added to the sequestered iron. This should be borne in mind when reading my comments, throughout the book, on mineral deficiencies.

In addition to the shortage of organic matter, which may be remedied by the means described in the last chapter, excessive lime may cause deficiencies in plant growth. The inability of the *Ericaceae* family to thrive in untreated alkaline soils is well known. What is less frequently realized is that many other plants suffer from nutritional deficiencies under similar circumstances. Roses, for instance, are happier in a slightly acid medium; flowering cherries which actually dislike too acid a medium, nevertheless frequently suffer from mineral deficiencies in alkaline clays. Apple and other fruit trees are subject to similar nutritional disorders.

Plants feed by means of their roots, taking in water and soluble mineral salts from the soil. Their leaves take in carbon dioxide from the air through breathing pores known as stomata. By the action of sunlight the green cells (chloroplasts) which give the leaves their colour, break down the carbon dioxide into carbon and free oxygen. The carbon is changed into sugar and starches to feed the plant while the oxygen is 'breathed out' and expelled via the stomata into the air. This process can be satisfactorily carried on only so long as the chloroplasts remain healthy. Their healthy green is maintained by the mineral elements taken in from the soil by the roots. Deficiency of one or more of these elements causes a yellowing of the leaves, known as chlorosis, with consequent loss of efficiency in their job of absorbing the sunlight to break down the carbon dioxide from the air and manufacturing the sugars and starches necessary to the healthy life of the plant. In cases of extreme chlorosis almost the whole of the leaf surface turns yellow. Consequently little or no carbon dioxide or oxygen can be obtained from the air and the plant sickens and eventually dies. A similar phenomenon can be seen in variegated plants which are slower in growth than their green-leafed kin.

What then are the mineral elements which are vital to keep up the green colouring of the leaves and so maintain the plant in healthy growth? The major elements are nitrogen, phosphorus, potassium, calcium, magnesium, iron and sulphur. Equally important to plant growth are the minor or 'trace' elements—manganese, boron, copper, zinc, molybdenum, sodium, chlorine and silicon. Small quantities of iodine and fluorine, also, are helpful to plant growth.

If the soil is short of nitrogen it will be shown in the plants by small, yellow-green leaves which drop prematurely as they age. This shortage may be corrected by a green manure crop of the *Leguminosae* family—clover, vetches, peas or beans—and by keeping up an adequate supply of organic matter in the soil. Sulphate of ammonia also is useful to correct the deficiency and may be used at the rate of 34 g to the sq m (1 oz to the sq yd).

Phosphorus deficiency produces similar symptoms to those caused by a lack of nitrogen. It is usually found in high rainfall areas where the phosphates are constantly being washed out of the soil. Where deficient, phosphorus is best supplied as superphosphate in late spring and early summer.

Potassium deficiency is often indicated by the condition of the potato and brassica rows. The plants show scorched leaf margins, curling leaves and stunted growth. Onions and shallots turn brown at the tips. Apples, gooseberries and currants die back and show a similar scorching of the leaves. This deficiency is particularly common on the chalky soils of the south, south-east and east of England. It may be cured by adding bonfire ash when available, supplemented on light soil by sulphate of potash in autumn. In the flower garden, magnolias often show chlorosis on limy soil as a result of potash deficiency. This may be cured by dressing with bonfire ash from time to time. On the other hand it must be noted that some lime-haters abhor bonfire ash. *Gentiana sino-ornata*, for instance, would quickly be killed by such a dressing. This is because the ash of a bonfire on which many plant remains have been burnt contains *all* the lime content of those plants and is very concentrated.

Plants growing on alkaline soils are not likely to suffer from calcium deficiency. However, magnesium deficiency is more common on alkaline soils than generally realized. It is shown by chlorosis or yellowing of the leaf. The pattern of chlorosis in plants tends to vary according to which element is deficient. In magnesium deficiency the centres of the leaves become pale and areas of dead tissue develop near the mid-rib. Fortunately, magnesium deficiency is easily and quickly corrected by an application of Epsom salts (magnesium sulphate) at the rate of 34 g to the sq m (1 oz to the sq yd). In the case of fruit trees and other established trees it is helpful to bore holes in the rooting area of each tree at distances of about a metre (a yard) apart and 60 cm (2 ft) deep. A teaspoonful of Epsom salts should be placed in each hole and the earth replaced. Epsom salts may also be watered in at the rate of a tablespoonful dissolved in 9 l (2 gal) of water and applied over the root area of each tree or large plant. This is a very simple corrective of soil alkalinity as magnesium is antagonistic to calcium and therefore prevents too much of the latter being absorbed by the plant. If applications of the solution are continued at fortnightly intervals it will render and keep the topsoil acid.

39

Such means may be used to cultivate shallow-rooted lime-haters such as *Gentiana sino-ornata* in alkaline soils. For this to be effective, however, it must be stressed that a suitable rooting medium in the form of a small bed of peat and leaf-mould must first be prepared and raised above the surface of the existing land.

A deficiency of manganese is common on alkaline soils. It causes a typical chlorotic pattern or yellowing of the tissue between the veins of the leaves. In our limy clay soil, Japanese cherries and roses were often affected as well as hydrangeas and rhododendrons. Hydrangeas will often grow quite well in limy and chalky soils. If they are suffering from any mineral deficiencies a yellowing of the leaves will quickly appear. This is usually quite easily cured by watering in a solution of sequestered iron. It is interesting to note that this does not, however, affect the colour of the flowers. Hydrangeas on acid soils generally have blue flowers while the flowers of those on limy soils are red or pink. (We treated our hydrangeas with sequestered iron and the flowers remained pink in the early days when sequestered iron was first introduced. However, the later form incorporated manganese and magnesium sulphate (see p. 37) and this, applied as a spray to the leaves, began to turn the flowers blue. Each treatment deepened the flower colour. Manganese is the element which—with aluminium—seems to affect the colour of hydrangea flowers.)

Aluminium, however, more certainly brings out the blue colouring in hydrangeas. My husband and I preferred our hydrangeas blue because that is the colour which shows up best against the green setting of a garden in which shrubs predominate, so every year in November we applied a dressing of aluminium sulphate, giving the really big old plants as much as 1·35 kg (3 lb) each applied dry over the root area and left for the rain to wash into the soil. For younger plants, however, 0·45 kg (1 lb) per plant is quite adequate.

On limy soils, aluminium and manganese suffer chemical changes induced by the high alkaline content and so the plants are unable to absorb them as they would in an acid medium. Magnesium shortages also occur as mentioned earlier. It is necessary, therefore, to supply extra quantities of these substances to any plants which show they are deficient of them by exhibiting the typical yellowing of the leaves.

Iron, too, remains locked in alkaline soils and so the so-called 'lime-haters' (all plants which need fairly large quantities of iron) are unable to grow.

In alkaline soil many of the elements which we add to correct deficiencies remain locked in the soil just as do the natural minerals. Iron, which is easily absorbed by plants growing in acid soils, becomes changed in alkaline soil to hydroxide of iron or carbonate of iron which is not soluble. Plants can absorb only soluble minerals and so they cannot take up iron in this form. The chemists therefore had to find a form in which iron, manganese and other elements would remain soluble and resist the chemical changes commonly induced by alkalinity and of course it was important, too, that such substances should not harm plant life.

Credit must be given to the Geigy Company for working upon this problem and for evolving the iron sequestrene—which remains stable and available to plants even in alkaline clays which hitherto had presented the most obstinate problem. Even so it must be placed as near the root zone as possible and watered well in so that the roots can absorb before soil action can render it useless. It cannot be stressed enough that the instructions supplied with the product must be followed exactly.

Results with fruit trees and roses have been startlingly good. In our own garden we treated *Pieris japonica, P. floribunda* and *Meconopsis betonicifolia*—the blue poppy—the blue of which is apt to become a muddy purple when grown in alkaline soils. The pieris quickly lost the pronounced yellowish tinge they had been showing, became a healthy green and grew and flowered well while the meconopsis achieved the dazzling kingfisher blue usually associated with acid soils of pH 4·5 or pH 5. A yellow and dying hydrangea in a neighbour's garden was also treated and within a month a healthy green began to creep back into its leaves. Within ten weeks the plant was a splendid dark green and the flowers, though still pink, were of a much richer colour. A chlorotic hydrangea in our own garden responded dramatically and so did a young plant of *Rhododendron (Azalea) albrechtii.* Both of these had forgetfully been planted near a pocket of builder's lime.

Although I saw and studied many of the reports received by the Geigy Company from gardeners who took part in their nation-wide trials on rhododendrons and allied plants, and in spite of my own experiences, I am not entirely convinced that this iron product, though extremely valuable, is the complete solution to the problem of growing lime-haters on alkaline soils. An easier solution is to grow calcifuges in tubs and other containers or to plant in raised beds of lime-free soil insulated from the rest of the ground by heavy-duty black polythene—as described in Chapter Fifteen.

In our garden the response of rhododendrons and azaleas to the early sequestered iron was mixed and it seemed as though mag-nesium and manganese were also necessary before chlorotic rhododendrons were completely cured. I propose to go more fully into this in Chapter Fifteen when discussing ways of growing lime-haters and of widening the plant range on alkaline soils.

A major difficulty caused by the excessive calcium content of a soil is the locking up of such elements as iron, manganese and magnesium so that plants cannot absorb them. It seems that the excessive lime does not harm the plants by poisoning them—it induces chronic starvation of mineral elements instead. Further-more, a very limy or chalky soil may be entirely deficient in potassium, ammonia and sodium. The problem is aggravated because added ammonia—and added phosphates, too, quickly lose their value when they come into contact with the lime. The vegetable garden in particular will benefit from a general spring dressing of one part of sulphate of ammonia, two parts of sulphate of potash and two parts of superphosphate applied at the rate of 50 g per sq m ($1\frac{1}{2}$ oz per sq yd).

By adding Epsom salts (magnesium sulphate) at the rate of a tablespoonful to 9 l (2 gal) of water and watering it into the ground at fortnightly intervals alkaline soil may gradually be rendered more acid although the alkalinity would increase when the dressing ceased. Roses do best in a slightly acid soil and rose lovers whose gardens are on limy ground will find that their plants benefit greatly by the application of a solution of Epsom salts. Strawberries benefit in the same way but care must be taken not to splash the leaves which might show scorch as a result. Magnesium sulphate or Epsom salts is a short cut to curing plants that are suffering from lime-induced starvation on alkaline soils. It cannot, however, cure lack of humus or moisture. Plants need organic feeding as described in the last chapter as well as chemical help and the one should be used to support the other. Organic materials—humus—act as buffers in the soil, helping the plants to tolerate a wider pH range.

Where mineral deficiencies are suspected, soil samples should be sent for diagnosis to your county local Horticultural Adviser, who will be able to assess the deficiencies accurately and to recommend treatment.

FOUR

Gardens on Chalk and Lime

To grow lime-haters in alkaline soils is a struggle to the end. A few of us do it and succeed but whether the trouble and expense justify the end is for the individual gardener to decide. When I look at the many beautiful gardens on lime and chalk which have been created without the use of any of the lime-hating plants I honestly wonder why we try. We have at our disposal hundreds of good plants which grow naturally and without trouble on alkaline soils. Why not use these? When one is old or ill or has left the garden, all one's cherished lime-haters will die. If one wants to make a beautiful garden or a garden which will last for centuries one should choose the plants which thrive unaided in one's soil. Such a garden may be small or large but provided it is filled with good plants it will have beauty and peace and give pleasure to all who know it over the years.

One has only to think of the cottage gardens of the Cotswold country to realize what loveliness may be created upon limy soil. Think of the roses and wistaria flowering against honey-coloured limestone walls. Remember how some of the clematis thrive, and how the lilacs and hawthorns embower the spring. Think of the irises and peonies, the delphiniums and Madonna lilies, bleeding heart, columbines, galega and hemerocallis; the foaming edges of catmint and pinks; the wallflowers, polyanthus and tulips; the stocks and nicotianas—the hundred and one scents and colours of delight—the jumbled, yet harmonious whole that makes an

44

English cottage garden at its best. Add honeysuckle and jasmine, variegated holly and clipped yew shapes, snowdrops and daffodils, winter-flowering iris, wintersweet—all these and never a lime-hater among them.

Most bulbs, with certain of the lily group excepted, do not object to lime. Herbaceous perennials, apart from lupins which are alleged to be lime-haters but with which we—at any rate—had no difficulty, thrive upon it and so do most of the alpines. Perennials, of course, need an adequate depth of soil with suffi-cient humus added as described in the first two chapters. In some limy gardens, however, very little depth of soil exists. This, fortunately, need be no deterrent as has been shown by the wonderful garden made in a chalk pit at Highdown, near Goring in Sussex, the home of the late Sir Frederick and Lady Stern, and by many other gardens in such downland areas where the solid chalk is covered by only a centimetre or two (inch) of soil. Where the chalk is hard-panned and seemingly solid it may be broken up by a pick-axe and the plants set amid the resultant rubble. This chalk rubble will be found to hold water well and plants set amidst such broken chalk will seldom suffer from drought. In Sir Frederick and Lady Stern's garden, which Sir Frederick des-cribed in his fascinating book *A Chalk Garden*, herbaceous and tree peonies thrive along with stately spired eremurus, lime-tolerant lilies, anchusas, alliums, everlasting peas, clematis, the more vigorous hybrid tea roses, old-fashioned roses and species, some primulas, many irises, snowdrops, species tulips, daffodils and the pretty-early flowering anemone species such as the sun-loving *Anemone blanda* from Greece with its large, shiny-petalled blue and pink 'daisies', followed by *A. apennina* from Italy—happy in semi-shade and bearing its blue and white rayed flowers over several weeks—the peacock hued *A. pavonina*, the brilliant red *A. coronaria*, our native wood anemones in white and blue and *A. ranunculoides* in yellow as well as the furry-budded pasque flowers and starry hepaticas.

Shrubs and trees, too, are to be found at Highdown. As might be expected they belong to such genera as prove readily adaptable to a well-drained and sunny situation. Similar problems arise in many other chalk and limestone gardens so to mention here some of the shrubs grown at Highdown may prove helpful. [Highdown is now carefully maintained by Worthing Borough Council and The Highdown Garden Advisory Committee. My descriptions of the plantings there were written in the early sixties and there will have been some changes since then. However, Highdown is such a famous and important garden on chalk that I felt those gardening in similar conditions would still like to read of it as it was in the owners' lifetime.]

In the dark days of winter *Prunus subhirtella* 'Autumnalis', November cherry, bursts into a starry cloud of white or pink, and flowers on and off until March, accompanied by the useful lime-tolerant winter-flowering heaths, *Erica carnea* (now *E. herbacea*) and *E. × darleyensis*. The wintersweet, *Chimonanthus praecox*, will also be in flower and will be followed in February by *Mahonia japonica* with its handsome pinnate, holly-leaves and arching sprays of lemon, lily-of-the-valley scented bells, *Viburnum grandiflorum*, which might be replaced in the average garden by *V. × bodnantense*, flowers too. Both these viburnums are more accommodating to hot, dry situations than the better known *V. farreri* (formerly *fragrans*) which, in our own garden, seemed to need quantities of water in summer to flower freely. *V. × bodnantense* on the other hand excels in full sun where its leaves take on all season a burnished reddish bronze leaf colour that makes a most effective background to pale blue, bearded irises and delphiniums before it bursts into heads of vanilla-scented, pinky daphne-flowers in autumn.

Forsythias and daphnes do well on the chalk, but the sweet-scented *Osmanthus delavayi* seems shorter lived than on peatier soils and is perhaps better replaced by the very similar × *Osmarea burkwoodii*. All the flowering cherries, peaches and almonds like chalky soil and for small gardens the dwarf Russian almond *Prunus tenella* 'Fire Hill' is particularly useful, forming a dense 1-m (3-ft) high, thicketed shrub freely covered in spring with its bright pink almond flowers.

All viburnums like the chalk and some even seed themselves freely. The evergreen *Viburnum* × *burkwoodii* is a good one for early bloom with large flower heads, apple blossom pink in bud opening to a chalky white. *V.* × *juddii*, a hybrid of the sweet-scented favourite *V. carlesii* is a more vigorous grower than its parent and generally more satisfactory than *V. carlesii* which is sometimes apt to die out. Few magnolias like a hot dry soil. The early-flowering *Magnolia stellata* will seldom grow although the similar, but much stronger-growing *M. kobus borealis* with lemon scented flowers makes a small tree. This species takes longer to flower than *M. stellata* but where one hopes to create an enduring garden it is a plant of such distinction that it should most certainly be grown. A hybrid between the two, *M.* × *loebneri*, introduced by Hillier's, is also an excellent early variety for chalk. The chaenomeles—or the cydonias, as they used to be known—present no problem and they offer a choice of vivid and attractive colours which might otherwise be lacking among shrubs in chalky and limy gardens. Apart from the geranium-scarlet, blood-red and orange-flame varieties there are also white and apple-blossom flowered sorts which associate well in a group with the others or, used alone, make a happier choice for a difficult red-brick wall.

Lilacs and flowering crabs, of course, enjoy lime and chalk. So, fortunately, does the uncommon handkerchief tree or ghost tree, *Davidia involucrata*, with its large white, dove-like bracts. It flowers in May along with *Magnolia* × *highdownensis* with pendant, bowl-shaped flowers centred by a telling crimson boss. Said to be a hybrid between the lime-hating *M. sinensis* and the lime-tolerant *M. wilsonii*, as often happens in crosses between lime-hating and lime-tolerant parents, it takes after the lime-tolerant side of the family and like *M. wilsonii* does well on chalk.

Most of the berberis family also do well on the chalk. The evergreen *Berberis linearifolia*, a compact shrub with a hint of apricot to soften the brilliance of its blossom—and the pretty hybrid *B.* × *lologensis* do not in the least mind even the chalkiest spot in the garden. The rare and striking Judas tree, *Cercis siliquastrum,* with its pinky purple pea flowers, heart-shaped leaves and fine autumn colour is another fine plant that is happy on chalk as is *Choisya ternata* the evergreen Mexican orange with its sweetly-scented white flowers in May and autumn.

As in all hot and sunny gardens with good drainage, the cistus family does well at Highdown. So do the various buddleias, deutzias and philadelphus or mock-orange blossoms. Brooms of the cytisus section do not tolerate well the very chalky soil but the genistas with their showers of golden firefly-flowers thrive. The pink *Kolkwitzia amabilis* which rightly earns its common name of beauty bush is often shy to flower in less sunny gardens but at Highdown it excels.

Many of the hybrid tea roses need a better soil than can possibly be provided in the shallow depth overlying the chalk but some of the lovely Riviera climbers, old roses, and the various species and shrub roses do well. 'Souvenir de Claudius Denoyel' is a lovely deep red climber with flat, full-petalled flowers, which is noticeable at Highdown and also in the limy garden at St. Paul's, Walden Bury, Hertfordshire, home of the late Sir David Bowes Lyon, President of the Royal Horticultural Society. I mention this rose particularly because almost everyone loves a deep red rose and this is one which has proved just as vigorous and very free-flowering in our own limy clay and in fact seems happy on all types of alkaline soil and on clay.

The American dogwoods or cornels do not like lime but Asian *Cornus kousa* grows and flowers quite satisfactorily at Highdown. Often it is the case that although the American and Japanese representatives of a genus are calcifuge their Chinese counterparts will accept lime and chalky soils readily as will hybrids between the two. Buddleias as a genus like both chalk and lime as does *Carpenteria californica,* a semi-tender evergreen which, however, will survive most winters in a sunny, sharply drained situation. July cherry-blossom flowers are supplied by the New Zealand hoherias followed by the handsome and colourful escallonia family and the potentillas. The common garden hydrangea does not like the extremely dry and alkaline conditions at Highdown but *H. villosa* does well and remains a good blue colour in spite of the chalk.

Hydrangea aspera also succeeds although its flowers become a mauvy red which is not nearly so attractive as the blue of *H. villosa*. *H. involucrata* 'Hortensis' does well and is attractive with its bunches of blush-coloured, miniature begonia-like florets. Senecios and the useful long-flowering hypericums with their golden rose-of-Sharon flowers are another feature of the garden while the tall-growing Corsican heath, *Erica terminalis,* is the one autumn-flowering heath which will grow well upon such chalky soil.

Eucryphias are popular these days on account of their very beautiful white, bowl-shaped flowers with a central freckling of red or tan anthers in late August. Fortunately, the fairly hardy *E. × nymansensis* does well on chalk. Hibiscuses, caryopteris, fuchsias, *Spartium junceum* and myrtle complete the August scene and carry on into September when they are joined by the various berried shrubs and trees in which Highdown is rich.

Euonymus or spindle trees, cotoneasters of all sorts, the scarlet-berried viburnums, crataegus, pyracanthas, fruiting crab apples, holly and the various mountain ashes with coral, orange, yellow, pink and white berries join the berberis in making a gay feast of autumn colour.

In November and December the autumn-flowering cherry again begins to bloom along with the golden *Coronilla glauca* and the winter viburnums. Junipers, which love the chalk, *Picea glauca albertiana* 'Conica', which make neat 2·4-m (8-ft) pyramids, and griselinia provide an evergreen background, while the cinnamon bark of the finest arbutuses—*menziesii* and *andrachne*—the snake-bark maples and the paper-barked *Acer griseum* add further interest.

Although many shrubs are grown, Highdown is not primarily a garden of shrubs. It is rather a connoisseur's garden where many rare bulbs and plants find a home. Furthermore it is a triumph of skill and determination that shows what beauty may be achieved on the seemingly harsh and intractable chalk.

49

Hidcote Manor in Gloucestershire—now a National Trust property—is a plantsman's garden of a different type. Highdown consists of rock gardens and pools in the famous chalk pit and of shrub borders, underplanted with bulbs, lining grassy glades. Hidcote, too, has an informal shrubbery area but the garden is better known for its magnificent mixed borders where little-pruned roses are allowed to make huge scented bushes and mock oranges, lilacs, chaenomeles (cydonia) and other shrubs mingle with such statuesque foliage plants as the giant crimson rheum, knit together by peonies, lilies, feathery plumed astilbes, agapanthus, poppies, sages, sedums, violas, hemerocallis, lychnis, kniphofias and verbenas; with half-hardies, such as dahlias, cannas and large-flowered fuchsias interplanted where needed to give colour emphasis. Hidcote is famous, too, for its series of small enclosures—each little bigger than an average suburban front garden yet so skilfully planned and planted to strike exactly the right note. Paving is plentiful in the Cotswolds and paving is well used in these enclosures—soft, honey-coloured tints of stone merged into the borders by the overlapping foliage plants. Hostas with their soft green, ribbed leaves, bergenias with their fleshy crimson paddles and the ivy-leaved cyclamen are used extensively as underplanting. These plants are all effective ground-cover and help to keep down weeds.

Many and charming are the Cotswold gardens, showing well what can be done on limy soil. Two more examples come to mind, Kiftsgate with its famous hedges of *Rosa gallica versicolor* ('Rosa Mundi') and other old roses and its mixed borders each with a different colour scheme, and a garden near Bibury where a broad central area of paving interplanted with pinks and thymes, lavender, helianthemums and other rock plants, slopes gently between twin borders in softly muted tones.

Rock and paving is of course a characteristic of many chalk and limestone areas where it can usually be obtained fairly easily and inexpensively and used to add distinction to any garden. Aubrietas, alyssum, dianthus, mesembryanthemums, lewisias and onosmas all love a sunny, dry wall but many people feel that the brilliant blue lithospermums are denied them if they garden on lime or chalk. This need not be the case. *Lithospermum graminifolium* will do very well on either, and we grew *Lithospermum* 'Grace Ward' quite happily on a north-facing rock wall in our own garden. Although lithospermums love the sun it is not always realized how much their roots resent dryness. A north-facing situation and a peaty, root run may well be the answer on chalky soils to growing them well—a wall or raised bank they must have. In my experience lithospermums will always die off if grown on the flat.

Highdown is a garden on dry, chalky soil in sunny Sussex. Hidcote and Kiftsgate are sited upon lime in the colder Cotswolds. The soil in both these gardens is comparatively well drained. At St. Paul's, the late Sir David Bowes Lyon had a different problem to overcome—that of heavy, alkaline clay. This he tackled by drainage, as described in the first chapter of this book and by putting in all the organic matter he could find. In a lecture before the Royal Horticultural Society on 13th October 1959, he described how he put in *'coal ashes, coke ashes, anthracite ashes, sawdust, paper—and of course leaf-mould, anything to break it up.'* Also he advised *'to burn as much of it as possible. I get all the old tree stubs, roots, big bits of wood and everything I can get in the winter and make an enormous fire and when there is a great heat in it I put the clay right on top of the fire. I build it up into a cone and let it cook slowly. The fire will come through here and there after a day or so, and as soon as it does the hole should be plugged up. In this way the fire can go on for sometimes three or four weeks, provided that one stops up the holes every day, and in the end there is the beautifully burnt clay which is lovely stuff. It is like brick dust and it handles well; it digs in beautifully and even in its pure state, plants seem to revel in it.'* The action of frost on clay was useful, too, he said, but above all he recommended choosing plants with thick coarse roots which would thrive naturally in the clay—plants such as the peonies, the irises and eremuri—all of which, you will have noticed, do well in the other gardens on alkaline soil that we have discussed in this chapter—even on the sun-baked chalk of Highdown. Notable among the trees to succeed on the limy clay at St.

Paul's are horsechestnuts, prunuses, lilacs, davidias and magnolias. In our own modest garden, my husband and I were surprised at how readily some of the magnolias grew in our limy clay. In properly drained alkaline clay many of those magnolias which dislike shallow chalk soils will thrive. This is, I think, because the clay supplies their demanding fleshy roots with more food and moisture than they can find on the chalk. At St. Paul's, Walden Bury, the small-growing, early *Magnolia stellata* succeeds as does *M. denudata* and the whole of the *M.* × *soulangiana* group. *M.* 'Lennei' is particularly outstanding. The June-flowering *M. wilsonii* grows well.

There, too, in an area of neutral soil in the woodland where the natural leaf-fall and decaying vegetation overlies the limy clay, rhododendrons and azaleas have been established.

Like Kiftsgate, St. Paul's is a garden of roses. The strong-growing hybrid teas are happy and many shrub and old-fashioned roses are grown as big, free-flowering bushes among other shrubs.

'Souvenir de Claudius Denoyel', the deep red, fruity scented climber, thrives here and as I mentioned earlier it seems to do well in all gardens on alkaline soil. The beautiful double yellow 'Lawrence Johnston' named after Major Lawrence Johnston who created Hidcote does better here than on lighter soils where it is often subject to black spot. 'Frühlingsgold' throws up masses of its butter-yellow blooms in May and the dainty flowered, sweet-scented hybrid musk roses also grow well.

Some lilies excel at St. Paul's; among them are the beautiful, pale-yellow-trumpeted *szovitsianum* which is also among the many outstanding plants grown well at Hidcote. The hybrid 'Golden Clarion' strain thrive as do 'Maxwill' and *Lilium testaceum* but although the golden-rayed *L. auratum* is grown it dies out after a few years and has to be renewed. This is a lily which really needs an acid soil.

Again the lesson is driven home. Plants which like one's soil endure, while those die out which can be grown only with difficulty and which have to have conditions artificially adapted to their liking.

On clay soils, strong-rooted plants do well. Luckily the hostas and bergenias, so much appreciated nowadays for their decorative foliage, thrive, and in areas where drainage is still difficult despite all one's efforts, the handsome ligularias will be useful. This genus has a great capacity for absorbing all surplus water, so it may be planted—along with moisture-loving irises—where it is necessary to drain the ground without the effort or expense of inserting pipes or cutting drainage trenches. Willows can also be used to mop up moisture. By carefully chosen planting near the margin of the grass, soggy, waterlogged lawns can often be improved without the necessity of lifting the turf and going to elaborate drainage procedures.

FIVE

The Mixed Border

A well-planned mixed border can be the mainstay of any garden where a sufficient depth of soil exists or where the underlying chalk or limestone can be sufficiently broken up (for gardens where this is impossible see Chapter Fourteen for the treatment of dry banks and rough dry ground).

A mixed border is a great improvement upon the old conception of the herbaceous border. By including shrubs and bulbs as well as herbaceous perennials it gives a much longer period of colour. In even a small garden it is possible to plant a mixed border to cover the four seasons giving spring, summer, autumn and winter interest. A proportion of evergreen shrubs and shrublets should be included so that an interesting pattern of foliage and texture remains in winter.

In summer when the border is at the height of its beauty such prodigally-flowering subjects as the shrub roses, philadelphus, lavender and hebes (veronicas) provide a weight of blossom to contrast effectively with the spires of the delphiniums, pentstemons and mulleins and to provide relief from the ubiquitous daisy flowers which although excellent in themselves when carefully selected and well sited are apt to overweigh the purely herbaceous border. In summer, too, there will be the restful foliage of those shrubs which have flowered earlier as well as of such plants as are grown purely for the effectiveness of their foliage, setting off and framing the bright patches of flower colour.

In even the smallest gardens room can be found for at least one good mixed border. In the back garden of a suburban plot a sweeping border may cover the length of one side, curving to take in the end while the rest of the plot is grassed. One might add a small deciduous tree to give shade in summer without obscuring the winter light or a low bed of lime-tolerant winter-flowering heaths or dwarf conifers to break the expanse of grass and give added interest.

Whether the garden be large or small, the mixed border should be allowed as great a width as possible. The edge may be straight or curved. My personal preference is for a curved border although care must be taken to get really generous curves and sweeps and to avoid niggling bays and promontories. Straight borders, too, are effective so long as no attempt is made to edge them with a single species of plant. Rather should the front of the border be irregularly broken by plants of widely different textures and effects—one might use a ground-hugging juniper next to a froth of long-flowering Allwoodii pinks, the grey foliage of which will make a useful contrast with the dark green of the juniper when flowers are over. Dwarf lavenders, clumps of catmint, dwarf bulbs such as the autumn-flowering schizostylis with their pink or red miniature-gladioli-like spikes, the bold ribbed foliage of hostas, or bergenias, sprawling mats of helianthemums, the attractive velvety-grey 'lamb's ears' of *Stachys lanata*—all these are useful for front-row planting. Even a group of the winter-blooming, lime-tolerant *Erica carnea* (now *E. herbacea*) may be included—its mossy foliage providing an effective green cushion when the flowers are gone.

Forming neat hummocks of grey all the year round, the lavenders are excellent for the mixed border. To keep them compact and prevent them becoming straggly and broken it is essential to shear them hard back as soon as the flowers are dead. 'Hidcote' is a fine, dark purple dwarf for the front of the mixed border while its counterpart 'Hidcote Pink' is no less useful. Much more dwarf but striking enough to form an incident at the border edge is the extremely sweet-scented *Lavandula spica*

'Nana Alba'. In well-drained soil in sun this dwarf will go on for years. For some reason the tall-growing white lavender is not long lived in many gardens. For sheer beauty it is worth growing, however, and young stock can be constantly kept coming along from cuttings which strike easily from ripe wood removed with a heel and inserted in a moist, shady spot in the open ground.

The fine, grey-leafed old English lavender is an asset to the mixed border. In fact I would never plant such a border without including bushes of both the old English lavender and the tall white lavender as middle row shrubs with a clump or two of the purple and pink 'Hidcote' varieties in the foreground to echo the grey colour note and habit.

Santolina chamaecyparissus, the cotton lavender, is another plant to give an evergreen—or rather ever grey note to the front of the mixed border but its yellow button flowers are poor and should be removed in the bud stage. *S. neapolitana,* however, has flowers of lemon yellow which go well with its grey-green foliage and so it may be allowed to flower.

The golden variegated form of the periwinkle, *Vinca major* 'Variegata', is a plant to use purely for the effect of its handsome, sunny-looking foliage as its blue-grey flowers are insignificant beside those of the purer blue, wine, and white of the dwarf periwinkles.

A taller semi-evergreen shrub to extend the season of the border so that it may give garden interest and flowers for cutting throughout the year is *Viburnum × burkwoodii* which bears its vanilla-scented heads of flowers as early as March in a sheltered position. With its elegant fringed tassels of pink-flushed, suede-grey catkins, in January, *Garrya elliptica* is a valuable, tall-growing evergreen for the back of the mixed border. It will grow away from a wall although it undoubtedly shows up best against stone or whitewash or even pebbledash. Another back-row shrub, worth including for the warm tints of scarlet and orange that its foliage assumes in winter is *Stranvaesia davidiana* with clusters of matt-finished coral-scarlet berries to add to its gaiety.

Cotoneaster salicifolius flocossus is another interesting evergreen with a weeping habit and dark, deeply-veined leaves shaped like those of a willow, with corymbs of hawthorn-like flowers in May and scarlet winter berries. It makes a small tree for the back of the mixed border. Its relation *Cotoneaster dammeri* is a front-row shrub with the arching, prostrate habit and fine berries of *C. horizontalis,* but unlike *C. horizontalis* it is evergreen.

Such evergreens as these should be used in the mixed border to form the outline of the bays in which herbaceous plants and bulbs may be grouped. A mixed border should be wide. A width of at least 2·4 m (8 ft) is essential if the border is to be effective. Three metres (10 ft) would be better and, if the border is made as long as possible, such a width would not look out of place in a small suburban garden.

I have mentioned the variegated periwinkle as an evergreen herbaceous plant for the border front. Quite different in character are the bergenias (megaseas) of which *Bergenia cordifolia* is still one of the best. Planted in sun and well-drained soil at the border-edge its fleshy, paddle-shaped leaves will make a handsome group while its fat, early spikes of pink, bell-like flowers are valuable to cut for the house. The leaves of *B. purpurascens* turn to crimson in winter, making a vivid colour splash to cheer the eye.

One of the greatest assets of the mixed border is its ability to add winter interest to the garden and for this reason wherever room can be found for it I would include the spreading, prostrate juniper—*Juniperus horizontalis* 'Douglasii'—the feathery, ground-hugging branches of which deepen their glaucous blue to violet-purple in the winter months. Junipers of all kinds do particularly well on chalky and limy soils and their autumn and winter leaf-colour seem to be enhanced in such situations.

For a silvery note, in well-drained soil, *Senecio greyi* makes a rounded, spreading bush, smothered with lemon yellow daisies in early summer. It is a valuable subject to site at the curve of a border or to give a finished appearance at either end. More tender than the senecio but very lovely *Elaeagnus macrophylla* has rounded silvery leaves and a low, sprawling habit. It is splendid for the front of a sheltered border on sharply-drained chalk or limestone where its silvery leaves will provide a foil for delphiniums, the early-flowering magenta *Gladiolus byzantinus* or the cherry-crimson China rose 'Fellemberg'. But the value of the elaeagnus does not lie solely in its foliage effect. Regularly in November, when established, the plant will put out myriads of tiny, silver fuchsia-bells that give off a most delightful fragrance. For colder, stiffer soils *E. macrophylla* is best replaced by its hardier offspring *E.* × *ebbingei* which makes a taller bush that is best placed towards the back of the border. Its leaves are almost as silvery though more pointed in shape. Towards winter the silver of the top surface is replaced by a lively, glossy green.

Handsome evergreens to flower in late summer are the escallonias. *Escallonia* 'Iveyi' is a fine shrub with dark green leaves and white, bell-like flowers. *E.* 'Apple Blossom' is said not to do well on chalk though it was perfectly at home in our garden on limy clay. *E.* 'Donard Gem' and 'Donard Brilliance' are good plants in clear pink and glowing crimson respectively. They will do well on any soil. All the escallonias mentioned are reasonably hardy south of the Trent. In very bleak districts the backing of a wall will help them to keep their leaves in winter.

One does not want, however, to overweigh the mixed border with evergreens. Their function is to provide the skeleton of the border so that it looks furnished and interesting throughout the year. In windy districts the evergreens also serve to help to break the force of the wind and protect the more flimsy herbaceous plants and bulbs. Flowering deciduous shrubs of the syringa (lilac), philadelphus (mock-orange), deutzia and weigela (diervilla) families also play their part and here a little discriminating selection may help to give the border added appeal. The Persian lilac—*Syringa persica*—is an excellent shrub for the mixed border. Lighter in character than many of the hybrids it is a shrub of graceful stature and its daintier panicles of sweetly-scented bloom are lilac in colour and very freely borne. *S. microphylla* 'Superba' is also good and although its narrow panicles of flower may not at once suggest a lilac to the uninitiated its delightful scent leaves one in no doubt as to its identity. Moreover, this species flowers twice, in May and again in September when its fragrance will be doubly welcome. Nearer the conventional garden lilac in appearance is one of the finest of the new hybrids 'Esther Staley' with large shapely trusses of warm pink flowers. 'Maud Notcutt' is a splendid single white, 'Prodige' an extra-large-flowered deep purple and 'Clarke's Giant', lilac blue. Other fine lilacs are 'Buffon' in soft pink, 'Primrose' a creamy-yellow which looks well with the dark red-purple 'Massena', 'Condorcet' a double lavender, 'Paul Thirtion' double claret-rose, and 'Blue Hyacinth' a distinctive, new-look lilac with the tubular flowers of the species held in a fine hyacinth-blue truss.

Of the mock-oranges, *Philadelphus* 'Virginal' is still one of the best of all doubles. 'Albâtre' also is good. More graceful bushes with single blooms are the milky *P.* 'Burfordensis' and *P.* 'Belle Etoile' which has large, distinctive, purple-centred, squarish flowers and makes a manageable shrub for the smaller border. For a really small garden the dwarf *P.* 'Manteau d'Hermine' and *P. microphyllus* are the varieties to choose.

Many deutzias are of an undistinguished appearance. However, there are some first-rate shrubs in the genus which is a particularly useful one on account of its ability to do as well in shade as in sun. The best hybrid deutzia in my opinion is 'Magicien' with comparatively large, fringed petals in clear pink. Other good members of the family are 'Joconde', × *kalmiiflora*, 'Contraste' with starry, lilac-pink blossoms, 'Veitchii' and *setchuenensis corymbiflora* with widely-bunched heads of cool-scented white.

A fine early-flowering weigela (diervilla) is the sulphur-yellow *Weigela middendorffiana*. This species, however, needs a sheltered and preferably a semi-shaded position. Of the related weigelas the bright pink 'Avant Garde' and 'Conquête' are good for sun and make arching shrubs which are attractive during their season of flower in May and June. Out of flower they are rather coarse in foliage. The crimson 'Eva Rathke' does not like limy soil and is to my way of thinking dull in colour compared with the pink varieties. Those who enjoy variegated foliage will find *W. florida* 'Variegata' worth planting. The flowers of this variety are of a soft coconut-ice pink and the fresh green leaves are edged with cream and useful to pick to accompany other flowers indoors. A charming shrub which needs full sun to flower freely is *Kolkwitzia amabilis*, the beauty bush, which does extremely well in chalky gardens. Similar to the kolkwitzia are the abelias with dainty, miniature, foxglove-like flowers. *Abelia schumannii* with soft, rosy-lilac flowers is perhaps the best for general planting, but for a sheltered, sunny border against a wall the semi-evergreen *A. floribunda* is lovely with large blooms of crimson-lake.

We have discussed the evergreen *Viburnum × burkwoodii* earlier in this chapter but there are two deciduous viburnums which are indispensable to even the smallest mixed border. They are the winter-flowering, foot-high *V. × bodnantense* and the spring-blooming *V. carlesii*. Both are deliciously scented and *V. carlesii* makes a handsome rounded shrub with its soft green leaves and rose-flushed, bun-shaped heads of daphne-like flowers.

Daphnes themselves do well on chalk and lime and no border should be without the well-known *Daphne mezereum* with its sweetly-scented, rosy-purple flowers. *D. m.* 'Album' is similar and is usually a vigorous bush with gold-eyed, ivory-white blooms that are just as fragrant as those of the type. Both these daphnes like to get their roots under a stone. Indeed so many small shrubs and bulbs appreciate the nearness of moisture-retaining stones that I like to edge the mixed border with either a flagged path or with a band of irregular paving. Such an edging seems also to help the doubtfully hardy front-row plants such as the large-flowered fuchsias, the crocus-like zephyranthes and schizostylis (which in spite of assertions to the contrary I have always found to do well in limy soil). Early species of crocus and thymes delight to seed in the cracks and the paving serves a double purpose by allowing front-row plants such as helianthemums and catmint to creep forward and soften the border edges without interfering with the mowing of the grass.

Towards the front of the border many bulbous and rhizomatous subjects may be grown. The brilliant little *Crocus chrysanthus* and *C. tomasinianus* should be planted in mixture for February colour. They may be followed by vivid tulips such as the *fosteriana* or *kaufmanniana* hybrids, with Dutch irises and groups of the lily-flowered tulips for later colour.

Tall bearded irises are wonderful border plants because their sword-like foliage adds a note of interest when the flowers are over. For this reason I like to plant them towards the border front where their leaves may be seen. Offers of older varieties of tall bearded irises should be firmly discarded. There are now many lovely up-to-date varieties to be bought; 'Patterdale', 'Galilee', the pale and sturdy 'Jane Phillips' and 'Great Lakes' are good. 'Desert Song' is a pleasing butterscotch-cream. 'Sable' and 'Carbondale' represent the popular 'black' irises and are fine to contrast with yellow or white. 'Zantha' is bright yellow, and 'Hi Time' a golden apricot, while 'Rocket' is almost orange. Whites such as 'Arctic Snow' look lovely set against the dark green foliage of subjects not in flower. Some of the pinks such as 'Pink Bountiful' and 'Pink Lace' blend well with blues and browns. These last tend to be more expensive, if really good varieties are wanted, but 'Troutbeck' is a not-too-pricy medium brown. A good red nearer claret in colouring is 'Garden Glory' although the superb 'Quechee' should be watched for, while 'Technicolor', too, is good. For the specialist I shall make further suggestions of irises in the next chapter.

Fuchsias are lovely in flower and graceful in habit. Although technically shrubs, they are so often cut to the ground by winter frost in the average border as to be ranked among the semi-herbaceous plants and placed in the front row. The well-known *Fuchsia* 'Riccartonii' and *F. magellanica gracilis* are hardy enough to survive in most gardens and even when reduced to ground level will throw up arching shoots to 60 or 90 cm (2 or 3 ft) high in the spring. Prettiest of all the small-flowered fuchsias is the ghost-pale *F. magellanica* 'Alba' which is in fact not white but the most delicate blush pink. 'Mrs. Popple' is a very hardy large-flowered red and purple fuchsia while 'Mme Cornelisen' has smaller but graceful slim droplets of flower in red and white. All these fuchsias will be helped to overwinter if a shovelful of ashes or a layer of bracken be placed over their crowns before the hardest frosts begin.

Most people will want to grow such favourites as peonies and delphiniums in the bays formed by the shrubs in their mixed borders. Lupins, however, are said not to do well on very chalky or limy soils although we grew them in our alkaline clay of pH 7·5 and found them reasonably permanent and the tree lupins are reliable even on pure chalk. In the small garden where space is limited one needs to choose mainly such herbaceous plants as bloom over a long period.

One of the most outstanding of these long-flowering plants is *Anthemis* 'Mrs. E. C. Buxton' with sulphur yellow daisies of a refinement of colour not often found in perennials of their class. Another striking yellow is to be found in *Lysimachia punctata* with wide blooms of treacly gold carried in upright spikes. Like the anthemis mentioned, this lysimachia is a sturdy middle-row plant reaching from 75–90 cm ($2\frac{1}{2}$ to 3 ft) in height and seeming never to be out of flower from early June until September. Golden yellow may be supplied by the feathery foliaged *Coreopsis verticillata*, with dainty starry flowers, and the larger brown-blotched flowers of *Coreopsis auriculata superba*. *Coreopsis* 'Badengold' is similar but without the brown blotch.

Valerian or centranthus is another long-blooming perennial that to my mind is not used nearly as much as it should be. Its red, rosy, pink and white flowers are delightful with the yellow mentioned above and when grown in a mixture have a light and frothy effect, showing up well against the greenery of border plants of which the blossoms have faded or which are not yet in flower.

Cynoglossum nervosum is a front-row perennial to provide that touch of brilliant blue that is always so welcome in any border, while its taller relation, *Anchusa* 'Morning Glory' will perform equally well and over as long a period at the back of the border.

A daisy flower with an unmistakable touch of quality is *Osteospermum jucundum* (*Dimorphotheca barberae* of gardens) with apple-scented foliage and dark-centred, shining-pink ray florets. Only 38 cm (15 in) high this is a subject for the front of the border. Although a South African it seems fully hardy in well-drained soil and is easily increased from cuttings pulled off and dibbled in a shady spot in early summer.

Quite different in character are the potentillas, of which the strawberry-leaved 'Gibson's Scarlet' with quite large flowers of true scarlet, black-centred, and the golden *P. recta* 'Warrenii' may be relied on for the longest flowering season.

With these a clump or two of the better day-lilies such as the yellow *Hemerocallis* 'Hyperion' and the apricot 'Pink Lady' and such newer hybrids as I shall deal with in the next chapter will, when established, provide a supporting cast of continuous flower throughout the summer months against which the more ephemeral border stars may take their turn upon the stage. The Madonna lily—*Lilium candidum*—enjoys lime and will tolerate the conditions of a mixed border if planted where sun and air can reach the stem. September is the best planting month and the green shoots of the lily will already be appearing. It should be planted not more than 5 cm (2 in) deep in well-drained but not too dry soil. This lily, like most of its genus, resents disturbance and should be lifted only when the clumps become crowded. In some gardens the Madonna lily has proved finicky and a myth arose that it would grow only in cottage gardens, always failing in grander domains. The explanation, I think, lies in the liberal doses of soapsuds, tea leaves and slops and the occasional dollop of horse manure to which cottagers treated their most cherished plants. Their simple recipe for success might be tried in other gardens and for many plants with advantage.

One of the best points of a mixed border is that it is not limited by the boundaries of convention to the growing of only one or two categories of plants. Anything may be grown that will do well in company with its neighbours, and help to make a pleasant picture. Floribunda or hybrid musk roses, the old-fashioned but free-flowering and long-blooming China roses and the 1·5-m (5-ft) rugosa varieties may mingle with bulbs, heaths, day-lilies and delphiniums. Polyanthus, primulas and wallflowers should be grouped to give spring colour and, when they are lifted, dahlias and petunias should take their place for summer flowering. To show something of colour and interest throughout the year should be the aim.

For a mixed border to be successful the drainage should be reasonably good. Marls and clays will probably need to be drained as described in Chapter One. On the other hand lime and chalk soils will need the inclusion of plenty of moisture-holding humus. Before the border is planted the ground should be trenched as deeply as possible (see Chapter One) and allowed to settle. Provided these preparations are followed and lime-tolerant plants are chosen the mixed border should be a success in all but the shallowest and driest soil.

Treated clays with their higher fertility level offer a good chance of success to a much wider plant range. The appealing blue omphalodes, golden trollius (globe flower) and doronicum will enrich the border in spring, to be followed in summer by the lime-yellow flower froth and beautiful leaves of *Alchemilla mollis*. The astilbes with their varied plumes of colour will be at home, as will be the graceful *Dierama pulcherrima* (wand flower), the geums, willow gentian, hardy geranium species such as 'Buxton's Variety' (blue), *G. alpinum* and the pleasing pink *G. endressii* 'A. T. Johnson'. Tall irises such as the yellow and white *I. ochroleuca*, the blue 'Monspur', the *Japanese kaempferi* hybrids and even the yellow *I. pseudacorus* of our riversides will also be happy. With them one might plant such striking ligularias as the orange-rayed 'Desdemona' or the shaggy-petalled 'Gregynog Gold'. With winter protection the scarlet lobelias should survive. Lysimachias, mimulus, evening primroses, with the handsome rodgersias, rudbeckias and thalictrums, offer an exciting prospect.

SIX

Many Herbaceous Plants Revel
in Alkaline Soils

Most herbaceous plants do not object to lime in the soil. Some such as scabious and the useful carnation family revel in it. Lupins are perhaps the most notable—and inconvenient—exception to the general rule. With the exception of *Lupinus arboreus* they do seem to die out on chalk. The odd thing is that they do very well indeed on the limestone uplands in the Colwyn Bay and Llandudno areas of North Wales—those same areas in which rhododendrons often succeed apparently against all the rules, probably in places where silica is present or where rotted vegetation has created pockets of acid soil. The South African schizostylis or Kaffir lilies are a similar case. Said to be lime-haters, with us they grew like a weed. In both these cases I think the truth may be that it is not the high calcium content of the soil to which the plants object—nor are they deprived of any essential elements therefrom—rather is it the dryness of the southern chalklands which starves the plants of essential moisture. Limestone seems often to hold more underground moisture than chalk and in the west, of course, rainfall is much heavier than in the south which accounts for the many flourishing clumps of lupins and schizostylis on the limestone hills of North Wales.

When planting herbaceous subjects in shallow soil over chalk or limestone each should have its site well prepared, the rock being broken into rubble with a pickaxe and a hole taken out much larger than the size of the plant at planting time would indicate.

Half a bucketful of loam well mixed with compost should then be tipped into the hole to give the roots a good start. This 'luncheon basket' of good soil and compost is vital to the success of the plant and if necessary a load of medium loam should be bought for the purpose.

Peonies are among the loveliest of plants and without exception they seem to do well in all chalky or limy gardens. The May-flowering *Paeonia officinalis,* the familiar peony of cottage gardens with its heavy, petal-filled heads is still a magnificent plant for any garden and variations may be found in crimson, cherry, pink, white and magenta. They all do well in sun but the flowers last longer in partial shade. Peony 'tubers' must never be planted too deep (5 cm (2 in) below the surface is ample) or they will not flower. Even when planted correctly, few, if any, flowers will be seen the first season after planting. Thereafter they should increase in beauty and vigour every year. It is a strange thing, I have noticed, that many of the most worthwhile plants require patience on the part of the gardener—a period of waiting before they give of their best. Hellebores, *Iris stylosa,* hardy cyclamen, eremuri all exact it. Perhaps that is why they are not more often seen in gardens. Some gardeners, I know, become impatient, discard the plants and replace them with something to give a vivid, instant show. This is a pity because in the long run many of the slow starters give the most pleasure.

Double and single Chinese peonies succeed the May-flowerers in June and among these are some splendid plants. 'Bowl of Beauty' (pink with a centre of creamy petaloids), 'Globe of Light' (rose and gold), 'Kelway's Glorious' (white), 'Solange' (salmon-orange), 'Sarah Bernhardt' (pink), 'Red Flag', 'Duchesse de Nemours' (flesh-pink), and the old frothy white 'Festiva Maxima' are among the best. For those who like to grow an uncommon plant, the early-flowering peony with the difficult name *Paeonia mlokosewitschii* is easy and delightful when its lemon yellow globes centred by pale pink carpels open above its sea-green leaves. This peony is sometimes expensive to buy, but for just over a pound one can usually buy a young plant the flowers of which will be well worth awaiting. My husband and I purchased such a young plant which took two years to flower but then gave us three blooms. The following year there were five, the next seven, and the year after it set eleven buds. Of course such a treasure should never be disturbed. You may split up lesser peonies if you must, though even with them the operation may well result in a season or more of flowerless sulks. If you have to move a clump of peonies September is the best time to do it and, contrarily enough, I have known removal at this season to cure an obstinately flowerless clump making it free-blooming thereafter.

Provided they are not disturbed, many of the species peonies are just as easy to grow as the hybrid ones. *P. lobata* 'Sunbeam' is another early flower and like *P. mlokosewitschii* should, in gardens subject to spring frosts, be given the protection of a north-facing wall or hedge. 'Sunbeam' lives up to its name with flowers of an uncommon cherry-scarlet lit by yellow anthers.

Most beautiful of all the peony species is the tall white *P. emodii* with gold-centred bowls of creamy loveliness. It is, however, slightly tender and should really be attempted only in sheltered gardens. Much tougher is *P. mascula* (syn. *P. corallina*) which has been found growing wild on the island of Steep Holm in the Bristol Channel where it is thought to have been taken by the monks. It is an attractive peony with glowing, rose-red flowers. The only peony suitable for the rock garden is *P. cambessedesii* from the Balearic islands. It is not very hardy and thrives best on one of those hot, south-facing dry banks that are so often found in gardens in chalk districts. This peony bears in April rather small, but very pretty, bright pink flowers above red-backed, silvery-green leaves. Its pods of coral pink and black seeds in autumn are also attractive.

Properly classed as shrubs, the moutans or tree peonies may, nevertheless, conveniently be dealt with here. They make large bushes of 1 to 1·2 m (3 to 4 ft) high in time and bear thirty or more sumptuous large flowers. They are among the most gorgeous of flowering plants for gardens on alkaline soil. The plants themselves are bone hardy but as they flower in May they might be caught by spring frosts. Although our garden was near the sea and so not subject to spring frosts we took no chances with these glorious flowers and grew them facing north under the lee of a rose hedge so that their blooms were somewhat retarded and shielded by the hedge from the morning sun which might have spoilt the flowers after a night of frost. Tree peonies should never be disturbed and so should be planted in well-prepared sites as deeply dug as possible, enriched by a half-barrow of compost per plant. Most tree peonies are grafted. They should be planted with the grafts 5 cm (2 in) below soil-level so that the scion in time will throw out its own roots. Of the old, well-known varieties 'La Reine Elizabeth' is a great beauty with petal-packed flowers as big as a dinner plate and of a glowing rose-red. 'Bijou de Chusan' is in the same style with flowers of a delicate blush pink and 'Comtesse de Tudor' has soft rose blooms. Of different ancestry are the *P. lutea* hybrids—'Souvenir de Maxime Cornu' with full-petalled, lemon-yellow flowers touched with red. 'L'Espérance' is a single yellow and a very beautiful flower. Lovely, too, are the newer tree peonies imported from Japan, many of which have single or semi-double flowers which show the great central boss of stamens and carpels that so much enhances the flower. 'Yano Okima' is a beautiful white—but it is not always possible to purchase these newer introductions by name and almost all are good.

Both herbaceous peonies and the moutans are liable to attack by botrytis. In the moutans this shows itself when healthy stems and leaves suddenly wilt and die. Such shoots should be immediately removed and the cut surfaces dusted with flowers of sulphur. Botrytis sometimes causes the buds of herbaceous peonies not to open. They turn brown and wither. Soft brown areas appear at the base of the shoots and eventually the leaves wilt and turn brown in a similar way to affected shoots of the moutans. A grey mould appears in damp weather. This annoying disease may be controlled if all dead shoots are removed and destroyed. The topsoil around the plant may be contaminated and should be scraped away and burnt. The plants should be sprayed with the fungicide captan, paying especial attention to the base of the shoot. Peonies of all types are best left un-mulched as mulching material lying over the winter promotes conditions in which this fungus thrives.

Like the peonies, many irises do well on lime or chalk. Iris is the Greek word for rainbow, and anybody seeing the present-day range of tall-bearded irises at Chelsea Flower Show or at the British Iris Society's Show in the Royal Horticultural Society's Hall might think that the genus is indeed well named. Modern tall-bearded irises range in colour from white and oyster, through pale shell-pink and butterscotch-yellow to turquoise, flax-blue and sapphire and to ruby and mulberry-red velvet. There are also browns, tans and near blacks as well as numerous bi-colours, blends, variegatas in which the standards are yellow or golden and the falls wine or red, edged with gold. Some of the most fascinating of all are the plicatas in which a pale ground colour is etched and stippled with markings of a deeper colour giving a wonderful almost translucent effect.

Tall-bearded irises do especially well on lime or chalk. They do, however, need shelter from strong winds which would tatter their petals and snap their stems. They must have a sunny position and well-drained soil. If your garden is clayey, then you will need to make a raised bed, incorporating plenty of sharp sand, peat and hop manure. In any soil they will benefit from the peat and hop manure but the raised bed is only necessary in really cold clays.

In the well-drained limy or chalky garden the tall-bearded irises are such a success that it is worth devoting a border especially to them. Such an iris border might be interplanted with daffodils and day-lilies with a background of Michaelmas daisies to provide later colour. Below are mentioned, colour by colour, some of the best varieties which may be slightly more expensive than those already suggested for the mixed border but are still not in the 'millionaires only' class.

Everyone likes a blue iris and nothing is prettier than a good clump of this colour seen in the sunshine of an early-summer day. Really exciting is the plumbago-coloured 'Blue Mohr' which is a hybrid descended from the exotic Oncocyclus group and inheriting some of its ancestors' lovely form. Yet it is no more difficult to grow than any other tall-bearded variety. 'Butterfly Blue' is a charming crisp, pale blue and 'Seathwaite' is another of light colouring. 'Pierre Menard' is deeper in tone—hyacinth-blue in fact and very attractive.

To contrast with blue, yellow looks well. If you like your yellows 'hot', 'Zantha' is a good one to choose. 'Gold Sovereign' is nearer to orange and ruffled in form. 'Sunray' is paler and 'Alfred Edwin' gives a particularly light effect with primrose standards and white, widely flaring falls. 'Pinnacle' is even better with reverse colouring—standards white and falls yellow.

Another colour that looks well with blue is brown and 'Tarn Hows' is a reddish, cedary brown that gives a warm effect in the border. 'Ballet Dancer' is beautiful in a blend of buff, gold, apricot and tan while 'Prior's Crag' is a free-blooming tobacco brown that combines well with such popular pinks as 'Cloudcap', 'Dreamcastle' and 'Party Dress'.

Black is a striking colour among irises. 'Black Forest' is a much-praised iris, but it is not a good 'doer' in every garden and rather subject to rhizome rot. 'Black Hills' is good where 'Black Forest' is weak, strong-growing and combining grand form, size and height; and 'Great Gable' is a good doer, a British raised iris that is more purple in tone.

White irises are difficult to place in an iris border although they look lovely in a herbaceous border or against the dark-green foliage of shrubs. 'Snow Flurry' and 'Cliffs of Dover' are two of the best of the newer varieties. Cream, too, is a lovely colour for irises and easier, perhaps, to place than white. 'Star Shine' is a good iris with a creamy cast and 'Bellerive' though cheaper to buy gives a first-class flower.

Deep red, like black, is a colour that must not be overdone in the iris border or it would create too heavy an effect. For an occasional deep note to highlight the brighter colours it is excellent. 'Ranger' is a fine red, though rather late to flower. For a mid-season variety, more likely to coincide with the flowering of the rest of the border, I would choose 'Technicolor' which is rich ruby velvet in effect.

Of the popular plicatas with their contrasting stitching and stippling there is a choice of colour. The blue and white 'Benton Fandango' is popular while 'Firecracker' in yellow and red and 'Minnie Colquitt' in white and purple are also good.

The later-flowering Siberian irises with their slender stems and graceful, butterfly flowers usually in soft, velvety blues will not do on hot chalky soils. In limy clays, however, they are happy and with the taller *Iris* × *monspur* 'Cambridge Blue', the white and yellow *I. ochroleuca* and the golden *I.* × *monnieri* make valuable plants for moist ground. If your garden is on the chalk downs or on rapidly-drained limestone and you covet these moisture-loving irises it is quite easy to grow them by sinking a plastic bowl into the garden, filling it with good, rich loam and planting your irises therein. It is then easy by regular watering to keep the soil suitably moist.

Like the peonies and irises, most plants which do well on chalk or lime have coarse, strong roots that are able to seek out any available moisture and nourishment in the soil. Such are the hemerocallis or day-lilies, a particularly accommodating genus that will do well in sun or shade, moist soil or dry.

American breeders have taken up the day-lily, producing many richly coloured forms. 'Carved Ivory', the golden 'Doubloon', 'Golden West', 'Red Torch', the bright red 'Ambassador', 'Pink Damask', 'Salmon Sheen', the peach-coloured 'Prima Donna' and 'Painted Lady' in cinnamon and yellow are among the most exciting of the new varieties while the older 'Pink Lady' and the older yellows 'Hyperion' and 'Sirius' are still worth growing, pleasing in colour and very free-flowering.

As might be expected from plants known as day-lilies, the individual flowers of the hemerocallis usually last but a day. Nevertheless each stalk bears a succession of ten or twelve heads and so the flowering period of an established clump is long, many varieties blooming for a month or more in June and July after the tall-bearded irises are over.

Eremuri, the fox-tailed lilies, are among the more exotic plants that do well on chalk or limestone. *Eremurus robustus* flowers in June and throws up graceful spires of pink flowers 1·8 to 2·4 m (6 to 8 ft) high while the spikes of *E. bungei* are 1·5 to 1·8 m (5 to 6 ft) and golden yellow. The Shelford hybrids and Sir Frederick Stern's Highdown hybrids also are good, their colours varying from pale to deep pink, lemon, deep yellow, apricot and white. Eremuri are somewhat expensive to buy, a single root costing from £2·00 according to variety. However, they increase quickly if given full sun and the perfect drainage which is to be found in most gardens on chalk and limestone. Division presents something of a problem but must be tackled before the clumps become overcrowded or they will not flower so well. Five spikes is the limit which each plant should be allowed to carry before being divided. The clumps are very heavy to lift so it is advisable for two people to tackle the raising together, standing on each side with forks which they push straight down into the ground before slowly raising the plant. This avoids breaking the brittle, starfish-like roots which do not spread but go deeply down into the soil or rubble. After lifting, the roots should be put into a shed to dry off. When dry they will divide easily into several crowns and should be replanted with the tops 7·5 or 10 cm (3 or 4 in) below soil-level. It is best, I think, to make a little mound on which the crowns can 'sit', rather as one does with the rhizomes of tall-bearded irises, so that the roots can stretch down into the ground all round. A covering of bracken should be given in winter to ward off frosts.

Border carnations and pinks do so well in sun-baked gardens that really no directions are needed for growing them. On the clay, however, the pinks do well enough but border carnations present a problem, needing full sun and a slightly raised bed if they are to succeed. A layer of ashes placed at ground level with a 7·5-cm (3-in) depth of soil above them is the best recipe for success in a flat, clayey garden. The Allwoodii or perpetual-flowering pinks are especially useful with their large single or semi-double flowers in clear, bright colours often beautifully zoned with maroon or chocolate at the centre. They are intensely fragrant, are seldom entirely without flowers in summer and often yield a few blooms at Christmas. The salmon pink 'Anne', crimson 'Barbara', white 'Blanche', yellow 'Goldfinch', lavender grey 'Hugh', silvery pink 'Margaret' and the lilac 'Susan' with a black centre are all good varieties to choose. The old laced-pinks, their petals edged and lined with a darker colour are popular, too, and may be raised from seed. All the plants from the sowing will not bear double flowers but all will be laced and well worth keeping.

Delphiniums do not as a rule dislike alkaline soils but it is wise to choose the more vigorous varieties. The weaker pinks tend to die out and the Pacific Giants often prove short lived. Poor, chalky soil needs enrichment if it is to grow delphiniums well and particular attention should be paid to watering and mulching with compost or rotted manure. It goes almost without saying that a good proportion of peat or other humus should be incorporated in the soil. Delphiniums, however, do well on treated clay.

Phloxes, those border standbys of late summer, will thrive in a deep limy loam but they are moisture-lovers and rarely succeed on chalk. We find that they give the best results when planted in semi-shade. Campanulas and anchusas, verbascums, veronicas, erigerons, rudbeckias, heleniums and coreopsis all do well on lime or chalk while the kniphofia, or red-hot poker, family is also satisfactory. All kniphofias need good drainage so, if they are to be grown on clay, weathered ash should be incorporated in the site. To my mind the smaller-growing varieties and species such as 'Gold Else', the orange-red *nelsonii,* yellow *galpinii* and ivory-white 'Maid of Orleans' are the most pleasing although a good clump of 'Royal Standard' or some of the tall-growing perpetual-flowering hybrids will give a showy effect. Verbascums are true chalk lovers and with their spiky growth are very effective in the garden scene. Among the best are the statuesque biennial *Verbascum broussa* with its flannelly, grey leaves and candelabras of yellow flowers, the medium-sized *V. nigrum* with green leaves and rich yellow spires, the dwarf *V. phoeniceum* with its spikes of purple, pink or white, the hybrid bronze and lilac 'Cotswold Beauty', 'Pink Domino' and the salmon and bronze 'Cotswold Queen'. Our native mullein, *V. thapsus*, a biennial, with flannelly leaves and tall yellow, single candlesticks, is also worth growing and allowing to seed where it will. It seems to choose the most effective spots.

Michaelmas daisies (asters), of course, are among the autumn standbys of any garden and in the most commonly seen *novi-belgii* section there have been many good introductions of recent years. Grown as they should be, divided each year and with each separate shoot replanted at distances of 15 cm (6 in) apart these will be magnificent indeed. Even with the more casual treatment that the majority of us find time to give they will make a splendid show. 'Mistress Quickly' violet-blue, 'Melbourne Belle' fuchsia purple, 'Orlando' large pink, 'Patricia Ballard' double pink, 'Ernest Ballard' enormous rosy carmine; the ecclesiastical family of the 'Archbishop', 'Bishop', 'Dean', 'Moderator', 'Sexton', 'Rector' and 'Cardinal'; the large-flowered 'Peace', 'Plenty' and 'Prosperity'; deep purple 'Eventide', gay claret 'Twinkle', the new fringed mauve 'Double One', ivory 'Blondie', and 'Choristers' with the shining white look—with none of these can one go far wrong. Some people find them rather tall and leggy, perhaps, for the smaller present-day garden, yet this difficulty can easily be counteracted and staking avoided if the stems are cut down to the height of a foot in June. This will result in an even greater display of flowers.

True dwarfs for the front row or the border of low-growing perennials are the delightful, double, lavender 'Audrey', the purple 'Jean', 'Little Red Boy' and 'Little Pink Pyramid'. These make charming cushions and hummocks of growth and need no staking. They are all better, however, for frequent division.

In very dry gardens many of the Michaelmas daisies succumb to mildew and grow but wretchedly. Here the *amellus* section will do well and are attractive with lighter, more feathery growth. Among the best are the old favourite 'King George' with its extra large single purple flowers, the light pink 'Sonia', 'Advance' in blue-purple, the near-red 'Brilliant' and the light blue *frikartii*. They grow only 60 cm (2 ft) high.

Some of the more informal chrysanthemums are ideal to associate with Michaelmas daisies and for outdoor growing we have found the rubellum varieties excellent. Favourites among them are the orange-vermilion 'Amberline', the brown-madder 'Duchess of Edinburgh', 'Lady in Pink', yellow 'Mary Stoker', deep pink 'Clara Curtis' and 'Red Ensign'. More permanent than the old Koreans they may be planted in autumn or spring and the colours are particularly clear and bright.

For a sunny border that is well-drained but not too dry schizostylis make free-flowering and uncommon clumps. The type bears colourful, glowing crimson flowers at the end of August but the pink 'Mrs. Hegarty' and the lighter, satiny 'Viscountess Byng' are true autumn flowers. They are delightful when associated with *Ceratostigma plumbaginoides*, the gentian blue flowers and spreading growth of which provide a splendid contrast.

Watering on dry, chalky soils and providing adequate drainage to prevent winter damp on limy clays are the main problems that face the grower of herbaceous plants on alkaline soils. Staking, however, is a problem which besets the gardener on any type of soil. Some people use canes and twine, others prefer brushwood, but we find the easiest and most effective method is to bend some strong wire into a circle, cutting off three lengths of similar wire and bending them over the circle to form legs. The length of the legs may be varied according to the heights of the plants it is desired to support and the circles may be saved from year to year. Quickly covered by the growing foliage, we have found these supports both neat and effective.

Herbs as a group mostly appreciate the well-drained light soil found in many chalk or limestone plots. The title 'herb garden' is apt to sound rather grand and perhaps some people may even think it sounds a little dull. They may picture a subdued arrangement of greys and greens—foliage rather than flowers—or feel it is not a sufficiently colourful subject to which to devote precious space.

Yet a herb garden need not be devoid of colour. Restfulness may and should be its keynote but along with the quiet greys of lavender and cotton lavender and the feathery greens of fennel and southernwood, the orange and gold of marigolds may mingle with the brilliant blue borage flowers. Clove carnations may rise from behind a foam of misty catmint, and at midsummer the red, pink, and striped gallica roses will bloom. These old roses have a place in the herb garden for their scent and to provide petals for pot-pourri, rose water and other delights. They will do well on limestone or alkaline clay but on chalk they will need plenty of moist peat around the roots to hold moisture. Mulches of lawn mowings will also help.

The design of the herb garden will depend, of course, upon the space available. The end of a small narrow garden, divided from the rest of the garden by a hedge of old English lavender would be an ideal site, or a herb garden would provide a dignified and delightful treatment for a small front garden, offering a pleasant change from the usual square of turf and narrow-bordered surround. Even the corner of a terrace or a square taken from the end of the lawn and enclosed by dwarf lavender would give room to grow herbs both for garden decoration and for culinary use. Pattern is important to the herb garden. The design, whether square, oblong or round, must be formal. It should be composed of several beds—four for the smallest square. A larger space might have a pattern of four outer beds around a central smaller square. A good lead or stone figure, a sundial or a bird bath would be ideal to make a focal point.

Paths will be easily maintained and look best if they are made of stone or paving, cemented at the joints but with pockets left to hold the delightful pink, red, white and purple prostrate thymes. Turf, gravel, and shingle are alternatives but where possible I would always use paving as the most durable and trouble-saving in the end.

So much for the design. The next question is to decide what plants to grow. These fall into two categories, the scented and decorative—such as the Madonna lilies, the old roses, carnations, catmint, lavender, rosemary, marigolds, the bergamots in purple and scarlet and pink, the various lavenders and rosemary, primroses and cowslips—and the culinary herbs. Some of course may be reckoned in either group. Borage of the gentian blue florets gives its leaves to add to cooling summer drinks. The petals of marigolds may be used in salad. Sage, invaluable in the kitchen, is decorative both in flower and leaf. The annual clary sage should always be grown, for its decorative purple, rose or blue bracts are useful to cut with clove carnations and old roses while the culinary sage may be preferred in its red-leafed or variegated form. *Salvia superba*, too, is invaluable with showy bright blue flower spikes followed by a cloud of red-violet bracts. Mints are many. They range from the round-leafed apple mint, delicious for sauce, to the fragrant eau-de-Cologne mint, peppermint, pineapple mint and the lowly pennyroyal. Thyme in bush form offers several choices. There are also fennel to flavour sauces used with fish, marjoram for forcemeats (both golden-leaved and plain), parsley, winter savory to use in mixed herbs, sorrel for salads and soup, tarragon, parsley, chives, Welsh onions for winter use, lovage for salads and stews, caraway to provide seed for seed cakes and bread, sweet bay, costmary that is good for salads with its taste of mint, angelica to candy, chervil for garnishes, basil, garlic, mace, horseradish, balm—the usefulness and delight of herb gardening is endless and nothing to my way of thinking can add more character and charm to a garden than its herbs.

Few of these herbs present any special difficulties in cultivation but the bergamots with their pleasantly-scented leaves and whorls of bright flowers need more moisture at the roots than most. If used in hot, dry gardens on chalk they should be planted in a sunken plastic bowl provided with drainage holes and filled with good rich loam. They will need frequent watering. In alkaline clays the bergamots will thrive so long as the drainage is good enough to prevent the earth from lying cold and wet in winter. Semi-shade suits them best. It is worth taking trouble to give them the right conditions because when well grown they will throw up strong tall flower stems up to 1 m (3 ft) high.

Clematis as a family are lime-lovers although the large-flowered hybrids find the shallowest chalk soils too arid and lacking in nourishment. There are, however, several attractive herbaceous clematis which will grow well in any alkaline soil provided they are given an annual mulch of rotted manure or good compost. Like all clematis they are coarse rooted and where the subsoil is hard or rocky it must be broken up with a pickaxe or mattock so that the roots may penetrate deeply.

One of the best known of the herbaceous clematises is *Clematis integrifolia* which sends up sturdy, erect stems to a height of 60 cm to 1 m (2 to 3 ft) bearing nodding, urn-shaped, thick-sepalled, flowers of velvety grey-blue. Even better is its offspring —a hybrid with the popular purple-flowered *C.* × *jackmanii*. This hybrid is known as *C.* × *durandii* and its flowers are really lovely, deep violet-blue and as much as 11 cm (4½ in) across. It blooms freely from June to September. As *C.* × *durandii* throws up shoots as long as 3 m (10 ft) in a season it should be given the support of a pillar or a tripod of pea sticks. Not truly herbaceous, the stems do not die down completely in the winter and should be cut back in February to within 60 cm or 1 m (2 or 3 ft) of the ground.

Also good is *C. recta* with masses of small, sweetly-scented white flowers borne in foaming panicles in June and July. In all but the windiest gardens it needs no support, growing sturdily to about 1 m (3 ft) high and each year becoming increasingly floriferous. In fragrance and flower it is a real winner for border interest and should be planted in all gardens on alkaline soil.

Often listed simply as *C. davidiana*, *C. heracleifolia davidiana* is another fine herbaceous clematis with corymbs of widely tubular, deep blue flowers. The variety 'Côte d'Azur' with sky-blue flowers and the pale azure 'Campanile' are two other good forms of this species. All three bloom in August and September and are valuable plants for late summer colour. In addition they are pleasantly scented.

All these herbaceous clematis with the exception of *C.* ×

durandii may be increased by division in early spring. Like all clematis their roots need shade so they should be planted towards the middle or back of the border where their roots may be shaded by smaller front-row plants. Support may be given by pea sticks or a tripod of canes or, in the case of *C. recta,* tall wire circles may be used as described on p. 75. In the mixed border the herbaceous clematis may be planted behind plants with an earlier flowering period, the long growths of the clematis being allowed to trail forward and cover the out-of-flower subjects in front.

SEVEN

Rock Plants and their Needs

Many of the best alpine plants grow in nature on limestone formations and so present little difficulty, so far as soil is concerned,
at any rate to the gardener on limestone or chalk. Most rock plants,
too, need sharp drainage as a protection against winter wet. This
again, on limestone or chalk, raises no problem although the
gardener with clay soils, which are apt to lie cold, will need to
pay particular attention to drainage and to the preparation of
suitable soil mixtures to fill at least those pockets on his rock
garden that are destined for the more tender plants. We find it
satisfactory to mix loam from the top spit which overlies the clay
with an equal quantity of fine chippings to three of leaf-mould or
peat.

Unlike most gardens in hilly limestone districts or on the chalk
downs, our garden was flat, so the more precious of our alpine
plants have to be grown on a raised 'table' bed. This is quite an
advantage because the retaining walling round the raised bed
offers a variety of aspects and homes for trailing plants and also
for such plants as the ramondas and some of the primulas whose
crowns must be protected from winter wet. We used a core of turves
as the centre of our 'table' bed, placing them grass side down and
building up a coffin shape to the height of 75 cm (2½ ft). Next,
using good loam we built the retaining walls, building with a
backward slope or 'batter' and filling in the space at the back with
loam. Each stone was laid as one might lay a brick, using the loam

as mortar, spread on top of each stone and ramming a generous quantity into each joint. We inserted the plants as we built, each in its pocket of good loam, leaving a wider crevice than usual between the stones and making quite sure that no air pockets remained at the back.

Suitable plants for walls at the sunny side of such a bed are *Campanula cochlearifolia*, alpine phloxes of the *subulata* group, *Thymus drucei*, *Sedum cauticola*, *Onosma tauricum* (the almond-scented golden drop with its hanging yellow bells), pentstemons, such as the deep pink *Pentstemon × newberryi* and carmine *P. roezlii* and *Saponaria ocymoides*.

In non-limy soils, of course, the brilliant blue lithospermum would be a 'must' for such a wall and in fact we grew *Lithospermum* 'Grace Ward' in ours without any difficulty. This variety is reputed to be less of a lime hater than the well-known 'Heavenly Blue' but I do not know how it would grow on chalk. It may be that, as in the case of schizostylis, dryness at the root rather than alkalinity is its real enemy and that is why it succeeded in our heavy soil and moderately damp climate. If tried on chalk or limestone it should be given a good handful of moist peat mixed with the soil in which it is planted.

Just as blue as these two species but without the attraction of their open-faced stars, *L. × intermedium* (now *Moltkia × intermedia*) is a lime-lover but it, too, needs humus to succeed.

We did not include rampant growers such as the aubrietas, alyssums and the more vigorous pinks in our low walls. An open pocket on the rock garden or in a slightly raised border is best for them. However, the smaller pinks such as the crimson and pink *Dianthus* 'Dainty Maid', the delightful *D. boydii*, the dense-growing *D. alpinus* with its 2-cm- (inch-) wide rose-coloured flowers, 'Little Jock' with double flowers of apple-blossom pink and the scarlet-crimson 'Fusilier' might be given a place. Oddly enough there are two members of this lime-loving family which will not tolerate lime. They are *D. glacialis* and *D. neglectus*.

Shady wall pockets are as easy to fill as are the sunny ones. Here the golden lambs' tails of *Chiastophyllum oppositifolium* (syn. *Cotyledon simplicifolia*) would be effective. *Ramonda myconi* is lovely with its soft, green leaves and golden-eyed, lavender-blue flowers that always remind me of an African violet. In a shady wall, and given plenty of leaf soil we have always found them easy to please. The haberleas are rather like ramondas but their flowers are borne in drooping umbels. *Haberlea rhodopensis* is a pretty lilac form and *H. virginale* a beautiful white. There are white ramondas, too, but often these are disappointingly muddy in tone. They should be seen in flower before being bought. Primulas as a family are shade-lovers and *Primula marginata* with silvery edged leaves and its varieties are no exception. We grew ours at the top of the wall so that we could more easily heap fresh soil over the stems when they became leggy as they inevitably do. The lavender-flowered *P. m.* 'Linda Pope', the white-eyed 'Marven' and the deeper lavender 'Prichard's Variety' are good ones to choose although they are all lovely. I do not think there is a dud among them.

Larger-flowered than *P. marginata* are the hybrids of *P. rubra* (*pubescens*). Of these I like best the lilac-flowered 'Mrs. J. H. Wilson', although 'The General' in crimson, 'Faldonside', carmine, and the terra-cotta 'Rufus' are also fine.

Drainage in a 'table' bed is naturally good, so for the top a 15-cm (6-in) layer of medium loam mixed with a quarter part of leaf-mould and just topped with chippings is adequate.

The top of a 'table' bed is an ideal place for the smaller saxifrages interplanted with tiny bulbs such as the 7·5-cm (3-in) daffodil *Narcissus asturiensis,* the hoop-petticoats—*N. bulbocodium* and its allies—and the taller, very graceful angel's tears, *N. triandrus albus.* Very early crocuses such as *Crocus ancyrensis* 'Golden Bunch' and the *C. chrysanthus* varieties are attractive, too. I shall go more fully into these in the chapter on bulbs but I would also like to suggest here planting the dwarf early-flowering, bulbous irises such as *Iris reticulata* in its varieties and the brilliant blue *I. histrioides major* on such a raised bed in full sun.

Of the saxifrages one might choose some of the smaller 'mossies' such as the densely tuffeted 'Cloth of Gold' which is named for the colour of its foliage as its flowers are white, and the crimson 'Pixie'. The kabschias or 'cushion' saxifrages are especially suitable for a partly shaded bed or even a north or west dry wall. Of these the sulphur-yellow *Saxifraga* × *elizabethae* is well known. *S.* × *haagii* is smaller, making dense green mats covered with tiny golden stars and *S.* × *jenkinsiae* is a favourite of mine with its close grey cushion above which are borne quite large flowers of a delicate pink. 'Cranbourne' too, is pretty with grey-green cushions and deeper rose flowers. The engleria section is the one over which many people enthuse more than over any other saxifrages but personally I do not care for the Englerias. They seem to me weird and interesting rather than pleasing with their silver-encrusted foliage and tufts of green and silver hairs protruding from their long-necked stalks and making them look like strange sea-monsters rather than flowers. I am sure, however, that my taste is at fault in this, so for those who would like to try them here are a few of the best varieties—*S. grisebachii* 'Wisley', the crimson and pink flowers of which—like those of the rest of the section—are enclosed in baggy encrusted calyces; *S. porophylla* with flowers in purple and pink; *S.* × *frederici-augusti*—claret and pink.

The silver-encrusted Aizoon saxifrages also are popular but not as much to my liking as the mossy and cushion sections of the genus. The flowers themselves are pretty enough but they rise on their slender stems from tiny rosettes of heavily encrusted, silvered foliage which seem either delightful or fussily Victorian according to one's taste. *S.* 'Minutifolia' (syn. *S. aizoon baldensis*) is a dwarf, only 7·5 cm (3 in) high with creamy flowers. *S. aizoon* 'Lutea' is taller with yellow flowers, and *S. a.* 'Rosea' has pink flowers. With more character and undeniably lovely are *S. longifolia* 'Tumbling Waters' with its 45 cm (18 in) spray of large white flowers and the cotyledon saxifrages with similarly long sprays of smaller, starry flowers.

Cyananthus are supposedly lime-haters but we find that the August-flowering *Cyananthus integer* does very well with us on the 'table' bed that I have described. Perhaps it will not stand chalk but it will stand a slight degree of alkalinity. It needs semi-shade and sends out long trailing stems with tiny leaves so that a well-grown plant will cover an area as much as 45 cm (18 in) square. Its flowers are really beautiful—periwinkle-blue and periwinkle-shape with a soft fringe of lighter-coloured hairs at the throat. It should, however, never be planted near gentians as the blues do not tone. I think it is the gentian that suffers by comparison.

Many gentians will not grow on chalk or lime. The August-flowering *Gentiana farreri* and its hybrid *G.* × *macaulayi* will tolerate lime but find chalk too dry. For the typical open rock gardens on sunny chalk or limestone slopes, *G. septemfida* is the gentian to choose and even this needs plenty of humus in the form of moist peat pressed around its roots at planting time so that they never dry out. The flowers of this species are smaller than those of the great asiatics but nevertheless striking, borne in profusion and being of a telling deep blue. *G.* × *hascombensis* is worth growing as it has a longer-flowering period, beginning in July with *G. septemfida* and carrying on well into October. *G. lagodechiana* is very like *G. septemfida* but to my mind of less garden value as its trumpets, carried singly, are not so freely borne.

The spring-flowering *G. acaulis* is difficult in many gardens, often growing well enough but obstinately refusing to flower. It is certainly not a lime-hater because it used to bloom and grow with exceptional freedom in the nearby garden of Gloddaeth Hall, the ancestral home of the Mostyn family, in a few centimetres (inches) of soil overlying pure limestone. I think, however, that limestone may suit it better than chalk. Certainly the limestone rubble seems to hold the water better and in the moist climate of North Wales never completely dries out. Whatever recipes may be given for success with *G. acaulis*, of two things I am sure: it must have full sun and sufficient moisture in spring. Without moisture the flower buds become blind.

One rock plant that is always happy on lime or chalk is the pasque flower—*Pulsatilla vulgaris*—a native of the chalk downs. Several lovely forms of this flower are in cultivation, including a miniature only 15 cm (6 in) high with modestly hanging bells that when pollinated upturn to reveal the depth of deep purple within, centred by its wonderful crown of golden stamens. *P.* 'John Innes' is a much larger form with blue-violet bells almost three times as big, opening from fat, silky-furred buds. There are several vinous-red forms in cultivation, a good large-flowered white, *P.* 'Budapest' which flowers very early and has big, silvery-blue bells and *P. caucasica* which is yellow. *P.* 'Mrs. van der Elst' is a very fine pink. It is rare in cultivation because it is more temperamental than the others. Seedlings from this form, however, are sometimes offered in varying shades of which the pinks are seldom much inferior to the type. The choice alpine species *P. alpina sulphurea* and *P. vernalis* are sometimes said to dislike lime. I have not tried *P. vernalis* but *P. alpina sulphurea* was happy in our former garden mixed with a low proportion of grit. In spring and autumn its silky-furred buds open to wide lemon-yellow bells. I believe that in the Alps this species is found on limestone formations.

The campanulas are on the whole an easy genus and most of them are happy on lime or chalk. An exception is the tiny light blue *Campanula cenisia* which in any case belongs to the more difficult section of scree-dwellers.

Among the irises the tiny *Iris gracilipes, cristata* and *lacustris* will not tolerate much lime; neither will *douglasiana* and *innominata* and their varieties. There is, however, a group of attractive large-flowered dwarf-bearded irises growing from 12·5 to 20 cm (5 to 8 in) high which is ideal for the rock garden. Recently this group has been taken up by the iris breeders and there is now a fine selection from which to choose. Of the reasonably priced varieties 'Blue Pygmy', the bright yellow 'Excelsa', 'Mauve Mist', the coppery-primrose 'Amber Queen', 'Rose Mist', and the petunia-purple 'Stylish' are all good. Of the older sorts still listed, *violacaea, azurea* and *cyanea* are still worth growing.

More difficult is the Juno group of bulbous irises, but a sharply drained pocket on a limestone or chalk rock garden in full sun is the nearest one can come to ideal conditions for them in this country. The Juno irises are rather unusual in appearance, their undeniably lovely flowers being carried above foliage which reminds one of a leek.

Earliest of the group, flowering in January is *I. planifolia* (syn. *I. alata*) with lowly but lovely flowers of lilac blue. It is one of the hardest irises to grow successfully. In warm, sunny parts of the country it may grow and flower reasonably well but should be covered with a flat pane of glass after flowering to ensure rest and ripening. The so-called *I. persica*, of gardens, is only 7·5 cm (3 in) high but exotically beautiful with waved falls of Prussian-blue, ridged with gold, and greeny-blue standards. It is even more difficult to grow than *planifolia* and so is the hybrid of *persica* with *sindjarensis* their turquoise-blue offspring *I.* 'Sindpers'. (Both need the protection of an alpine house or frame. However, the later-blooming *I. magnifica* with bluish-white flowers, *I. bucharica* with satiny-white and yellow blooms and *I. graeberiana* will do quite well on the open limestone or chalk rock garden. They flower from March to April and need a sunny, well-drained, high pocket. They may also be grown under a south-facing wall. Lime-loving, in neutral soil, they need added lime in the form of ground limestone. When happy these three Junos will increase and will need dividing every three years. As soon as the leaves have withered, give the pocket a thorough soaking. This is essential, because if you try to lift the Junos dry, the long, fleshy, carrot-like store roots will break off. Lift the irises carefully from the wet ground, wash the earth from their roots and leave them in a shed or garage for a day or two to dry off. It is then possible to separate the bulbs, carefully disentangling the roots.

Some members of the convolvulus family are particularly suitable for cultivation on lime and chalk rock gardens. Like the irises mentioned they need full sun and sharply drained light soil. *Convolvulus cneorum* is fairly well known for its glistening silver foliage and pink-flushed flowers but the lovely *C. mauritanicus* is not often seen. It is said to be more tender than *C. cneorum* so, for safety's sake, it should be planted with its back to a large, south-facing, sun-reflecting rock. Then, in a sharply drained pocket in full sun it should survive most winters. Against accidents, cuttings may be struck—taking semi-ripe wood with a heel in late July and placing the cuttings in a sand frame or in a pan of sandy compost under a bell-jar or in an indoors window. *C. mauritanicus* may also be easily raised from seed sown in slight heat (the living-room window ledge or the top of a wireless set will do) in spring. *C. mauritanicus* is so pretty that it is worth any amount of trouble. Its convolvulus flowers are periwinkle-blue, about 2 cm (an inch) across and freely borne from the end of July until well into October. In fact, as the season advances the blue seems to deepen. Sending out trailing stems sometimes a yard long in a season this convolvulus is particularly useful to grow behind clumps of aubrieta or arabis so that it may cover their late-summer shabbiness with its neat, small leaves and adorable flowers.

Neither of these convolvuluses is in the least likely to prove invasive but a warning must be given against the commoner *C. althaeoides*. This should never be planted near any small treasures that it might smother. It can become a weed in some gardens.

There are several varieties of clematis too, that can be most attractive in the rock garden, particularly if allowed to scramble over an established bush of rosemary or lavender or to cascade down a large rock. *Clematis alpina* with its pendant, somewhat bell-shaped, blue and white flowers is an obvious choice. Even lovelier are the shaggy-petalled doubles—the powder-blue *C. macropetala* and its pinky lavender variety 'Markham's Pink'. More prostrate is *C. scottiae* with clear pink bells and attractive silvery foliage.

The androsaces or rock jasmines are a choice genus beloved by the collector of alpines. Some, however, dislike lime (notably *Androsace primuloides, carnea* and *wulfeniana*). The more commonly seen *lanuginosa* and *villosa arachnoidea* are less exacting.

Most people know some at least of the delightful mossy phloxes which flower with the androsaces in later spring. The old-fashioned *Phlox subulata*, so often seen, is rather a harsh magenta and I do not care for the newer *P. s.* 'Temiskaming' of similar hue. However, there are some treasures among the softer colours. *P. s.* 'Betty' is pretty in warm soft pink and the cool lavender

P. s. 'G. F. Wilson' is also good. Then there are the *douglasii* varieties which make similar mats of foliage but with finer, needle-pointed leaves. Of these I would choose the silvery-pink *P. d.* 'Rosea', and the pale lilac 'Eva' and 'Boothman's Variety' with telling dark eyes. The lovely shade-loving *P. adsurgens* does not like lime or chalk, but *P. stolonifera* 'Blue Ridge', carrying its delightful flowers on stems 15 cm (6 in) high, will do well enough provided it is planted in peat and leaf-mould with a small rock placed over its roots to prevent them drying out.

Later colour is too often missing in many rock gardens. The rock scabious—*Scabiosa graminifolia* with lavender pin-cushion flowers and silver foliage, and *S. pterocephalus* (sometimes listed as *Pterocephalus parnassii*) with attractive lilac flowers over a mat of grey foliage—are useful to supply late-summer flowers. Lime- and chalk-lovers, they need full sun and will not mind a rather dry place. Sedums are not among my personal favourites but they are undeniably useful as they will grow in the driest and hungriest spots. *Sedum cauticola* with purple flowers in autumn and *S. spathulifolium purpureum* which makes pleasing purple rosettes of foliage and *S. spurium coccineum* are among the best. The scutellarias or skull-caps do well in light chalky or limy soil in sun. They are uncommon and interesting and look much more difficult to grow than in fact they are. *Scutellaria alpina* with violet-blue caps and the bright blue *S. scordiifolia* flower in July and August and are reasonably trouble-free.

Blue flowers always attract notice in the rock garden and some of the best are to be found among the veronicas. *Veronica prostrata* makes sheets of upright 10-cm (4-in) flower spikes in a clear and brilliant blue from May to July. *V. p.* 'Mrs. Holt' is a rich pink cultivar for contrast. *V.* 'Spode Blue' is dwarfer—only 5 cm (2 in) high—and has charming deep blue flowers. Paler in colour with china-blue flowers that are pretty above its prostrate blue-green foliage, *V. telephifolia* is a real treasure while *V.* 'Trehane' has golden leaves and 12·5-cm (5-in) light blue spires. Not strictly a veronica, as the shrubby members of the family now fall under the genus *Hebe*—*Veronica* (or *Hebe*) *hulkeana* is an enchanting rock-shrub for mild areas. With neat, oval leaves and spikes of delightful lavender-blue flowers it is a gem for a well-drained pocket in a sunny spot. Definitely frost tender—it cannot be grown safely in many gardens in Surrey—it should not be attempted away from the sea-coast.

Of the hardy geraniums, many are too vigorous for the average rock garden. However, the following will not grow too big; the pale pink *Geranium farreri* with its dusky, chocolate anthers; *G. sanguineum lancastriense*, a rare native plant, with salver-shaped flowers of a delicate pink; the creeping *G. pylzowianum* with cup-shaped pink flowers; the clear pink *G. dalmaticum* and its white cultivar *G. d.* 'Album'. Interesting, too, is the white herb robert from Wales, *G. robertianum celticum*, with its ferny, filigree foliage and endearing little white flowers.

Long-flowering and ideal for a crevice on the sunny or shady face of a wall is *Asarina procumbens*, a little plant that is full of quality, with decorative hairy leaves and pale yellow snapdragon flowers.

Small shrubs give character to any rock garden and some of the best, the dwarf brooms, find a sun-baked limestone or chalk rock garden very much to their liking. Some of the cytisus genus of the broom family will not grow in chalk but *Cytisus × kewensis* is one that does well. It should be planted just above a large rock where its trailing branches may waterfall down to become in spring a foam of pale, creamy, moonlit flowers. Plant nearby the soft blue-flowered *Ceanothus prostratus* which also needs a sunny, well-drained spot and the the two will give you a memorable colour effect for May.

Genista lydia is another dwarf broom. Of unusual and attractive arching growth it bears bright golden-yellow flowers in late May. Planted nearby, the soft purple *Cytisus purpureus* will make an effective colour contrast.

A similar type of shrublet is *Erinacea pungens*—the hedgehog broom—for which no slope can be too hot and dry. Making a 30-cm- (foot-) high mound and prickly as a porcupine this exceptionally spiny little bush will, when established, become studded beneath the protection of its quills with comparatively large broom-flowers of a lovely violet-blue. Also interesting is the tiny *Carmichaelia enysii*, the many graceful branchlets of which freely carry tiny pea-flowers of lilac-purple.

Most of the daphnes will do well on limy soils. *Daphne cneorum* is a pretty shrublet for a sunny place. It likes to be planted in a peaty pocket and to have its roots under a stone. Then when, in course of time, its stems become leggy and bare, a dressing of good loam and leaf-mould should be sifted over them. The stems then layer as they go giving longer life to the old plant and yielding rooted pieces for new. *Daphne retusa* and *D. tangutica* are taller, reaching 60 cm (2 ft) or more in time but remaining always compact with dark, glossy evergreen leaves and fragrant white and purple flowers in May and earlier. Of the two, *tangutica* is the faster grower and eventually makes the larger plant but both are delightful. *Daphne collina* is another delightful rock garden shrub forming a low, evergreen hummock covered with sweetly-scented pink flowers in spring and again in autumn. These last three are among the most reliable daphnes in cultivation.

With dwarf lavenders, creeping rosemary and perhaps a prostrate juniper or two, these shrublets will help to give the rock garden a furnished look. On the larger rock garden many of the more vigorous alpines may be grown. Helianthemums, hypericums, thrift, iberis, blue and yellow flaxes (linums), gold and lemon alyssum, double arabis, 'Dresden China' daisies and larger pinks of the type of 'Highland Queen', 'Waithman's Beauty', 'Oakington Hybrid', 'Emil Paré' and 'Dubarry', will give lasting colour for most of the season.

An attractive idea is the alpine border. On shallow soils this will not need to be raised, but on clays it should be raised to a height of at least 15 cm (6 in) or more to improve drainage. The soil should be mixed with stone chips, crushed brick or mortar rubble. Then, when this has been thoroughly worked together, about a quarter the bulk of leaf-mould or moss peat should be added. Such a border may follow the line of a path or may outline a herbaceous bed or a bed of shrubs. In it, among strategically placed rocks, the easier and more spreading alpines—aubrieta, alyssum, phloxes, dianthus, campanulas, sedums, and so on may make a delightful pattern of colour for much of the year.

EIGHT

Bulbs, Corms and Rhizomes

Bulbs are usually associated in the mind with spring but there are bulbs that flower at other seasons, too. In fact the bulb gardeners' year might be said to start in August with the writing of the bulb orders. At this time, too, the lovely autumn-flowering section of bulbs begins to bloom.

Suited to a sunny place on marl and clay as well as to the garden on chalk or limestone, the imposing crinums are bulbs that need plenty of room. Well-grown bulbs are nearly the size of a football and throw up a correspondingly large mass of handsome soft green, strap-shaped leaves. Massive umbels of trumpet-shaped flowers open above the stout stems in August. *Crinum* × *powellii*, the hardy member of the genus, is a clear and shining pink. There is a deeper, rose-coloured form and also a white, *C.* × *p.* 'Album' that is lovely against the dark green mass of cypress or yew or the decorative pinnate foliage of some of the larger mahonia species. Like many South African bulbs, crinums need moisture if they are to do their best. They are fully hardy but need a sunny spot in rich deep soil. In extremely cold gardens they might benefit from being planted in front of a sunny wall. Such positions are usually dry and so a bucket of water should be thrown over the clump at least twice a week. Shallow soils should have the underlying rock well broken up and plenty of compost and loam added before planting.

I have seen it stated that South African bulbs will not tolerate lime. This really is nonsense. Crinums, agapanthus, amaryllis, all flourish in several extremely chalky gardens while in our own limy clay we grew these and others without any difficulty. As I said earlier when talking about another South African genus, schizostylis, it is the need for moisture which is often not understood and this leads to failures for which the calcium content of the soil is wrongly blamed.

In warm gardens, the watsonias also may be tried and with their loose spikes of scarlet or rose tubular flowers and gladiolus-like leaves they are very handsome. In heavy soils, sand should be mixed with the soil during planting. They are not fully hardy, however, and should not be attempted in colder areas or soil which lies wet in winter although like most other South Africans they need summer moisture.

The amaryllis or belladonna lily is not as reliable in flower as are the crinums. It flowers in August and September before the leaves appear and the pink and white, funnel-shaped flowers, though attractive, always seem to me to have a naked and unfinished appearance. Like the crinums, the amaryllis needs moisture and a sunny spot. In fact it is lack of one or both of these that often leads to failure to flower. Unfortunately, sunny places in the garden are often dry, so to help achieve the necessary moisture a deep mulch of damp peat should be given before the ground dries out in spring. By acting like a blanket the mulch will help them to retain the moisture in the soil.

Nerines are more certain in flower than the amaryllis and with loose heads of rich pink flowers with curling narrow petals they have a more graceful and airy appearance than the rather stolid-looking belladonna lilies. *Nerine bowdenii* is not absolutely hardy in all districts and should be given a site at the base of a south wall where the soil has been enriched with well-rotted manure. The bulbs should be planted with their necks just above the surface—so a covering of leaves or dried bracken should be given in winter as protection against frost. In late August when the bulbs are preparing to flower they will need water.

Agapanthus praecox is hardy with protection in most districts and does well in soil that can be kept moist during the summer months. A covering of bracken loosely applied during the winter will give protection and rot down to provide food. The Headbourne Hybrids do not need even this care.

In cold districts it may be safer to delay planting South African subjects until spring.

Delightful to edge a bed of the taller bulbs such as the crinums and nerines, the little flower of the west wind, *Zephyranthes candida,* will grow and yield an increase of its white crocus-like flowers in a sunny spot where sand should be added if the soil is heavy. The clumps divide easily and the bulbs flower better if the clumps are frequently split up. *Sternbergia lutea,* sometimes alluded to as the lily of the field of the Bible, yields larger crocus flowers of daffodil gold. Not all forms are free-flowering and *S. l. angustifolia* is the variety upon which to insist. Loving a hot, dry ledge where it can be sunbaked, a pocket in the chalk or limestone rock garden is the ideal spot for the sternbergia where it should be allowed to remain undisturbed until it becomes overcrowded.

In October in a similar spot that unseasonable snowdrop *Galanthus nivalis reginae-olgae* comes into flower before its leaves. It comes from Greece and like all the eastern members of its genus does best in full sun with sharp drainage. Whether or not the idea of snowdrops in October appeals to you, the autumn crocuses have been with us so long that they now seem natural and right at that time of the year. Here, however, some confusion exists because the name autumn crocus has so often been attached to the colchicum or meadow saffron, which is a member of the lily family, instead of to the true crocus of autumn which, like those of winter and spring, belongs to the iris group.

Crocus speciosus is one of the stars of autumn, with its large chalices of deeply-veined bright blue, each lit by flaming orange stigmata. There is a charming white variety *C. s. albus* while the china-blue *C. s.* 'Aitchesonii' and the darker *C. s. globosus* flower later, so giving a succession.

C. kotschyanus (*zonatus*) flowered in early September, just before

C. speciosus, in our garden, but its rosy-lilac flowers are washy in effect compared with the vivid and lovely blue of *C. speciosus*. *C. sativus*, the crocus from which saffron used to be gathered, flowers in November and is useful for that reason. Its purplish lilac flowers are delicately feathered with violet and enhanced by the long blood-red stigmata. With it a few of the more expensive snowy-white *C. niveus* give a splendid contrast.

Unfailing in flower these crocuses of autumn are rather frail in petal and should be planted in a spot sheltered from the wind but where every gleam of the autumn sun will catch them and make them expand their dancing cups.

The colchicums are sturdier than the crocuses. Sturdier, too, are their foot-long, thick, strap-like leaves which rise in May and June and may become a nuisance in tidy garden-beds or even on the rock garden. Beneath shrubs their leaves will not be noticed or one may plant the bulbs in grass, but where this is done cutting must be postponed until the last of their leaves has completely yellowed and died down. Colchicums are more expensive to buy than most of the crocuses but each bulb when established yields many flowers and they increase freely. From half a dozen bulbs of one species a colony will soon be formed and they are lovely indeed when their jewelled chalices expand in the September sunshine.

Colchicum speciosum bornmülleri is one of the earliest and best, with large flowers of rich rose-lilac with a white centre. *C. speciosum* is also good, while its later-flowering white variety, *C. s. album*, is very fine indeed. *C. agrippinum* is a chequer-board flower, its petals tessellated in rose-purple and white, giving a very pretty and showy effect. However, *C. autumnale*, the true naked ladies of the countryside, seem leggy, thin of cup and poor in quality beside these other gems.

Colchicums need better soil than the crocuses and where this is poor and shallow as on chalk they should each be given a 20-cm (8-in) flowerpotful of good loam to start them off.

The soil can scarcely be too poor for the delightful, winter-flowering *Iris unguicularis* (*stylosa*). High lime-content and a sun-baked place on the rockery or beneath a south-facing wall are ideal and there this iris will, from among its clump of narrow, untidy leaves, freely produce a succession of large, delicately scented, wistaria blue flowers splotched at the hafts with ermine and lined and powdered with gold. This iris is such a gem that it should be in every garden. Watering in summer prevents the rest and sunbaking that are essential to its flower production. A rich soil promotes foliage growth at the cost of flowers. Slugs and snails are its enemies and for them a death feast of powdered meta fuel or metaldehyde slug pellets, mixed with bran or tea-leaves should be put down at the end of October. Then in November or December, according to the season and situation, the tightly furled buds appear and may be pulled (not cut) to open indoors or left to decorate the garden.

Other winter-flowering bulbous irises will do well on the rock garden. Both *I. histrioides major* and *I. reticulata* are easy to grow, provided you have a sunny, well-drained spot in which to plant them. There the bulbs must remain undisturbed to receive the summer rest and sun-ripening which will ensure their flowering freely next year. In the west and north, or in a wet season, this aim may be furthered by placing a pane of glass over the bulbs when the foliage has died down.

Even a small group of *I. histrioides major* will make a splash of brilliant blue to dispel the gloom of early February and three bulbs of *I. reticulata* Cantab make a useful contrast with a group of the cheaper reddish-purple *I. r.* 'J. S. Dijt'. Violet-scented, *I. reticulata* flowers a month later than *I. histrioides major* and is pleasant grouped with the snowdrops and early crocus of the *chrysanthus* type.

These little *chrysanthus* crocuses are among the merriest of winter flowers and like the little irises they enjoy a limy soil. We grow them in grass that is cut with shears or scythe when the leaves die down but they will do just as well in the rock garden, in paving, on top of a dry wall or to border a path or bed. If they are set in grass it is as well not to use a mower on the area. The little bulbs lie very near the surface and may be pulled out by the machine.

There are many lovely named varieties of *Crocus chrysanthus* in blues and yellows, cream and marigold, white feathered with purple, and yellow varnished almost all over with brown so that it is not until the flower expands in the sun that one sees the glowing gold of the interior. We have found, however, that a purchase of mixed seedling bulbs gives all these varieties. Perhaps they are not quite so fine as the named forms but nevertheless they give us a lot of pleasure and for my part I think one would find it hard to differentiate between the best of our seedlings and the flowers of named bulbs at more than double the price.

Earlier to flower than *C. chrysanthus*, *C. ancyrensis* (often listed by the less botanically minded of nursery men simply as 'Golden Bunch') is a tiny but very bright golden crocus that yields from ten to twenty flowers from a single bulb. Liking a hot, well-drained place, it is one of those bulbs adapted by nature to a sun-baked pocket on a limestone or chalk rock garden.

Best known of these little early crocuses is probably *C. tomasinianus* with chalices of soft amethyst that look ghost-grey until they open. Plant these pale forms and also the deeper purple 'tommies' in a sunny, well-drained spot and three years later they will give you the most delightful of garden surprises by flowering from odd crevices and crannies all over the garden. They will also succeed in grass.

Some snowdrops, like the species crocus, enjoy hot, dry positions. Others, including *Galanthus nivalis* that sheets the ivy-covered floor of so many Welsh woodlands with white, prefer semi-shade and a leafy soil. All snowdrops are more easily established if planted in February or March as soon as the flowers have faded instead of as dry bulbs in autumn.

If your garden is one of those hilly downland gardens with soil that quickly dries out you are more likely to succeed with the large-flowered, grey-leaved *G. elwesii* than with *G. nivalis*. However, the Christmas-flowering *G. n. cilicicus* will do well on a sunny ledge or at the edge of a droughty, sun-baked border. So will *G. caucasicus*, a fine, large-flowered snowdrop with broad, grey-green leaves. There is a January-flowering form of this species and another which flowers later, in March.

Snowdrops like lime and chalk and there are many from which to choose if you want to specialize in these enchanting flowers. *G. byzantinus* flowers in January and February and like the other easterners it needs full sun. The shorter-stemmed *G. ikariae* and its subspecies *G. i. latifolius* also like rock garden conditions.

Among the shade-loving *G. nivalis* varieties there are some particularly fine forms. Not everyone likes double flowers but the double snowdrop has an old-world charm and, moreover, is not expensive to buy. Endearing, too, is *G. n.* 'Scharlokii', its long, divided spathe giving the effect of a donkey's or rabbit's ears above the drooping bell. *G. n.* 'Viridapicis' is distinctive with a green spot at the tip of each petal. In *G. n.* 'Merlin' and 'Colesbourne' these markings extend from base to apex of the inner segments giving the effect of a snowdrop with a green inner bell. *G. n.* 'Allenii' is a splendid large-flowered form with solid petals of great substance, its flower three times the size of that of the common type. *G. n.* 'Atkinsii' is another well-known form but the flowers are sometimes imperfect. The 'Straffan' snowdrop is not quite so large in flower but often yields two blooms from each bulb. But perhaps the giant *G.* 'S. Arnott' is the most reliable and attractive of all. All these 'giants' increase best in a sunny place but they do need some leaf-mould in the soil to hold moisture. *Leucojum vernum*, the more substantial snowflake, appreciates similar conditions to the *nivalis* section of snowdrops.

Winter aconites, like snowdrops, find chalk and limy soils agreeable. Like the snowdrops, too, they are difficult to establish unless moved just after their flowers fade. In our garden the common winter aconite *Eranthis hyemalis* never flowered. We tried again with the larger *Eranthis × tubergenii* and found this more ready to oblige. It was worth persevering because the sunny golden flowers above their green Toby ruffs are a happy sight. It should be noted that while *E. hyemalis* enjoys the shade, *E.* × *tubergenii* does best in a sunny place.

Another early flower which enjoys sun and lime is *Anemone blanda* with its wide-rayed, 'daisy' flowers in blues and pinks which look particularly gay in the February sun. Its Italian cousin, *A. apennina,* flowering a month later, has flowers of bright blue or white and does well in sun or shade.

Grass is surely the best of all settings for daffodils. The dancing gold of some of the trumpet varieties, the creams and oranges of the 'red-cups', and the ghostlier whites, are seen to perfection against a background of green.

To get the best effect the drifts should be roughly boat-shaped so that the mower will pass by easily on either side. Most of us fall back on the old trick of throwing the bulbs gently forward and planting them where they lie. However, when choosing a site for a natural planting it is important to remember that the grass in which the bulbs are set should not be cut until the foliage has died away in June. This is essential because the bulbs need the nutriment from the dying leaves if they are to flower well the following year.

Some daffodils naturalize better than others. Fortunately, these are usually the older and cheaper varieties.

The yellow, large-cupped 'Carlton', and 'John Evelyn' with its pale perianth and attractive ruffled apricot cup, are two reasonably-priced varieties that succeed in grass. The sturdy white-trumpet, 'Mount Hood', thrived well with us. Although old-stagers now, 'Winter Gold', 'Flower Carpet' and 'Golden Spur' are as effective as any. They are strong and reliable and increase easily. Of the late-flowering narcissi, the old 'Pheasant's Eye' is splendid when naturalized. Slow to start, after a year or two it increases freely to yield its white, sweet-scented, gently-recurving blooms.

Lovely though these large kinds are, my favourites are among the smaller daffodils. *Narcissus obvallaris,* the Tenby daffodil, is one of the earliest, flowering before the larger varieties have crooked their heads. Only 25 cm (10 in) high, its smaller, golden flower is perfectly formed with a pleasingly rolled-back brim to

BULB PLANTING LIST

Genus and species	Order	Plant	Depth	Distance apart	In flower
Agapanthus praecox	Nov. to Feb.	April	cover crowns with soil	45 cm (18 in)	June–Sept.
Alliums	August	Sept.–Oct.	9·5 cm (3 in)	7·5–15 cm (3–6 in)	Summer
Amaryllis belladonna	July and Aug.	September	10 cm (4 in)	23 cm (9 in)	August
Anemone blanda	July	September	5 cm (2 in)	7·5 cm (3 in)	Feb. and Mar.
Anemone apemina	July	September	5 cm (2 in)	7·5 cm (3 in)	April
Colchicum	June and July	July–Aug.	5 cm (2 in)	10 cm (4 in)	Sept.–Oct.
Crinum × powellii	Nov. to March	April	15 cm (6 in)	30 cm (12 in)	Aug.–Sept.
Crocus (autumn flowering)	June and July	July–early Aug.	7·5 cm (3 in)	7·5 cm (3 in)	Sept.
Crocus (winter flowering)	July and Aug.	September	7·5 cm (3 in)	7·5 cm (3 in)	Jan. and Feb.
Crocus (spring flowering)	August	September	7·5 cm (3 in)	7·5 cm (3 in)	Jan. and Feb.
Eranthis (winter aconite)	July and Aug.	Sept. (Spring is better if you can get them)	2·5 cm (1 in)	5 cm (2 in)	January
Fritillaria	August	September	7·5 cm (3 in)	15 cm (6 in)	April
Galanthus (snowdrop)	January	Spring	7·5 cm (3 in)	7·5 cm (3 in)	Jan. to Mar.
Galtonia candicans	Jan. or July	Mar. or Sept.	15 cm (6 in)	30 cm (12 in)	August

Gladioli species	Jan. or Feb.	March (Lift and dry in October in heavy soil or cold areas)	7 5 cm (3 in)	15 cm (6 in)	July
Iris unguicularis	Nov. to Feb.	Spring	Cover rhizomes with soil	30 cm (12 in)	Nov.–April
Iris histrioides and *reticulata*	August	September	5 cm (2 in)	5 cm (2 in)	Early Feb. and March
Iris Oncocyclus and Regelia sections	July–August	October	2·5 cm (1 in)	30 cm (12 in)	April and May
Iris (Dutch, etc.)	August	Sept. and Oct.	7·5 cm (3 in)	15 cm (6 in)	May
Lilium candidum	July–August	September	2·5 cm (1 in)	30 cm (12 in)	June to July
Other lilies	July–August	November (May also be planted in spring)	10 cm (4 in)	30 cm (12 in)	Summer
Narcissi	July	Aug.–Sept.	10–15 cm (4–6 in)	10–15 cm (4–6 in)	Spring
Nerine	June–July or February	Aug.–Sept. or March	10 cm (4 in)	45 cm (18 in)	Sept.–Oct.
Tulip species	August	Sept.–Oct.	12·5 cm (5 in)	15 cm (6 in)	Spring
Sternbergia	July	August	10 cm (4 in)	15 cm (6 in)	Autumn
Zephyranthes	July	July–August	7·5 cm (3 in)	23 cm (9 in)	Autumn

the trumpet. The Tenby daffodil is quickly established. It will flower from the first year of planting and increases well. With us a dozen bulbs yielded forty flowers within four years of planting.

Just as appealing, though by no means perfect of form, the Lent lily, *Narcissus pseudo-narcissus,* is usually shy to flower for a season or two. It is happy on a grassy bank, or in light woodland. When once it is really established it will give plenty of its pale perianthed blooms on their lowly 15-cm (6-in) stems. In North Wales where it is happy it grows in its thousands. Sheets of the small, dancing flowers on the slopes of Tal-y-Fan in the Conway valley have earned it the name of 'Daffodil Mountain'.

Unfortunately, *Narcissus cyclamineus* does not do well in dry, limy soils. It needs a moister, peaty spot. Its hybrids 'February Gold', 'March Sunshine' and 'Peeping Tom' are more accommodating. They are not, however, bulbs for grass. At the front of a bed or in good soil at the forefront of shrubs is the place for them. Like most daffodils *N. cyclamineus* and its hybrids do well in clay.

The little hoop-petticoat daffodils do not succeed in dry, chalky or limy soils but *N. triandrus albus*—the angel's tears daffodil with its elfin, turned-back ears and drooping creamy bell is more likely to succeed. Its hybrids, 'April Tears' and 'Raindrops' take kindly to the chalkiest soils and are very real treasures for any gardener who appreciates charm and grace.

Sunny, well-drained chalky gardens are ideal for many of the species tulips. Coming as they do from Eastern Europe they need such a position if they are to flower and increase freely. This does not mean that they will not succeed in more acid soils. It is the sharp drainage and sun-baked position that is essential. These tulips vary in size from the 7·5-cm (3-in) high *Tulipa tarda* (*dasystemon*) with its short-stemmed starry white and yellow flowers to the large blazing scarlet bloom of *T. eichleri* and of *T. fosteriana* and its hybrids. In between come the lovely little *T. chrysantha*—buff and rose-carmine on the outside and buttercup gold within—the coppery *T. hageri, T. clusiana,* the pink and white 'sugar-stick' tulip, the taller *T. marjolettii* with its dainty primrose blooms, the pink *T. saxatilis* which increases by underground stolons, and the earth-hugging *T. linifolia,* the glossy scarlet flowers of which associate so well with the yellow of *T. batalinii.* There is also the whole race of *kaufmanniana* hybrids in their various attractive shades.

In clays such as ours was, it is the ordinary garden tulips which do well. We could plant a group of Darwins or Cottage Tulips and leave them undisturbed for years, confident that they would increase and flower each season. I am not sure, however, whether this would work so well in colder districts.

The gay and useful Dutch and Spanish irises do well in most soils provided they do not lie too wet and cold in the winter but the later-flowering English iris needs a moist and shady spot if it is to become established.

Not so often seen as they might be, the interesting and attractive fritillarias are at home in alkaline conditions. With its 'crown' of drooping yellow or orange bells surmounted by a tuft of grassy foliage, the crown imperial, flowering at daffodil time, is just the type of stately and uncommon plant to add character to a border of cottage flowers. *Fritillaria meleagris,* the fritillaria of certain Oxfordshire meadows, is of a meeker charm. Its white or chequerboard bells might well have been carried by any of the fairy lantern-bearers in the illustrations of one's childhood books.

Less glamorous, perhaps, but with a charm of their own, many of the alliums or ornamental garlics with their tasselled or spherelike heads of starry flowers strike a note of distinction in the garden. Hardy, long-lived and accommodating in any soil they deserve to be planted much more widely than they are at present. One of the first to flower, in May, is *Allium karataviense* with broad flat leaves and globe-like heads of rosy-pink flowers. Also in May blooms the taller purple-lilac *A. aflatunense* with densely rounded heads. *A. moly* was a favourite in old-world gardens with handsome glaucous leaves and umbels of bright yellow flowers on foot-high stalks in June. Much taller and rather imposing is *A. rosenbachianum* with its light purple flowers on 1-m (3½-ft) stems while the 60-cm (2-ft) *A. azureum* and *A. albopilosum* in sky-blue and lilac respectively flower still later at the end of June and well into July.

There are few gardens in Britain where the exotic Oncocyclus irises may be said really to succeed. Usually they dwindle and fail to flower but in the chalk or limestone gardens in sunny parts of the country there is more chance of establishing them than anywhere else. True lime-lovers, a calcareous soil suits them well. They should have the sunniest place in the garden—a bed against a south wall is ideal—and perfect drainage. Then, in spring, when they are beginning to grow freely, they should be given frequent drenchings with water—a bucketful at a time.

In some upland gardens the drainage will be sharp enough even for these eastern natives. Elsewhere a raised bed should be prepared, rising on a foundation of broken bricks or stones and ashes. On top of this drainage layer add 20–23 cm (8 or 9 in) of good soil mixed with ground chalk or limestone rubble, bringing the bed to a height of about 45 cm (18 in) above the soil level of the surrounding garden. This may be attractively edged with a low retaining wall in which onosmas, *Lithospermum × intermedium* (now *Moltkia × intermedia*) and the more compact dianthus will do well. The rhizomes should be planted in October, being set about 2 cm (inch) below the surface and covered with cloches to keep off the winter damp. In March the cloches should be removed but they should be replaced again as soon as flowering is over to concentrate the sun's rays on the plants and ensure the thorough baking of the rhizomes essential to the next year's flower production as well as to keep off summer rain and so enforce the complete rest that is necessary.

Iris susiana, the mourning iris, is probably the best known of the Oncocyclus irises and is much sought after by flower arrangers. The large flowers of this iris are borne on stalks only 30 cm (a foot) high. The standards are rounded and immense, and the falls slightly drooping. These striking blooms are soberly coloured —veined and dotted with black on a grey ground with a diffuse hairy beard and the dark signal patch on the falls that is the badge of the group.

Still more exotic and even more difficult to grow is *I. gatesii,* its flowers veined and dotted with purple on a ground of greenish white giving an effect that is more appealing in its strangeness, to my eye at any rate, than *I. susiana's* widow's weeds.

I. lortetii is the easiest to grow of the Oncocycli and is one of the most pleasing, with flowers of pale lavender thickly speckled with reddish-violet to give an effect of silvery pink overall.

The Regelia irises are a little easier than the Oncocyclus group and will do well on a sunny well-drained limestone or chalk rock garden. Even these will flower better if covered with a cloche after flowering to ensure ripening and rest.

I. hoogiana is a beauty with gold-bearded, smooth-petalled flowers of lavender-blue on 45-cm (18-in) stems and there is a form with pale bronze standards and purple blue falls, taller and equally attractive.

I. stolonifera is striking with light violet standards veined and edged with brown, and white-veined, purple-brown falls with bright blue signal patches. It has all the strange appeal of the Oncocycli but is much easier to grow. *I. flavissima* is a dwarf of this section and holds its yellow flowers on only 7·5-cm (3-in) stems. It is a gay and sparkling little iris, its horizontally-flared falls being set off by a brilliant orange beard. If left undisturbed in a dry, sunny place it will flower freely for years.

I. korolkowii needs moister conditions and should be planted at the bottom of the rock garden with peat added to the soil to retain moisture. It is beautiful, but cold, with a white ground veined with purple-grey and with dark velvety signal patches at the base of the falls.

Hybrids between the Oncocyclus and Regelia sections are in commerce. Most of them have the more amenable and more freely-flowering disposition of the Regelia parent combined with the exotic distinction of the Oncocycli. 'Isis', 'Charon', and 'Luna' are three good ones and it is possible to purchase mixed hybrids at a cheaper rate. They flower with their parents in late April and May.

Some of the species gladioli flower in early summer and are not difficult to grow in well-drained soil in the milder parts of the country where they need not be lifted at the end of the season. These wild gladioli are slender and graceful, more like the *colvillei* hybrids in appearance than the monsters of late summer which look more at home in the vegetable garden than elsewhere. The hybrids, however, look well among shrubs. Usually obtainable are the cream-coloured *Gladiolus tristis* which has a very sweet scent, the rose-pink *G. communis,* carmine *G. segetum, G. byzantinus,* showy in unashamed magenta and its lovely white form, *G. b. albus.*

Supreme among lime-loving bulbs is the Madonna lily. Yet, even on the limestone it loves, *Lilium candidum* can be a temperamental beauty. Botrytis is its enemy. The Salonika form is the type to plant to avoid this menace. Cottage gardens used always to grow this lily to perfection—the secret, I suspect, being the liberal doses of slops, tea-leaves and soapsuds administered to it in turn with other cherished plants. Certainly the soapsuds would help to combat botrytis and tea-leaves are a tonic which I find never fails to improve any ailing plant. *L. candidum* should be planted no more than 2·5 cm (1 in) deep in September when growth begins. It need full sun and an airy position.

Lilium regale will succeed in either acid or alkaline soils so long as its basic needs are met. *L. regale* is vigorous and trouble-free, reliable in bloom, attractive in scent, and has large open trumpet-flowers, gold-throated and lined outside with pink. The rules for success with this lily are simple but strict. If you follow them, provided that you have purchased sound bulbs—well supplied with basal roots—from a reputable bulb merchant you cannot go wrong. First, drainage: all lilies need good drainage. In a heavy clay soil a raised bed should be prepared. In loamy soils the digging of a hole 60 cm (2 ft) deep by 60 cm (2 ft) square will give a site for three lilies. At the bottom of the hole place a layer of stones, broken crocks or clinker and fill in with a compost of turf loam, leaf-mould or moist peat and grit. On shallow chalk or limestone omit the drainage layer. Well-rotted manure may be added under the bulbs. Each bulb should be placed on its own little cone of sand. This will help to prevent rot and I always like to put sand around and over the bulbs as well. The tops of the bulbs should be about 10 cm (4 in) below soil level. November is the best time to plant and it is wise to choose a site among dwarf shrubs which will protect the young lily growth from frosts as well as supplying necessary shade to the lower part of the stem. *L. regale* is stem-rooting—that is, the stem sends out feeding roots as it grows so it should not be planted too deeply, 75 cm (3 in) is ideal and a nourishing mulch of leaf-mould or compost, added in spring after growth begins, will be beneficial.

The popular tiger lilies will grow only on acid soils. There are, however, some hybrids between the tiger lily and lime-tolerant species which will grow in alkaline soils. Known as the Mid-Century Hybrids they are vigorous and easy. They flower earlier than the old *tigrinum*, in June and July. Unfortunately, some of the newer varieties are still expensive to buy, but one of the best, 'Enchantment', which may bear as many as sixteen upright flowers of vivid nasturtium red, may usually be bought at a modest price.

Hybrid lilies like many other hybrids often prove more vigorous than the species from which they are raised. Two strains which were successful in our garden were the Bellingham Hybrids and the *Marhan* crosses, both of which bear generous candelabras of recurving turkscap flowers in varying shades of buff and orange. Similarly reasonable and vigorous is 'Edna Kean', one of the Preston strain with dark, healthy foliage and re-curved flowers of deep orange red.

More expensive, the Golden Clarion strain is a fine breed of yellow trumpet lilies of the *regale* type in colours ranging from clear lemon yellow, through champagne and buttercup, to deepest gold. Some are self-coloured and others striped on the outside with brown and claret.

L. henryi is an autumn-flowering species which succeeds on lime and with its orange-yellow turkscaps spotted with brown it may be used to replace the calcifuge tiger lilies. *L. speciosum* and its varieties *rubrum*, *melpomene* and *roseum*, exotically spotted and shaded with varying degrees of rose and wine colour, surprisingly enough did well in our limy clay. Both this species and *L. henryi* flower too late to be successful in cold northern districts.

For those who admire lilies with an upturned trumpet, the *maculatum* group offers an easily-grown range of attractive bulbs. 'Alice Wilson' is an old favourite and a very good flower in clear golden yellow with chocolate-brown anthers. 'Mahogany' is a self-coloured mahogany crimson, while *bicolor* is vivid orange shading to scarlet. *Alutaceum* is popular and free-flowering with black-spotted flowers in apricot to light yellow. All flower in early June and may well be followed by the equally easy and accommodating *umbellatum* group. Ranging in colour from yellow and apricot to orange, gold, vermilion, and mahogany, all are good and any specialist catalogue will list a number of varieties from which to choose.

A very easy race of lilies, bred from the Canadian hybrids mingled with the Connecticut strains, has recently been introduced by a group of young enthusiasts in Cheshire. Propagated on their land, these bulbs are now available in variety to British gardeners. Hardy and extremely easy, they will do well in almost any soil, provided they are given a rich, friable compost. Well-rotted garden compost or stable manure mixed with moist peat, leaf-mould and rotted bracken suits them well. Heavy clays should be lightened with sand. Once suited, these lilies, which flower in succession from June to early August, will increase readily, building themselves up into one of the most spectacular successes of the garden. Catalogues may be obtained from Cheshire Bulb Farms Ltd., Maynestone Rd., Chinley, via Stockport, Cheshire.

Easier to grow, however, than the easiest lily, the summer hyacinth *Galtonia candicans* is a majestic flower for any garden. I think, though, that its 1·2-m (4-ft) spikes of solid-textured bells look best grouped at the forefront of shrubs so that the dark background may throw their ivory spires into full relief.

Opportunities to use bulbs in garden planning are often neglected because ordering is forgotten and so the necessarily stringent planting times are missed. Reliable bulb merchants often will not despatch bulbs once the optimum time for planting is past. Late planting of bulbs such as daffodils and narcissi which are widely obtainable until too far into the winter may lead to disappointing results. It is particularly important to order and plant the summer- and autumn-flowering bulbs at the correct time, too, so for this reason I have included a bulb planting list (pages 100 and 101), with notes as to the latest reasonable time for ordering the bulbs.

NINE

Lime-tolerant Trees

As a lover of shrubs and trees, I think the garden is always at its most interesting in the winter because then, undistracted by vivid colour, one can appreciate the few subjects that are in flower to the full. Some of the finest trees for lime and chalk, flower in the winter, in all but the bleakest districts transforming the dead months of the year into a time of promise and delight. There are of course people who are not interested in winter gardening but most true gardeners think as I do and consequently get great pleasure from their gardens in winter.

One of the most pleasing of winter-flowering trees is an evergreen and particularly striking in the fact that although a member of the great *Ericaceae* family, along with the rhododendrons and heaths, unlike them it has no dislike for lime. *Arbutus unedo* in common with other arbutuses thrives on alkaline soils. Its flowers are waxen ivory urns which it carries among its warm green leaves in December while at the same time bearing the previous season's orange-red fruit. There is a pink-flowered form of this tree known as *A. u.* 'Rubra' which is lovely with its rose-pink bells and dark red 'strawberries'. Even more beautiful is the autumn-flowering *A.* × *andrachnoides* with similar dark leaves and showier clusters of ivory bells but making a tall tree with particularly handsome shaggy, reddish bark.

All the flowering cherries like lime and one of the most delightful flowers in November, *Prunus subhirtella* 'Autumnalis' is seen up and down the country in a few gardens but although it is frequently mentioned in articles and books it is not planted nearly as widely as it should be. Opening in bursts of bloom in any mild spell throughout the winter, the November cherry gives much pleasure. There are two forms; the type with frilly white flowers and *P. s.* 'A. Rosea' which blooms in a cloud of rosy blush. Although sharp frosts kill the open blossom there are always more buds to follow, yet at no time does the flowering seem sparse. Blooming as it does through the winter and finishing its season with a grand burst of bloom in March, there are few small trees more worthy of garden space.

For favoured gardens or to grow against a sheltered south wall *P. mume* 'Beni-shi-don' is a Japanese apricot that flowers in February, its branches spangled with shapely cream-stamened flowers of deep, velvety, cherry-crimson. To add to its delights this apricot has a strong fragrance of hyacinths. The buds will open in water and the flowers last well. Its branches should be pruned back by a third after flowering and this can pleasantly be achieved by cutting bloom for the house.

The flowering peaches do not take kindly to chalk but on deeper soils do not resent the presence of lime. For a reasonably loamy soil the February-blooming *P. davidiana* 'Alba' is beautiful with rounded white blossoms followed by slim pale green leaves. This is not a tree for bleaker gardens. In such exposed places *Cornus mas*, the cornelian cherry, although not necessarily a lime-lover, and certainly not a cherry, will thrive equally as well on alkaline as on acid soils. Of bushy form, this cornus species may grow in time to 6 m (20 ft) and so must rank as a tree. Its flowers take the form of tiny yellow stars, very freely borne. The flowers are followed in summer by the round, red, cherry-like fruits that give the tree its English name.

I am not a champion of almonds, despite the beauty of their blossom, because in so many districts, together with the peaches, they fall victim to peach-leaf curl that curls and bloats the leaves with disfiguring blotches of red. Spraying with lime sulphur in the tight bud stage and again in the autumn, just as leaf-fall starts, helps to prevent this affliction, and a copper-containing spray also is effective. However, in districts where other almonds and peaches are grown, yearly spraying is a tiresome necessity. For those who are prepared faithfully to carry out this chore *P.* × *amygdalo-persica* 'Pollardii' is the tree to plant. Slightly earlier than the common almond, it has larger flowers of richer pink enchanced by a deep chocolatey bark.

In March, the earliest and some of the very best cherries begin to flower. They are true lime-lovers and on such soil usually add to their merits by following their prolific spring blossom with brilliant autumn tints. Many of the early blooming cherries have single flowers that are much smaller than those of the later so-called 'Japanese' cherries of garden origin. Their flowers are full of individual quality and perfection and at the same time so freely borne as to give a truly worthwhile garden effect. Of these, *P. subhirtella* 'Beni Higan' the spring-flowering form of the November cherry, if planted as a bush-shaped tree makes a compact cylinder of rosy bloom. *P. sargentii* has larger, single pink flowers and is one of the finest trees for autumn colour. Its leaves turn to glowing crimson in later September. For warm gardens *P. cyclamina* makes an interesting small tree. Its flowers have long, reflexing sepals reminding one of the petals of the cyclamen from which it derives its specific name. The warm pink of the flowers takes on an added glow from the bright copper of the unfolding leaves.

In recent years several valuable hybrid cherries have been added to this early-blooming group. One of the best of these is *P.* 'Okamé' with semi-double flowers of vivid rose-crimson approaching in colour the carmine of its tender parent *P. campanulata*. From *P. incisa*, its other parent, *P.* 'Okamé' derives its undoubted hardiness.

Among the larger-flowered cherries are many well-known beauties, among them the too vigorous, too bright, pink *P.* 'Kanzan', *P.* 'J. H. Veitch' ('Fugenzo') which is just a little paler in colour and more suitable for small gardens on account of its more moderate growth and *P.* 'Amanogawa', slim and upright—resembling a maypole in spring when wreathed with its large

flowers of apple-blossom pink. Less well known are the shell pink
P. 'Ichiyo', *P.* 'Jo-nioi' with a profusion of sweetly-scented white
blossom, *P.* 'Tai Haku' with magnificent single white flowers
sometimes as much as 8 cm (3½ in) across, *P.* 'Ukon' with creamy
semi-double flowers that look yellow against the bronze of its
unfolding leaves, the pure white *P.* 'Shirotae', *P.* 'Shirofugen'
with coppery leaves and blush-pink flowers fading to white then
blushing pink again as they fade and *P.* 'Shimidsu'—one of the
best of all with long-stalked, frilly, double white blooms. For a
lawn tree where there is plenty of space none is more lovely than
the March-flowering *P.* × *yedoensis,* its arching, wide-spread
branches bearing a heavy crop of almond-scented, pale blush
flowers which quickly fade to white but last long in beauty. Those
who like weeping trees, myself among them, will rejoice in the
early rose-bud cherry *P. subhirtella* 'Pendula', its deeper pink
form 'Rubra', and 'Kiku-shidare sakura'—the chrysanthemum
cherry of Japan with its very double, rosy-pink blooms.

Lime-loving, too, and useful to accompany the cherries are the
crab-apples. Everyone knows *Malus floribunda* with its arching
branches and fountains of apple-blossom, flowers, while even
more popular are *M.* 'Lemoinei', *M.* 'Eleyi' and *M.* 'Alden-
hamensis' with their dark purple leaves and crimson flowers. *M.*
× *atrosanguinea,* too, is attractive with crimson buds and rosy
flowers. The leaves of this species are bright green and it makes
a modest, mushroom-shaped tree that is useful for limited spaces.
When considering crab-apples, however, autumn fruit is almost
as important as spring flowers. So, whether to make crab-apple
jelly or for the glow of their colourful little apples in the garden,
the orange-and-red fruited *M.* 'John Downie', *M.* 'Cheal's
Crimson' or the yellow-fruited *M.* 'Golden Hornet' should be
planted. All these varieties have white flowers. *M.* 'Hopa' is a
handsome tree where space is not short. Vigorous growing and
with greyish-purple foliage it bears large deep pink flowers that
are conspicuous for their beauty and followed by small but bright
red fruits.

For those who like coloured foliage, the ornamental plums—

Prunus cerasifera 'Nigra' with a cloud of small rosy flowers and the rosette-flowered, smaller-growing *P.* × *blireana*—are good.

To strike a picturesque note in a mixed border or to place as the focal point on a lawn, or in a garden of old roses, the silver-leafed weeping pear *Pyrus salicifolia* 'Pendula' should be grown for the beauty of its habit and silvery leaves and the modest charm of its blossom. Its fruits, however, are hard, tasteless and quite uneatable.

The lovely genus of magnolias has been mentioned already in Chapter Four. To go further into the matter: species may be selected for almost any soils. Some, notably the summer-flowering *Magnolia sieboldii*, demand an acid soil. There are, however, substitutes for this species in the rather sprawling *M. sinensis* and the more upright-growing *M. wilsonii* which is the better plant for small gardens, with similarly pendant, saucer-shaped flowers with an effective boss of dark red stamens, a honey and lemon scent and the additional distinction of brown-furred buds and young shoots. *M. stellata*, an early-flowering bush magnolia with numerous waxy strap-shaped petals, is said by some not to tolerate lime. This is not true. It does well in alkaline clay and there are old specimens in limestone gardens in North Wales. But it will not succeed in hot, chalky gardens. There *M. kobus borealis* is a wiser choice. However, this species takes rather longer to flower than *M. stellata* (but not impossibly long) and will in time become a fairly large tree.

Magnolia denudata, one of the parents of the well-known *M.* × *soulangiana*, is even more beautiful than its offspring, bearing on its bare grey branches many vase-shaped blossoms of purest white before the leaves appear. This magnolia does well in many gardens on limestone and alkaline clay. The white, purple-flushed *M.* × *soulangiana* succeeds on such soils as does the desirable *M.* 'Lennei', with large, solidly textured, scented flowers that are pinky-purple on the outside and white within. This magnolia was particularly happy in our previous garden.

Flowering in May, the Judas tree, *Cercis siliquastrum*, is a real lime-lover, to be seen at its very best in the hot, chalky gardens of the south of England. In such places *C. racemosa* will also succeed. This species makes a taller tree than the bushy *C. sili-quastrum* with similar rosy-lilac flowers (paler than in the best forms of the Judas tree but very pleasing all the same) borne in drooping racemes instead of wreathing the stem as in the better-known species. *C. siliquastrum* 'Alba' is the white variety of the Judas tree and lovely if planted with the rosy purple type where the branches may overlap.

Laburnums and hawthorns do well on lime but the latter need a poor soil if they are to flower freely. On our limy clay, enriched by ten years' added humus, the 'Paul's Scarlet' thorn grew vigorously, making many leafy branches but bearing relatively few flowers. This is regrettable because hawthorn blossom whether single or double, pink or red, or the scented white, is delightful and the sparse flowering of our tree was a keen disappointment. At the time of writing root-pruning was being carried out and this did effect some improvement.

A very graceful tree for small gardens, reaching no more than 3·6 m (12 ft) in height after many years, is the semi-pendulous *Caragana arborescens* 'Lorbergii'. Bearing a profusion of golden pea-flowers in May, it is nevertheless for its beautiful foliage and attractive bearing that this species is mainly grown. Its leaves are compound and composed of narrow, light green, linear leaflets, giving the effect of fine lace. Not too hardy in exposed gardens, this species should be planted where it will be sheltered from the north and east in well-drained but fertile soil.

Horse-chestnuts are usually thought of as stately trees for parkland and large estates but one which is quite suitable for modest gardens is *Aesculus pavia* 'Atrosanguinea', which bears its 15-cm (6-in) crimson candles in June.

Unfortunately, three of the loveliest genera of summer-flowering trees—the stewartias and the snowdrop-flowered styraxes and halesias will not tolerate lime.

The Chinese fringe tree, *Chionanthus retusus*, is quite at home although the American fringe tree will not grow. *C. retusus* is an attractive small tree, its long, fringe-like racemes of white flowers drooping from the leafy branches in July and having a faint but sweet fragrance.

Making big trees in time but not flowering for many years, *Kolreuteria paniculata,* with handsome pinnate leaves and panicles of golden flowers, and the paulownias with their foxglove blooms are fitting trees for larger gardens. They need full sun and shelter. The paulownias flower in May and the kolreuteria in August.

Autumn colours and berries often seem to be particularly fine in hilly chalk and limestone districts. Outstanding both for leaf colour and berries is the mountain ash family. Choice ranges from the native rowan with its bright orange berries, which, unfortunately, in many districts are all too quickly stripped by the birds, to the white and pink sorbus species from China.

For small gardens, the ideal mountain ash is *Sorbus scopulina* often listed as *S. decora nana* or *S. americana nana* or sometimes even as *S. decora.* This is a slow-growing tree reaching perhaps to 4·2 m (14 ft) in height over many years and certainly becoming no more than 2·4 m (8 ft) across. The comparatively large leaves are glaucous and handsome and the big sealing-wax red berries are borne in heavy clusters, making this a really outstanding little tree. Also compact is *S. cashmeriana* with white fruits the size of marbles and graceful ferny foliage, while for the rock garden *S. reducta* is a beauty, seldom reaching more than 60 cm (2 ft) in height and bearing bright rose-pink berries. Larger-growing than those so far mentioned but really taking up little space, the lovely *S. hupehensis* is distinctive with grey-green foliage and large bunches of currant-size white berries tinted with pink. Also good is *S. h. obtusa* with grey-blue leaves and rose-pink berries. The white and pink berried forms do not seem to tempt the birds as much as do the more familiar orange scarlet of the native mountain ash, so in districts where bird damage is heavy these are the species to choose. For areas where feathered robber friends are less troublesome it is worth planting *S. matsumurana* with the most vivid autumn leaf-colour of the genus and heavy clusters of brilliant red fruits.

Among other notable berry-bearing plants the spindles are

shrubs rather than trees and with the hollies must be left until the next chapter. The only spindle-berry which becomes a real tree with age is our native *Euonymus europaeus* and nothing is more effective in late October than its show of rose-coloured capsules dangling from the branches like little square parcels spilling their orange-red seeds.

Of the cotoneasters, the hybrid 'Cornubia' must be dealt with here. Although of bushy growth it rapidly reaches 6·6 m (20 ft) or more, and very gay it is. Its bright red berries are perhaps the largest of the genus. However, the bright berries are 'Cornubia's' only real merit because, attractive though this cotoneaster is when young, its habits becomes ungainly as it gets older. On chalky banks its growth is checked and so becomes more manageable. *C. salicifolius* may be grown as a small tree with its lower branches removed. It seldom reaches more than 2·4 m (8 ft) in height with an umbrella spread of slightly weeping branches. Its leaves are slim and evergreen and its berries very bright. A prostrate cotoneaster that may be purchased as a standard grafted on the tall stem of a different species is the beautiful *C.* 'Hybridus Pendulus'. Evergreen with neat glossy leaves, like many of its genus, it is attractive in summer when bearing its clusters of hawthorn-like flowers. In exposed places, however, its display of berries may prove disappointing on account of weather damage.

Ornamental trees appeal to the gardener not only by their beauty of blossom or berry but on account of their foliage and habit as well. Pleasing in growth, sometimes with attractively coloured young foliage, sometimes with interesting or beautiful bark and always with splendid leaf colour in autumn, the acers or maples rank high in garden merit. Unfortunately the small-growing group often referred to as the Japanese maples—*Acer palmatum* and its varieties—do not grow well on limy or chalky soil. Nor do the much more vigorous *A. rubrum* (the scarlet Canadian maple), *A. pennsylvanicum* and *A. saccharinum* from America. However, the following will succeed without difficulty: the Chinese *A. davidii* with its white and green 'snake-bark' trunk; *A. griseum,* the paper-bark maple which is very attractive with its red-brown peeling papery bark and vivid autumn colour; the large Norway maple, *A. plantanoides,* with conspicuous yellow flower clusters in spring and yellow autumn leaf colour except in the varieties 'Crimson King' and the purple-leafed *A. p.* 'Schwedleri'. These Norway maples are fast-growing and make very big trees. They are not suitable for small gardens but where there is room *A. p.* 'Drummondii', its leaves margined with white, and the cut-leafed *A. p.* 'Lorbergii' are very distinctive. Of our native sycamores *A. pseudoplatanus* 'Brilliantissimum' is a slow-growing form suitable for the smaller garden and worth planting for its spring foliage of coral pink.

Graceful and pleasing though the birches are at all times of the year, it is in winter perhaps that we appreciate the beauty of the family to the full. Then, stripped of leaves, there is little to distract the eye from the beauty of stem and bark.

The wild *Betula pendula* is as garden-worthy as any of the birches, its silvery whiteness enhanced by the rough black corky ridges that show here and there on the stem. In winter the delicate tracery of its branches is hazed with the purple of incipient buds and catkins. Tall-growing though it is, the silver birch is never really out of scale, even in the smallest garden. To set off a larger space, the taller *B. p.* 'Tristis' lets fall its shower of weeping branchlets from an impressive height. In smaller gardens a weeping effect can be more suitably obtained from 'Young's Weeping Birch' which makes a mushroom-headed tree, its pendulous branches becoming in summer a veil of leaves sometimes reaching to the ground and making a green tent, enchanting to children and no less delightful to grown-ups.

Yet another form of the silver birch, *B. p.* 'Dalecarlica', is the Swedish cut-leaf birch with a smooth white trunk and daintily cut green leaves. Good, too, is the upright-growing *B. p.* 'Fastigiata' which is similar in growth to the Lombardy poplar and a useful tree for screening. All these are true silver birches.

Different in its appeal is the black birch—*B. nigra*—a North American tree. Loving damp ground, in its native land it is known as the river birch. Unlike those of the *B. pendula* varieties, the trunks of which become silvery as they near maturity, the stem of the black birch retains its light brown colouring, neither does it shed its bark yearly as do the other birches. Instead the old bark is retained to make a shaggy mass round the branches, giving a black effect in the wintry sun.

One of the loveliest of all birches, the Chinese *B. ermanii,* reaches a considerable height in time, although taking up but little lateral space, and is not a tree for the suburban garden. In the right setting it is magnificent when fully grown with a smooth soaring trunk the colour of palest, milky coffee. Another birch, the bole of which gives the same creamy-fawn effect, is *B. jacquemontii.* Unfortunately, this birch is but little known but Messrs. Hilliers of Winchester list it. It is a most attractive tree and although the specimens I have seen are only young they seem likely to make smaller trees than *B. ermanii* and so to be more generally useful.

The bark of *B. platyphylla szechuanica* is particularly gleaming in its whiteness and, lovely though the warmer tinted boles of *B. ermanii* and *B. jacquemontii* may be in the autumn garden when showered by the golden rain of their spent foliage, in winter there is little more pleasing than the cold white stems of a group of *B. platyphylla szechuanica* perhaps rising from behind a spread of rosy winter-flowering heaths. The canoe birch of Hiawatha, *B. papyrifera,* has the smoothest white trunk of all.

All the birches attain their greatest beauty when showing a considerable expanse of stem. This is best achieved by the removal of the lower branches in youth. The trunk should be left clear to a height of at least 3·6 m (12 ft).

In the garden eucalypti have a similar effect to birches, with their graceful growth and pretty trunks. They are evergreen and therefore doubly valuable. However, the only one which is reliably hardy inland in the British Isles is *Eucalyptus gunnii* although on the western coast *E. globulus* will often succeed. *E. gunnii* does not mind lime and will in time become a very tall tree. Luckily it does not mind pruning and lopping and so is worth planting even in quite small gardens. It is better left unstaked and so forced to anchor itself securely against the winds.

Another tall-growing tree but one of very slow growth and so also a possibility for the smaller garden is the beautiful *Ginkgo biloba*, the maidenhair tree—a true lime-lover. Although cone-bearing and therefore a conifer, the ginkgo is not in the least like other conifers in appearance. Elegantly branched, it bears fan-shaped leaves of a lovely soft green that call to mind the fronds of the tender maidenhair fern. These leaves become pale yellow in autumn before falling.

More conventionally coniferous in appearance the junipers come at once to mind as a genus of lime-lovers. Here, however, there is sadness because *Juniperus recurva* and *J. r. coxii*, the most handsome of all with their shaggy, reddish, soft-barked trunks and drooping blue-green foliage, will thrive only in moist, acid soil. Regrettable though this is, the genus nevertheless has a wide range of distinctive evergreens to offer the limy garden. Among the best are *J. communis*, a native of the chalk downs; *J. c.* 'Hibernica', the Irish juniper, of close, columnar growth forming an upright pillar that makes it particularly useful for formal planting and *J. virginiana* making a tall but slender pyramid of bluey-green.

As do the junipers, the yews, also, thrive on limy ground. They are good, too, for seaside gardens and are surprisingly resistant to spray and salt-laden winds. For small gardens, the Irish yew—*Taxus baccata* 'Fastigiata'—is the best choice, making a narrow dark column that remains neatly furnished to the ground with growth. There is also a golden variety, *T. b.* 'Aurea', which is a golden flame in spring but later in the season loses most of its distinctive colouring. This, to my mind, is an advantage rather than otherwise because to see bright gold foliage in the same place the year round can become tedious, as many inheritors of golden privet find. Unlike those of many columnar growers, the yew's branches remain closely upright and near the main stem so that the tree seldom needs corseting with wire as the cypress family often does.

Most of the better-known false cypresses (chamaecyparis)—

especially the *lawsoniana* varieties with their blue, silver, green or gold foliage—will grow on lime or chalk and so will the Monterey cypress, *Cupressus macrocarpa* which in its lesser-known form, *C. m.* 'Donard Gold', is compact and of a pleasantly deep golden colouring.

Many of the firs (abies) dislike lime and require a deeper, moister soil than is to be found in most calcareous gardens. Two that will succeed even on chalk are the Spanish fir, *Abies pinsapo* and its hybrid offspring *Abies × vilmorinii*. These, however, are trees for big gardens and need plenty of space. Another large tree, the Grecian fir *Abies cephalonica*, also will grow on lime.

The spruce family (*Picea*), to which the Christmas tree belongs, is not as a whole suited to shallow chalk. It should be noted, though, that it is the poor soil and lack of depth to which the spruces object and not to the calcareous content. On soils which are deeper and which hold more moisture, even though the ground be alkaline, most of them will succeed.

When planting trees on solid chalk or limestone, it is important to prepare the sites thoroughly. Holes at least twice the diameter of the present spread of the trees should be excavated with a pickaxe, deep enough to accommodate the trees in such a way that the soil marks on the trunks, which indicate the depth at which they have previously been planted, will come level with the top of the soil. Below this depth, the chalk or limestone must be broken with a pickaxe for a further foot, leaving a spongy, moisture-retentive rubble.

On clay soils it is important to pay attention to drainage before trees are planted. Few will do well if standing in cold, water-logged soil or if the clay cracks and dries out during the summer. Any hard pan of clay must be broken up before improving the soil in the immediate planting site. Otherwise the water will drain through the more porous material and then, reaching the impermeable layer, will be halted and the planting hole will fill like a bowl, literally drowning the tree.

Once the pan-layer has been broken up, coarse drainage material such as broken crocks, large cinders, stones, etc., should be incorporated in it. The planting hole should then be filled with a mixture of good soil, bonemeal, river sand and moist peat. This material should also be mixed to some degree into the surrounding soil, rendering it more porous and also allowing the roots to penetrate as they extend. It is important, too, that drainage pits should be dug at the lowest parts of the surrounding ground, or else the whole area drained as described in Chapter One.

Provided attention is paid to these points, most genera will thrive. One tree that has come to the forefront in recent years is the golden-foliaged *Robinia pseudoacacia* 'Frisia'. Making a tree of small to medium size, it is a great garden asset. Its leaves are rich yellow from spring to autumn, making it particularly effective if associated with the rounded outline and vinous leaves of *Cotinus coggygria* 'Royal Purple'. It should be planted where the sun will shine through the leaves.

Up on the Downs, and in other windy areas, especial care needs to be paid to staking. The stakes are best placed in position before the trees are planted. Pointed stakes are easiest to drive well into the ground. In really solid chalk, however, even the holes for the stakes may need to be pickaxed, the stakes being then wedged into position with stones or bricks. A barrow-load of good soil mixed with well-made compost should be used around the roots of each tree when filling in the hole.

Stakes should always be placed to windward of the prevailing wind. Most people know their own prevailing wind but if there is any doubt about this a quick glance at the surrounding trees will settle the question. My husband and I always thought that the prevailing wind of our garden was south-westerly until an almond tree at an exposed corner of our land began to take on an irregular shape, the north-west side of the tree being almost bare of branches and the remainder, their leaves streaming like tattered lance-pennants, growing towards the south-east, thus plainly indicating that the winds mainly affecting our garden came from the north-west.

Tom's Rubber Tree-Ties or *Rainbow Plastic Ties* are reasonably priced and efficient. Home-made ties may easily be improvised from stout wire threaded through a piece of rubber or plastic hose-pipe, or an old bicycle tyre, and twisted into a figure-eight. The important thing is to secure the tree firmly to its stake without chafing and to be able to adjust the tie easily as the tree grows, otherwise the tie may cut into the bark causing injury and sometimes an unsightly scar with consequent bulging of the tree below the tie.

TEN

Accommodating Shrubs

Having begun the last chapter with winter-flowering trees, perhaps in this one we should be conventional and start with spring. Certainly no two shrubs speak more of spring than the forsythia and the chaenomeles (cydonia) which will be, to many gardeners, for ever known as 'japonica', however much the botanists despair.

Both the forsythia and chaenomeles have long flowering seasons. Varieties may be chosen which will bloom from February and earlier. Planted together, choosing varieties that really will flower at the same time, such as *Chaenomeles* × *superba* 'Knap Hill Scarlet' and the popular *Forsythia* × *intermedia* 'Spectabilis', they provide a colour contrast which will not easily be forgotten.

Earliest to flower of the forsythias is the pale yellow *F. giraldiana* which may sometimes open at the end of January but which can always be counted on for February bloom. This is followed by the Korean *F. ovata*, which is deeper in colour and makes a spreading bush about 1·2 m (4 ft) high. Provided a free-flowering form is chosen, this is one of the best forsythias for the small garden.

Later come *F.* × *intermedia* 'Spectabilis' in all its brazen brilliance, and the more subtle *F. suspensa* with its trailing growth and paler yellow flowers. Both these should be grown in any garden which has room for them. *F. suspensa* makes an effective standard on a 90- or 120-cm (3- or 4-ft) leg when its arching growths can shower down in cascades of starry lemon bells. These growths, however, must be cut back by about two-thirds after flowering or they will become straggly and the flowers will be sparse. *F. suspensa* is satisfactory on a wall—even a north wall will do—or to cover an arch or screen.

Of the chaenomeles, 'Aurora' is the most reliable early-flowering variety. It may bloom even before Christmas and has typical apple-blossom-shaped flowers in coppery salmon which appear freely throughout the winter, especially when the shrub is grown on a south wall. The common *Chaenomeles speciosa*—the typical cottage 'japonica'—is next to bloom and this too will yield very early flowers in a sunny, warm aspect. The rule for early bloom is to grow the chaenomeles on a south wall, but for later bloom, often continuing all spring and summer, a west or north wall is best.

If your walls are red brick then you will probably want to grow the white-flowered *C*. 'Nivalis' form, or one of the apple-blossom pinks. Against cream, white-washed, or stone walls, the scarlets cannot be beaten.

Of course there is no need ever to grow the chaenomeles against a wall unless you want to. In the open they will form picturesquely gnarled, free-flowering bushes.

Generally speaking the *C. speciosa* forms are tall-growing. Of the dwarfer forms the blood-red *C*. 'Simonii' is one of the best. Of the taller *C. speciosa* varieties, good ones to choose are the double-flowered *C*. 'Lady Moore', the salmon-pink *C*. 'Cardinalis', *C*. 'Moerloosii' in pink and white, *C*. 'Nivalis', *C*. 'Rowallane' with large, rose-crimson flowers and 'Knap Hill Scarlet' and 'Boule de Feu' of which both blood-red and apricot-terra-cotta forms exist, the red being the most suitable for wall-training.

Also useful as companions to the forsythias are the berberis. Most of this genus tolerate lime and *Berberis darwinii* grows vigorously and flowers well on our limy clay. The even more vivid *B. linearifolia* is quite happy on lime and even chalk and so is its beautiful hybrid offspring, the apricot-flowering *B.* × *lolo-*

gensis. I have seen it stated that these two berberises are not fully hardy, but both do well in a garden near Chester in a frost-pocket on cold, limy, Midland clay. A berberis the hardiness of which has never been in doubt, is *B.* × *coccinea,* a lime-tolerant hybrid between *B. darwinii* and the golden-flowered *B.* × *stenophylla.* *B.* × *coccinea* is a better shrub for the small garden than either of its parents, reaching to no more than 90 or 120 cm (3 or 4 ft) in height, and remaining compact in habit. It has deep bluish-green leaves and fiery scarlet-vermilion buds opening to flowers that are similarly brilliant without and golden-orange within, making a display that is glowing and vivid without being garish.

Yellow, crimson, orange and gold—so far the shrubs suggested for our limy garden have been vivid in colour. One needs the contrast of white to cool the flame. Many white-flowered shrubs have the added blessing of scent and in this respect two genera at once spring to mind for alkaline soil. They are the osmanthus and the viburnums. The first of these offers the delightful *Osmanthus delavayi,* a neat, dark evergreen with tiny holly-like leaves. In spring it bears myriads of white 'daphne' flowers with a powerful vanilla scent. A good shrub for the south and west, *O. delavayi* might be replaced in bleaker parts by its bi-generic hybrid × *Osmarea* 'Burkwoodii' which has similarly scented white flowers and lacks but little of its parent's quality.

The viburnums are true lime-lovers and among them the compact *Viburnum carlesii* stands supreme. Its offspring *V.* × *juddii* is very similar but slightly stronger-growing and should replace its parent on the colder clays. *V.* × *carlcephalum* is another child of *V. carlesii* but one that unfortunately has little of its parent's refinements to recommend it. Strong in growth, it sends up ungainly stems to a height of 2·4 m (8 ft) and its flower trusses are coarse and heavy. *V.* × *burkwoodii,* however, another hybrid of *V. carlesii,* is an excellent viburnum. Exceptionally hardy it will do well in all gardens. It is semi-evergreen and given the protection of a west wall will bloom all through the winter, ending with *V. carlesii* in spring. Even better is *V.* × *burkwoodii's* sister seedling 'Park Farm Hybrid' with larger chalk-white flowers more richly tinted with pink in bud. Later on in the year *Viburnum plicatum* 'Lanarth' is one of the most spectacularly pleasing shrubs for chalk, lime or even clay; a stronger grower, with tiered branches that become snow-like in late May with wide platters of ivory-white flower-heads. For smaller gardens its place should be taken by the less vigorous *V. p.* 'Rowallane'.

In the cytisus genus of the broom family the chalk garden loses a valuable section of later spring bloom. Yet most of the hybrid brooms will do well on limestone. For pure chalk the choice must fall on the genistas which thrive even on the hottest, chalkiest banks.

To replace the white broom and the coloured cytisus hybrids on chalk, the Spanish gorse, *Genista hispanica,* is the best the genistas have to offer. Very useful it is, too, making a dome-shaped bush up to 90 cm (3 ft) in height that becomes a mass of rich gold in May. It will grow in the poorest, driest soil and when so grown is extremely hardy. Dwarfer in growth are the hairy *G. pulchella* and *G. lydia,* the soft green shoots of which combine well with the bright yellow flowers. Genistas of other colours there is none but its violet-blue flowers make *Erinacea anthyllis,* the 'hedgehog' broom, a useful associate. Also on hot, dry banks the blue-flowered, evergreen ceanothuses will often prove hardy, particularly if placed with a large rock behind them and a heavy stone over their roots to prevent windrock. *C. thyrsiflorus* is one of the hardiest and is a tall, erect-growing shrub bearing dense, thimble-heads of pale to deep blue flowers in May. The prostrate form of this species is particularly valuable in exposed, windy gardens. Other good evergreen ceanothuses are the rich blue 'A. T. Johnson' which flowers in both summer and autumn, *C.* × *burkwoodii* which flowers almost continuously through the summer and on into the autumn and the late-flowering 'Autumnal Blue' with large flowers of a particularly telling bright cobalt.

In the bladder nuts, the staphyleas, we have some uncommon yet delightful subjects for alkaline soils. The finest of all, *Staphylea holocarpa* 'Rosea', does not seem to be obtainable in commerce at the present time. This is a great pity because it is hardy in the south and west and is a fine shrub which may in time reach the proportions of a bushy tree. It is beautiful in April when covered with its shell-pink flowers. I am sure it would be worth the while of the more discriminating nurserymen to propagate this species.

S. colchica makes a tall shrub of up to 3·6 m (12 ft) in height with conspicuous erect panicles of creamy flowers and a scent of coconut-ice. *S.* × *elegans* 'Hessei' is a hybrid of *colchica* with large drooping panicles of red-tinged flowers giving a rosy effect.

Many of the prunus family have been dealt with in the preceding chapter. There are, however, several shrubby members of the genus which should be considered when planning a garden on lime or chalk. One of the best is the crimson-pink dwarf almond *Prunus tenella* 'Fire Hill' which flowers in April. Blooming in March, *Prunus incisa*, the 'Fuji Cherry', bears a cloud of white blossom, rosy with the glow of the unopened buds and calyces. Sometimes a small tree, this cherry can easily be kept by regular pruning to a bush of manageable size. For those who like double flowers there are *P. glandulosa* 'Albiplena' and *P. g.* 'Sinensis' in double white and double pink. April-flowering, they reach to a height of 1·2 or 4 or 1·5m (5 ft). With the forsythias, chaenomeles, berberis, genistas, staphyleas and dwarf prunuses the garden on lime or chalk need never be short of colour in spring. The colour can continue all summer too. With the shrub roses and other lime-tolerant genera the alkaline garden can be decked with bouquets of flowering shrubs the summer long—at a time when the acid-soiled garden of the rhododendron fan is going through a quiet patch. Lilacs, deutzias, philadelphus, weigelas and abelias have all been discussed in the chapter dealing with the mixed border. The abelia-like *Kolkwitzia amabilis* with larger soft pink foxglove-like flowers must be mentioned again as one of the most satisfying of all summer-flowering shrubs for full sun. Unless it can be so sited, however, it will not flower freely and in the north and west, at any rate, would not be worth planting. In *Dipelta floribunda* we have another shrub with foxglove-like flowers. The dipelta is a tall shrub reaching perhaps to 3 m

1. *Cyclamen coum.* A pretty winter-flowering cyclamen that is happiest on well-drained soil. In clayey gardens it should be given the benefit of a raised bed or rock-garden pocket.

2. *Daphne cneorum* 'Variegatum'. Like all daphnes this species appreciates moisture at the roots. The variegation, however, renders it more tender than the type. When grown on cold clays, *Daphne cneorum* and its cultivars should have the soil lightened by the addition of grit or peat. A flat stone over the root area will then enable the roots to seek moisture in summer.

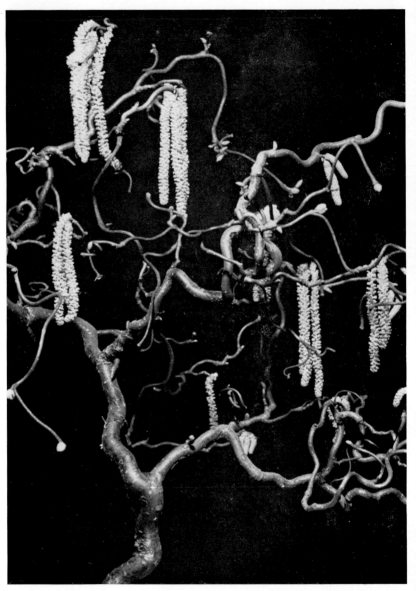

3. *Corylus avellana* 'Contorta' makes an interesting talking point in any garden. It is attractive in catkin and the twisted stems are useful for indoor arrangement. Perfectly happy on most soils, it does well on lime, chalk or clay.

4. *Euphorbia wulfennii*. A handsome shrub for chalk or limestone and it will even succeed on clay. It needs plenty of room but its lovebird green and gold flowers and architectural structure give it great appeal.

5. *Deutzia chunii* is one of the most elegant species in the genus, with large flower panicles and lance-shaped leaves that are grey beneath. Like all deutzias it will succeed in partial shade.

6. *Helleborus niger,* the well-loved Christmas rose, does well on clay. On poor chalky soils it needs the addition of well-rotted manure or compost. A mulch of forest bark or peat applied in late autumn will keep the flowers clean.

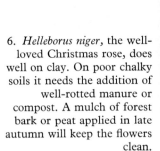

7. *Galtonia candicans* is a lily-like bulbous subject. Tall and graceful with hanging ivory bells of some substance, it is at its best in the mixed border or among shrubs. Coming from South Africa, it needs sunshine and good soil which does not lie wet in winter.

8. *Magnolia × loebneri* is a hybrid which does well on chalk.

9. *Pulsatilla vulgaris.* A downland native, this charming spring-blooming plant does well on chalk or lime. On clay it needs rock-garden conditions. Known as the pasque flower, it earned its name by providing the dye with which Easter eggs were coloured.

10. Potentillas are always useful. The newer, more unusually coloured cultivars such as 'Tangerine' and 'Red Ace' need a semi-shaded position if they are to give full value.

11. 'Frau Dagmar Hästrup' is one of the finest rugosa rose varieties. Its shapely pale pink single flowers are followed by large tomato-shaped fruit which colour well.

12. *Viburnam plicatum* 'Lanarth' with the cultivars 'Mariesii' and 'Rowallane' are among the finest shrubs for chalk. 'Lanarth' is taller and less branching than the other two and so is useful for the shrub border. The others, with their tiered habit of growth remain dense to the ground and are worthy of specimen planting in grass or paving. 'Rowallane' is the least vigorous of the three and so best for small gardens.

(10 ft) but occupying little lateral space. Blooming in June, its flowers are pale pink flushed with yellow in the throat. Its bark is attractively shaggy and, like the kolkwitzia, to give of its best the dipelta should be given a place in the sun.

An uncommon and interesting summer-flowering shrub for the garden on chalk or lime is *Deutzia chunii* which bears in July 1-cm ($\frac{1}{2}$-in) reflexed flowers that are pink on the outside and white within borne in large panicles on willow-leaved branchlets. A Chinese mock orange, *Philadelphus brachybotrys,* is good too, making a tall, arching shrub spangled along the length of its weeping branches with myriads of scented, creamy flowers.

The summer-flowering viburnums are among the most useful shrubs for alkaline soils. Lime-lovers though they are, however, most viburnums do need a certain amount of moisture in summer if they are not to flag. When planted in hot, dry gardens or on chalky banks care should be taken to break up the rock and to incorporate plenty of damp peat of as coarse a grade as possible so that it will not disintegrate too quickly but will last long to act as a sponge and hold reserve moisture for the plants.

The summer-flowering viburnums are of two types. One type carries its flowers in snowball-like inflorescences. The other bears flat heads composed of tiny fertile florets and showy sterile ones rather like the flower heads of the lacy hydrangeas.

One of the most easily grown of the summer-flowering viburnums is the common guelder rose, often seen in the hedgerows in chalk and limestone country. Its main garden value, though, lies not in its flower heads but in the brilliant scarlet berries it bears in autumn. The sterile form of the guelder rose, *Viburnum opulus* 'Sterile', however, is a valuable garden shrub. It is very hardy and thrives in most soils and situations. It is worth its place, too, for the scarlet tints which its leaves assume in the autumn. In time this form makes an enormous bush but it can be kept to a manageable size by pruning, which should be carried out as soon as the flowers are over. Even more vigorous is the Chinese *V. macrocephalum* with snowballs of 23 cm (9 in) or more in diameter. This species is rather tender and needs the shelter of a wall—a west wall is ideal. In shallow chalky soil it will not do itself justice. In deep, rich loam it is a magnificent sight.

Hardier and of more restrained growth the Japanese snowball bush, *V. plicatum tomentosum*, is full of quality with wide-spreading, horizontal branches and smaller but very shapely flower-balls. The fertile form of this viburnum is one of the finest of all hardy shrubs, its spreading branches adorned in late May with flat-topped, lace-cap flower-heads. There are several forms of *V. plicatum* and all are good, *V. p.* 'Mariesii' being the large-flowered form most often seen. *V. p.* 'Lanarth', already mentioned, is stronger-growing, becoming almost tree-like in time and having larger, very ornamental leaves while *V. p.* 'Rowallane' is much more dwarf with small leaves and flowers that are tipped with pink when in bud. All forms of *V. plicatum* colour splendidly in autumn.

An effective contrast in form to this last group of viburnums is to be found in *Buddleia alternifolia*, a graceful shrub with arching branches that is particularly effective if trained to a single stem when it will affect the habit of a small weeping willow. Willow-like, too, are its slender leaves. Its flower clusters are composed of lilac-coloured flowers and are sweetly fragrant. There is also a grey-leafed form of this buddleia but it is more upright in growth. Another delightful buddleia, flowering in the later summer, is *B. fallowiana* with woolly white leaves and large panicles of very fragrant, pale lavender-blue flowers. *B. f.* 'Alba' has similarly tomentose leaves but its flowerlets are white with an orange eye. It is especially lovely against a dark green background. *Buddleia davidii* 'Nanhoensis' also is lightly built and graceful and bears long spikes of lavender-mauve flowers. I like all these buddleias better than the coarser-growing cultivars of *B. davidii* which have the bad failing that parts of their heavy panicles of flowers invariably brown and die even before the last flowerlets have opened. A colour variant in buddleias comes from a hybrid *B. × pikei* 'Hever', bred by Mr. A. V. Pike when head-gardener at Hever Castle. This buddleia bears a profusion of airy and graceful flower-spikes over 30 cm (a foot) in length and of a pretty pink-lilac.

Brilliant colour may be given to the limy garden by some of the pink, red and violet-headed *hortensia* hydrangeas (the mopheads), but with the exception of *Hydrangea villosa* which makes a very large shrub and the even larger *H. aspera*, both of which need partial shade, no members of the genus retain their natural blue colouring on alkaline soils.

Hydrangeas in the past have suffered from almost as much misunderstanding as have camellias, being thought to thrive only in greenhouses or in mild, seaside areas. This is far from the case. Hydrangeas will succeed in many inland gardens. In the bleakest districts they should be given the protection of a wall—a north wall will do perfectly well. Hydrangeas in cold districts should be covered with large polythene bags in winter to keep off the frost.

When growing hydrangeas against a wall the builder's rubbish and limy rubble should first be removed and replaced with soil as good as is available. At the same time plenty of peat, garden compost, or other humus should be incorporated. Bearing in mind that plants against walls often suffer from drought, hydrangeas so situated should be given a thrice-weekly soaking at the rate of a couple of buckets full at least to each established plant. In hot weather a careful watch should also be kept on any hydrangeas grown in the open garden. These plants need a great deal of water and if their needs are not met the flowers quickly wilt and the large leaves flag.

In milder areas, or away from frost pockets and where there is good air drainage, selected varieties of hydrangea may be grown away from a wall and in the open garden. In the south of the country and in hot, chalky upland gardens it is as well to plant them in semi-shade if at all possible. Often gardeners like to cut away all flower heads to tidy up in autumn. This instinct should be resisted where hydrangeas are concerned as the old flower heads give very real protection to the next year's buds.

Although hydrangeas will grow and flower well in alkaline soils they may sometimes show symptoms of iron deficiency. The leaves become chlorotic, yellow and sickly looking. This may be speedily remedied by watering the prescribed dose of *Sequestrene Plant Tonic* over the root area. Care must be taken, however, not to splash the leaves or scorching may result. I have used this sequestrene with great success on some very chlorotic and almost dying plants. Within a month the plants were green and healthy but the flower colour was in no way affected, remaining a clear, rosy pink and not turning to muddy purple as often happens when attempts are made to 'blue' some shades of pink hydrangeas in limy soils.

One of the best of all hydrangeas, 'Altona', with fimbriated petals and very large flower heads of deep rose-pink that turn to crimson in autumn, is unfortunately suitable only for seaside gardens. Inland its place should be taken by the similarly coloured 'Gertrud Glahn'. 'Blue Prince' on limy soils becomes a vivid rosy-red. 'Heinrich Seidel' is a glowing cherry-red with fringed petals while 'Niedersachsen' is paler—clear pink with large florets—and 'Parsifal' is a very fine crimson pink. A selection of these might be used with 'Princess Beatrix' or 'Ami Pasquier', treated with aluminium sulphate (0·45 kg (1 lb) to a three-stemmed plant scattered over the root area in November) to give a contrasting violet, and 'Mme E. Mouillière' a charming white, button-centred with rose. For the front row the very dwarf red 'Vulcan' is ideal.

The lace-cap hydrangeas are lovely and have quite a different appeal. Very decorative with a central mass of bead-like fertile flowers surrounded by a few showy sterile florets, they are the artist-gardener's delight. They need semi-shade and a moister, deeper soil than the mop-heads. On limy soils they are not quite as effective as on acid because the vivid blue of the fertile florets is lacking. The old *H.* 'Mariesii', however, is attractive in rose and lilac and *H.* 'Rosalba' with its rosy beads and large white, deckle-edged florets that flush to crimson as they age is one of the finest of all shrubs for limy soils. It will stand drier conditions, too, than most of the lace-caps.

The shrubby veronicas or hebes are good for limy gardens. True, the leathery-leaved *Hebe speciosa* varieties in rich purple and claret and crimson are too tender for most gardens. *H. salicifolia*, too, does best at the seaside. This leaves as 'hardies': *H.* 'Midsummer Beauty' with handsome *speciosa*-like foliage and rich-lavender flower spikes making a bush of about 1·2 m (4 ft); the later and dwarfer-growing 'Autumn Glory' with rich violet flowers and 'Hielan Lassie' with bishop's purple spikes that are borne much earlier—from July to September in fact. To these must be added the race of *H. elliptica* hybrids which occur so freely in western seaside gardens and greatly surpass their *elliptica* parent, often having the magnificent *speciosa* for their other parent and inheriting dark, lustrous green coupled to the elliptical foliage shape that gives *H. elliptica* its specific name. Low and mounded in growth, their attractive foliage renders them valuable as garden furnishing even when out of flower. Some bloom early in summer and again in autumn. Others tend to an autumn- and winter-flowering habit. One outstanding seedling in our old garden had flowers of lavender-blue forming a dense compact spike. This seedling regularly flowered in June and September. Another had a pyramidal spike of deep rosy-mauve, the colour of the deeper forms of ling. This was a true winter-blooming plant in our district, flowering from November to April and covering its shapely, green hummocks with flush after flush of blooms whenever there was a reasonable spell of mild weather. It is a pity that nurserymen do not concentrate more upon the *elliptica* hybrids. Their spikes are not so large and heavy as those of the *speciosa* but they are colourful and very freely borne. The bushes, too, are more compact, offering less resistance to wind and seemingly unperturbed by the strongest gale. Severe winters, however, scorch and even kill the hebes in many gardens, and so they should never be used as backbone plantings but rather as interesting fill-ups that will not leave serious gaps if killed.

With the purple and wine-coloured veronicas, the yellow daisy bush, *Senecio greyi* (now *S.* 'Sunshine') is effective, handsome at all times of the year and making a spreading hummock of grey foliage. Other effective yellow-flowered shrubs are the evergreen hypericums with golden, bowl-shaped flowers and neat green leaves. The low-growing *Hypericum calycinum* (rose of Sharon) is the one most often seen and is useful to cover dry banks and rough patches of rooty ground where little else will grow. It is, however, extremely invasive and might be replaced in restricted areas by *H.* × *moseranum* which is hardy in most districts if planted in a sharply-drained, stony place in full sun. *H.* × *moseranum* has flowers that are quite as showy as those of *H. calycinum* and is non-invasive. It makes a compact bush of about 45 cm (18 in) high. There is a variety of this called 'Tricolour' with leaves that are pleasingly variegated in white, pink and green. Taller-growing, *Hypericum* 'Hidcote' is the finest of the hardy hypericums with flowers almost 6 cm (2½ in) across. It is usually seen as a bush of about 90 cm (3 ft) high although, if planted against a wall it will reach to 1·8 m (6 ft). However, if you can spare a place against a wall, the magnificent but slightly tender *H.* × 'Rowallane' is the most deserving of it. This hybrid has very shapely flowers of a richer gold and greater substance.

Less often seen even than the hypericums, the potentillas are attractive shrubs of moderate size. They like lime, are happy in sun or shade, and will thrive in almost any garden. Belonging to the rose family, their flowers are like small single roses, infinitely appealing in lemon, gold or white, against pleasant foliage, rather like that of a greatly refined tree lupin in shape. I would pick *Potentilla fruticosa purdomii* with sulphur-yellow flowers and light green foliage, *P.* 'Katherine Dykes' with golden flowers, and *P.* 'Vilmoriniana' with creamy flowers against silvery leaves—a shrub of moonlight and roses. These three make lightly-built bushes of about 90 cm (3 ft) high. *P.* 'Vilmoriniana' is more upright in growth than the other two which are mounded, spreading shrubs. More compact, and beautiful with silky-furred foliage is *P. arbuscula rigida*. It has bright yellow flowers while *P.* 'Maanelys' ('Moonlight') has the longest flowering season of all, from May to November, when it bears a continuous succession of soft, yellow 'roses'. Dwarfer-growing and making a spreading mat, suitable to hug the rocks on a limestone slope is the grey-leaved *P. mandschurica* with chaste white flowers and purple stems. The newer apricot-shaded 'Day Dawn', the well-named 'Sunset', 'Tangerine' and 'Red Ace' are now available.

Blue is a valuable colour in the late summer garden and there are several shrubs which may be used to supply it. Purest in colour—a piercing gentian-blue—is *Ceratostigma willmottianum*; its clustered flowers open in a succession so that there is but seldom a real flush of bloom. Nevertheless that keen blue is telling and the reddish stems help to make a shrub of quality and charm. Excellent while in bloom but with a comparatively short flowering period is the early September-flowering *Caryopteris × clandonensis* which bears spiraea-like plumes of hyacinth blue flowers. On acid soil I like to see these contrasted with the leaves of the deciduous azaleas as they begin to assume their autumn crimson. On lime the nearest we can get to this is to use the purple-leaved *Berberis thunbergii atropurpurea* as an associate.

Powder-blue in tone, the large, fat thimbles of *Ceanothus* 'Gloire de Versailles' are effective in the mass. This ceanothus is quite hardy. It may be grown against a wall if that is where you want it but it will do equally well in any sunny, well-drained border. Another good blue is *C.* 'Topaz'. The *C.* 'Ceres' is similar with lilac-pink flower panicles while *C.* 'Perle Rose' is deeper in colour, almost rose-carmine. All the ceanothus in this group are deciduous.

In late June, the tall, silver-leafed *Genista cinerea* bears its showers of gold. In August, *G. aetnensis*, the Mt. Etna broom, veils itself with scented, golden fireflies. Both these are 'tree' brooms, growing 1·8 or 2·4 m (6 or 8 ft) tall. Their main stems need to be securely staked in an upright position. *Cytisus battandieri* from Morocco is truly hardy and one of the few members of the cytisus family of brooms that will grow on chalk. Pineapple-scented, it has silky, laburnum-like foliage and bears in July chubby upright cones of golden bloom.

Seldom seen are two other pea-flowered shrubs: the quiet but graceful, August-flowering, *Indigofera gerardiana* with purple-rose flowers and elegant sprays of foliage and *Lespedeza thun-*

bergii which blooms in September with more showy panicles of brighter rosy-purple.

Loving a sunny position *Romneya coulteri* and *R. trichocalyx* are beautiful deciduous shrubs with handsomely cut foliage of greyish-green and silky, white, gold-centred flowers like huge poppies.

Another sun lover is the broom-like *Spartium junceum* with rush-like foliage and spikes of golden pea-flowers that emit a heady narcissus fragrance. This shrub should be cut well back after flowering and kept to 60 or 90 cm (2 or 3 ft) in height to encourage strong bushy growth otherwise it is apt to become leggy and is liable to suffer from windrock.

Autumn is the time of the many lovely berries which do so much to brighten our gardens. Useful to cover a bank or wall are the deciduous *Cotoneaster horizontalis* and the evergreen *C. dammeri*. Taller, humping itself into a low mound, *C. conspicuus* 'Decorus' is very free with its brilliant berries. A shrub of distinction is the evergreen *C. lacteus* with larger, leathery leaves that are felted beneath with grey wool. It bears glowing berries. Two cotoneasters whose berries last longer than any of these, reaching their full beauty after Christmas, are the tall-growing *C. pannosus* with small leaves and downy, orange-red berries which later become polished and *C. glaucophyllus serotinus* with larger, rounded evergreen leaves.

Stranvaesia davidiana salicifolia is a tall evergreen, matt, red-berried shrub. *S. d. salicifolia* will reach to 3 m (10 ft) in time so where a lower-growing bush is wanted the 1·2-m (4-ft) *S. undulata* would be a better choice. The berries of this species are orange scarlet in the type and there is a yellow-berried form which makes an unusual but pretty contrast.

Spindleberries such as *Euonymus alatus* and *E. yedoensis* give vivid leaf colouring as well as their most attractive seed cases and seeds. The yellow-berried holly, *Ilex aquifolium* 'Bacciflava', also is good while the freest berrying of the red-berried hollies is the handsome foliaged *I.* × *altaclarensis* 'J. C. van Tol'. Neither of these needs the presence of another holly in order to fruit and both will help to fertilize such females as the paradoxically named *I*. 'Golden King', the broad, flat leaves of which are widely edged with gold. *I*. 'Argenteomarginata' is the silver-edged holly to plant for berries. Both 'Golden Queen' and 'Silver Queen' are male and therefore do not bear berries although their pollen is useful to ensure a good crop on neighbouring female bushes.

Both sexes of *Skimmia japonica* must be planted to ensure crops of the holly-like berries. The bi-sexual *S*. 'Foremanii' is the one to choose for an isolated position. In some gardens old female bushes of *S. japonica* do not berry because they lack the presence of a male. To be sure of getting a male bush the sweetly-scented *S. j*. 'Fragrans' should be ordered by name. Another male which has been rightly commended for the excellence of its flowers is a form of *S. japonica* known as 'Rubella'. Unfortunately, this, like *S. fortunei* itself, does not do well on alkaline soils.

The pyracanthas are a family of berrying shrubs most commonly used as wall plants. With the exception of *Pyracantha angustifolia* which when heavily laden with fruit is not hardy in the coldest districts, this genus does not need a wall. Excellent as free-standing shrubs are the yellow-berried *P. atalantioides* 'Aurea' and *P. rogersiana* 'Flava', the fruit of which will last through the winter long after the better-known *P*. 'Lalandei' has been stripped by the birds.

The brightly berried berberises form another group of berrying plants which does very well on alkaline soils. One of the most colourful is the deciduous *Berberis wilsoniae* which adds the scarlet tints of its dying leaves to the bloomy rose-red of its berries. This species is a dwarf-grower of about 60 cm (2 ft) in height. One of the best of the taller berberises is *B*. × *rubrostilla* with larger, oblong berries of a more vivid rosy coral. Also good is *B*. 'Pirate King' which makes a vigorous, erect bush and bears a crop of fiery orange-scarlet fruit. Closely allied to the berberis and formerly reckoned among them is the group of shrubs now known as mahonias with handsome, widely-toothed, pinnate leaves and sprays of yellow flowers. Best known of these is *Mahonia aquifolium* which carries its short, bright cockades in

March and is useful to cover an awkward dry bank or to clothe the ground under old evergreens. More valuable in winter is *M. japonica* with long sprays of lemon bells and a wonderful lily-of-the-valley fragrance. For really warm corners in sheltered gardens the November-flowering *M. lomariifolia* is still more splendid in foliage and bears strong clusters of showy, upright racemes in bright yellow. Unfortunately, it is not scented.

Shrubs for every garden are the winter-flowering viburnums which were discussed in Chapter Five, but *Hamamelis mollis* and *H. japonica*, the witch hazels, are not for limy or chalk soils. In the alkaline garden their place can well be taken by the winter sweet, *Chimonanthus praecox*, with scented, yellow, purple-centred flowers that are parchmenty and subdued in the type but which become truly beautiful in *C. p.* 'Luteus'. The winter sweet may be grown as a bush in the open but it flowers earlier and more freely against a west or south-west wall. Its one drawback is that it takes several years to come into bloom. Its flowering may, however, be hastened if it is planted in good soil, watered during dry spells and spur-pruned after the fashion of an apple or pear tree.

The winter jasmine is everybody's shrub. It can be grown against a house wall or a fence or allowed to cascade down a bank or retaining wall. Pruning is apt to interfere with the production of long flower shoots. I find that cutting of these sprays for the house is sufficient pruning even for a big, old plant.

Associated with the jasmine or the winter sweet, a clump or two of the rosy winter-flowering heath—*Erica carnea* (now *E. herbacea*)—give brightness. Unlike many of the heathers this species does very well on lime or chalk and even relished our limy clay. Its season begins with the small-growing *E. c.* 'Eileen Porter' in November, followed by 'King George', 'Winter Beauty', 'James Backhouse' and 'Ruby Glow' carrying one on until March. All these form close mats of colour, followed by pleasant green foliage for the rest of the year. There is a vigorously spreading white variety known as 'Springwood', which with us began to flower in January, and a counterpart known as 'Springwood Pink'.

Taller-growing *E.* × *darleyensis* reaches 45 cm (18 in) with long sprays of lilac mauve. There is an excellent white heather—*E. mediterranea* 'W. T. Rackliff' which makes a 60-cm (2-ft) bush and bears pure white bells that are particularly striking against the fresh dark green of the foliage.

In February and March *E. mediterranea* begins to flower. Of this the best form, 'Superba', makes a bush of 90 cm (3 ft) or more and makes a fine show with its rosy-lilac bells. The dwarfer form 'Brightness' is also good.

In February, a relative of the forsythias comes into bloom with sweetly scented, white, tubular flowers that are just flushed with pink. *Abeliophyllum distichum* does well against a west wall and carries on until the yellow of the first forsythias greets the arrival of spring.

Beloved for their promise of spring, the earliest catkins of the year are eagerly awaited by gardeners and their households. Fortunately, most catkin-bearing shrubs are indifferent to lime. Perhaps the most pleasing is one of the first to bloom—*Garrya elliptica*. The garrya is a tall evergreen shrub with dull, dark leaves and infinitely decorative ropes of catkins, the individual flowers of which are suede-green flushed with rose and dove and delicately fringed. The male form of this shrub bears the finest catkins: they may be a foot long when fully developed. A well-grown bush in full flower is a most desirable possession in the dreary months of January and February.

Often planted as a wall shrub, the garrya will do well on a west or even on a north wall. It shows to its best advantage against stone or creamwash, the light background throwing the pattern of matt leaves and dangling catkins into relief. I have seen it used atop a bank, where the dripping pale green ropes were magnificently effective as they overhung a path below. To the flower-arranger the garrya is a gift—showy and dramatic when placed in a cream or white jug against a neutral background or on a window ledge so that the light illumines the gold pollen dust on the catkin fringes.

Probably the 'pussy willow' is the most familiar form of catkin, and there is no need to wait until Palm Sunday for this silvery, silky-furred delight. *Salix caprea,* the true palm or goat willow, yields occasional early forms which may be found in flower in the lanes in January. This species, however, is too big for most gardens. *S. gracilistyla* (from Japan) is of a more convenient size and yields quantities of slim, silvery 'pussy' catkins on attractively woolly twigs. This willow needs a dampish spot. For the dry, sandy garden, *S. irrorata* (from Arizona) is a more satisfactory choice. Its catkins are prettily tinged with pink when first they open, and like those of *gracilistyla* they will be freely borne in January and February. A small, compact, slender-branched cultivar of the purple osier known as *S. purpurea* 'Gracilis' might be planted. This variety has the added charm of bright, purple bark and plentiful, slender catkins.

Stachyurus praecox is a shrub which must be included here, for its stiff ropes of creamy bells are true catkins in appearance and are borne in February. This shrub also has reddish bark to enhance its appearance.

Corylus avellana 'Contorta' is a hazel with twisted branches, whose hanging 'lamb's tail' catkins are likely to appeal as indoor decorations. Of similar charm, but later to flower is *Corylopsis spicata,* a member of the witch-hazel family and one of the most subtly pretty shrubs in the spring garden. Its small, primrose-yellow flowers are carried in pendent racemes of about 3 cm ($1\frac{1}{2}$ in), consisting of perhaps eight flowers to the raceme. Unlike most catkins, those of *C. spicata* are sweetly fragrant. In time the shrub may reach 1·2 or 1·5 m (4 or 5 ft) in height and a greater spread, with attractively drooping branches. It is amazingly floriferous and the lightness and airiness of its tight little racemes make it a charming sight in the March sunshine. Unfortunately, its flowers are susceptible to spring frosts; it therefore needs a sheltered and partly-shaded situation.

A favourite with us for its fragrance is *Osmaronia cerasiformis*. Unfortunately this is apt to become chlorotic on shallow, chalk soils but it will grow well in all kinds of clay. Making a thicket of erect stems about 1·2 m (4 ft) high, the deciduous osmaronia produces racemes of almond-scented white, ribes-like flowers in February and March. One bush will scent a large area of garden. On shallow, alkaline soils an unrelated shrub with a similar name, the bigeneric × *Osmarea* 'Burkwoodii' will perform the same service. It makes a mounded dense bush of 90 cm (3 ft) or more across with neat dark evergreen leaves and milky-white, small, tubular flowers in April or May.

The bladder sennas are useful hardy shrubs that will grow anywhere. The two best are *Colutea arborescens* × *media* with grey pea-like foliage and rich, bronze-yellow flowers, and *C. a.* × *orientalis* with attractive glaucous leaves and coppery flowers. In both cases the flowers are followed by the large inflated seed pods that have given the genus its common name.

ELEVEN

Roses on Lime, Chalk and Clay

Many people think that one needs clay to grow roses well. This is not the case. Hybrid tea roses certainly prefer a heavy soil, yet in our limy clay they often suffered from mineral deficiencies and had to be sprayed with manganese sulphate and watered with Epsom salts to supply magnesium. It is a fact that roses do best in a slightly acid soil but this need deter nobody from growing them on any soils the pH of which is not above 8. Soils of greater alkalinity are not usual in the British Isles although it is possible that they could occur locally where very heavy liming had artificially raised the pH or where vast quantities of bones had been buried.

On all alkaline soils, as also on alkaline clays, the plants which do best are those with the coarsest roots and this is particularly true of roses. Most hybrid teas of the vigorous 'Peace' family, for instance, will succeed on shallow chalk soils or in the limiest of clays provided that the ground has been reasonably well prepared before planting. Weaker growers such as the old 'Mme Herriot', 'Ena Harkness', 'Mme Dieudonné', 'Margaret', 'Grand'mère Jenny'—which although related to 'Peace' lacks its vigour—and 'New Yorker', to name only our own failures, are not likely to succeed, nor are roses with much pernetiana blood. On the other hand 'Peace' itself, the raspberry red 'Karl Herbst', 'Monique' and 'June Park' in deep pink, 'Eden Rose' with its vivid colouring and silvery reverse, the carmine red 'Opera', pinky-red 'Fragrant

142

Cloud', scarlet 'Konrad Adenauer', 'Pink Favourite', bicolour 'Rose Gaujard' in carmine and silver, and the brilliant 'Super Star' are all strong enough to succeed on any clay or even pure alkaline soil, while the pink and gold 'Shot Silk' seems to like lime but succeeds better in the north of the country.

Most of the new floribunda roses do well on limy soils and one may enjoy slightly smaller and more refined blooms of similar shape to those of the hybrid tea roses from such varieties as the pretty 'Pink Parfait', orange-scarlet 'Korona', orange-yellow 'Telstar', the subtle 'Lilac Charm' and 'Queen Elizabeth' in clear pink and the salmon-pink 'Elizabeth of Glamis'. With looser blooms of more informal shape which open flat to reveal the centres of golden stamens, 'Evelyn Fison' (scarlet), 'Fervid' (deep red flushed with orange), 'Shepherd's Delight' (sunset colours of pinky-orange and red), 'Golden Fleece' and the lovely semi-double 'Iceberg', also succeed. Useful too are the old hybrid perpetuals—the white 'Frau Karl Druschki', the sumptuous crimson 'Hugh Dickson' and the silvery-pink 'Mrs. John Laing'.

Other roses which do well under alkaline conditions are the vigorous climbing sports of some of the hybrid teas. 'Climbing Shot Silk', 'Climbing Picture' and 'Climbing Madame Butterfly' in pink, and the glorious, fragrant 'Souvenir de Claudius Denoyel' with very large flat blooms of velvety crimson-red.

Most of the ramblers do well enough on lime and chalk but in choosing them some discrimination should be exercised. There is little excuse these days for planting the aggressively pink 'Dorothy Perkins' or the blatant crimson-pink and white 'American Pillar'. Nobody could tire of the creamy 'Alberic Barbier' or the coppery-pink 'Albertine'. The pinky-fawn 'François Juranville' is also good as are such yellows as 'Easlea's Golden Rambler' and 'Emily Gray'. Some rather newer climbing roses of this type bloom on and off from May until frost. Some of the best of these are the scarlet 'Danse du Feu', 'Golden Showers', the dark scarlet 'Guinée' and 'Meg' which is a very good semi-double pink rose with yellow shadings. Older climbers with similarly long seasons of bloom are the pale pink, very vigorous 'Mme Alfred Carrière', 'Zéphirine Drouhin' which is practically thornless and bears a profusion of rather floppy, sweetly scented flowers in raspberry pink, and the incomparable single yellow 'Mermaid' with its wonderful amber stamens.

Uncommon ramblers which flower at midsummer only are 'Flora' with nodding lilac-pink flowers, 'Felicité et Perpétue' with masses of white flowers rather larger than those of the average rambler, and the creamy-pink 'Adelaide d'Orléans'. These three have the advantage of retaining their glossy, healthy-looking foliage for most of the winter.

A treasure for warm walls in mild localities is the May-flowering double yellow Banksian rose—*Rosa banksiae* 'Lutea'—with its clusters of silky yellow rosettes.

On warm, sunny walls, too, will thrive such gems as the well-loved 'Gloire de Dijon' with quilted flowers in warm buff-apricot, 'Desprez à Fleur Jaune' with old-fashioned, richly-scented flowers in apricot-yellow, traditionally centred by a pretty button-eye, the pure crimson, silky velvet 'Cramoisie Supérieure', the rich pink 'La Follette' from the Riviera and the deep pink Australian-bred 'Kitty Kininmonth'. These last two, with the Banksian rose, are very vigorous, growing to a height of 7·5 m (25 ft) or more. They are ideal for the south or south-west wall of a house.

Vigorous though they may be, none of these roses will grow without adequate soil preparation. Where shallow soil overlies chalk or limestone, individual holes for each rose should be prepared. The sub-stratum must be broken up with a pickaxe to small rubble and half a barrowload of good loam, freely mixed with rotted manure or compost, should be added for each rose. Alternatively, I have seen it suggested that one might make raised beds, importing loam to give a depth of at least 30 cm (a foot) of good soil. My opinion is that such beds would dry out rather quickly and that the buying in of sufficient loam would be expensive.

Clay soils, on the other hand, may waterlog and so must be

drained before planting as no rose will grow well in waterlogged conditions. If you are able to start off your roses with a load of farmyard manure, so much the better. Roses thrive on manure and good though compost may be it cannot quite replace a load or two of honest farmyard 'muck'. All roses benefit from an early-summer mulch consisting of a 7·5-cm (3-in) layer of moist peat, chopped green bracken, or even lawn-mowings, applied when the soil is wet after rain. Care must be taken, however, to keep the mulch a few centimetres (inches) away from the actual plants. The mulching material should be spread over the root area and between the bushes, blanketing the soil and keeping in the moisture. The soil is benefited, too, when eventually the mulch rots down to form humus.

Where roses are grown in formal beds they should be mulched also in January or March whenever pruning is finished. This mulch should consist of manure and well-rotted compost, reinforced with bone meal or hoof and horn, or hop manure.

However much trouble one takes, though, the growing of exhibition hybrid tea roses on pure chalk is a chancy affair. Where the aim is generous quantities of bloom for garden decoration and for cutting, the varieties suggested earlier in this chapter will give good results.

For a prodigal display of blossom in sunny, well-drained gardens on chalk or limestone slopes the China roses are ideal. So sited they will send out great wands of growth, generously covered in bloom and they will continue flowering, on and on, one burst of blossom following another from late May until December. Good varieties to choose are the 'Old Blush China', cherry-crimson 'Fellemberg', 'Comtesse du Cayla' with deep salmon-pink flowers with a gold reverse and the chamaeleon-flowered 'Mutabilis', the blooms of which change from chamois-yellow to pink and finally to crimson with a softer and less garish effect than that of the modern 'Masquerade'.

Pleasant to include in mixed borders are some of the old garden roses. Here again, one must choose the vigorous growers —moss roses such as the charming pink 'Common Moss', 'Com-

tesse de Murinais' with beautifully quilled and quartered white
flowers, the bright pink 'Duchesse de Verneuil' and the maroon-
crimson 'Capitaine John Ingram'; centifolias, the 'cabbage' roses
of cottage gardens, such as the crested pink 'Chapeau de
Napoleon', the delicate blush 'Juno', 'Robert le Diable' with
richly-coloured flowers in violet, purple and cerise; the sturdy
semi-double pink damask, 'St. Nicholas', and 'Trigintipetala',
another damask and one which was used at Kazanlik to produce
the original attar of roses; some of the stronger gallicas such as
the old red rose of Lancaster, *R. gallica officinalis* and its striped
counterpart *g. versicolor* ('Rosa Mundi'), the gay, light crimson
flowers of which are slashed with blush-white. These old roses
are full of character and scent. They are true gems of the rose
world yet to eyes accustomed to the hybrid teas with their high-
centred form and modern colours they may at first come as something of a shock. Stop thinking of them in conjunction with the
moderns and one becomes enchanted by their gentle colours, the
clear soft pinks, creamy blush, darkest black-crimson, sumptuous
purples lit and splashed with maroon and scarlet and those smoky
lavender-greys sought after today by would-be breeders of a
'blue' rose. The shape, too, of these roses appeals—whether they
are full of a hundred petals like the centifolias, flat and lit with a
great boss of golden stamens as are many of the semi-doubles, or
tightly quilled and quartered, and button-eyed.

The Alba group, too, offers a choice for the most difficult sites,
flowering well even on north walls and growing vigorously in the
poorest of shallow soils overlying chalk or full of tree roots. Of
these I would choose 'Maiden's Blush' with small, attractively
muddled flowers of flesh-pink, which blush rosily towards the
centre, 'Celestial' with larger, truly lovely flowers of a warm silky
pink, 'Königin von Dänemark' of an even warmer pink with rosy
shadings and, for its associations, the double white Jacobite rose
R. alba maxima.

Particularly suited to heavy soils, regardless of their lime content, are such Bourbon roses as 'Mme Isaac Péreire' with large,
superbly scented, quilted flowers of rosy carmine which blue as

they age, making the modern rose-lover shudder but delighting those who have given their hearts to these older roses; 'Variegata di Bologna' which is white with neat purple stripes and splashes, the more vividly marked 'Commandant Beaurepaire' in pink and white and carmine, the superb 'Boule de Neige' its snowy petals rolled back from its high centre like some magnificent camellia, the rose-pink 'La Reine Victoria' and its famous sport, the creamy blush 'Mme Pierre Oger'. These roses, with the exception of 'Variegata di Bologna' and 'Commandant Beaurepaire', can be relied upon to flower again in autumn as can the attractively-scented hybrid musks, all of which are good. Such varieties as 'Felicia' (silvery-pink), 'Francesca' (pale yellow), 'Moonlight' (lemon-white with bronze foliage), and 'Will Scarlett' (scarlet), have a long season of flower and are useful to make large, free-blooming bushes in the mixed border or to plant as self-support-ing hedges spaced 90 cm (3 ft) apart and sheared hard back each February or March so that they grow sturdy and bushy and will remain well-clothed to the ground. *Rosa gallica officinalis* and *g. versicolor* may be planted alternately to form a striking, summer-flowering hedge. They should be given similar treatment.

The Burnett roses or Spinosissimas (*R. pimpinellifolia*) are useful on account of their early flowering. They bloom in May but like many of the older roses have only one season of flower. They are, however, most charming and very distinctive, making small mounded bushes of dense growth with the typical small, greeny-grey foliage and reddish stems of the Burnett rose. With their thicket-forming habit they may easily be propagated by division in autumn. A hedge of these divisions would make a charming feature in any garden and might be used to edge a terrace or other formal area.

All the Burnett roses are pretty but my especial favourite is 'William III' which grows to only 60 cm (2 ft) high and makes a dense hummock of grey-green leaves freely sprinkled with plum-crimson, double, rosetted flowers which quickly fade to a wonder-ful lilac-pink. 'Mrs. Colville', too, is pleasing with decorative single flowers of a rich, crimson-purple with a white centre. A special advantage is its lack of tiny thorns. 'Falkland' is a semi-double of warm creamy pink with very grey leaves. With the old 'Williams Double Yellow' rose we return to the typical yellow colouring of the group. An added distinction is a bunch of green carpels in the centre of the flower giving a pleasing buttony effect.

True these Burnett or Scots roses flower but once a year yet that is little enough drawback for the pleasure of having roses in May. They take up less room than most other flowering shrubs and their blooms last longer.

'Harison's Yellow' is almost double-flowered with large sulphur-yellow blooms. It makes a slender bush of some 1·5 m (5 ft) and is thought to be a hybrid between the Burnett Rose—*Rosa spinosissima*—and *R. foetida*, the Austrian briar. Easy, trouble-free and with a good scent, 'Harison's Yellow' or *R.* × *harisonii*, is a valuable rose for any garden.

A modern *spinosissima* hybrid, 'Frühlingsgold' (Spring Gold) is one of the loveliest roses I know. Its loose, semi-double flowers are immense and of a luminous butter-yellow. It makes a big, sprawling bush 2·1 m (7 ft) high and as much across. Where there is room, you could choose no better shrub to bridge the gap between May and June.

At the same time flowers the deeper coloured 'Canary Bird' (from *R. xanthina spontanea*) the hue of the flowers of which match the soft yet brilliant yellow of the breast feathers of the bird after which it is named. The flowers are single, as big as an old-fashioned five-shilling piece and shapely. Its foliage, too, is attractive, fresh, green and fern-like. 'Canary Bird' is a rose to treasure.

I have seen it stated that the Japanese *rugosa* roses are lime-haters. This statement is utterly unfounded in fact. While many Japanese plants are undoubtedly calcifuge, the *rugosa* roses are not among them. They thrive in any alkaline soils ranging from the alkaline clay of our former garden to the sheer chalk cliffs of the late Sir Frederick Stern's garden at Highdown. Making big bushes of 1·2–1·8 m (4 to 6 ft) with an equal spread, the rugosas are ideal roses for shrub beds or to grow as isolated specimens in cut-out circles in grass. In fact, the growing of sturdy shrub roses such as these, together with groups of peonies, drifts of bulbs such as daffodils, narcissi and the later-flowering, starry blue camassias is one of the most attractive ways of coping with upland gardens on chalk or limestone. Such a garden is practically trouble-free. Paths may be cut with the mower and the coarser grass scythed, when the bulb foliage has died down, in summer and again in November. Spacious treatment of this sort is ideal for the rugosas which need plenty of light and air around them if they are to remain furnished to the ground. Given sufficient room they will form shapely-green mounds of handsome foliage, liberally studded with bloom from May until October. The true *rugosa* varieties have not merely one season of flower, nor two, nor yet even three. They bloom on and on throughout the summer, each cluster of faded flowers being quickly replaced by fresh buds and requiring only the service of dead-heading.

In our old garden three or four varieties of *rugosa* roses provided a more solid display of flower than that offered by any bed of hybrid teas and their flowering was more continuous than that of any roses other than Chinas. The flowers of many varieties, too, are bigger than those of the China roses. The buds are shapely, opening to flat, single, or loosely double, blooms of 7·5 to 10 cm (3 to 4 in) across, and they never have too many petals to conceal the central cluster of gold or cream-coloured stamens. Another attraction of the *rugosa* roses is their scent—honey-sweet in 'Blanc Double de Coubert', heavier and more fruity in 'Roseraie de l'Haÿ'.

It is important, however, to get varieties of the true *rugosa* species as against the hybrids, crossed with other roses, which although excellent in flower become leggy and ungainly and will seldom remain furnished to the ground.

My favourite rugosa is the white 'Blanc Double de Coubert' which although officially designated double has more of a semi-single look about its flat, gold-centred, paper-white flowers. 'Belle Poitevine' is similar with flowers of a gentle, lilac-pink. 'Roseraie de l'Haÿ' is of that triumphant crimson-purple beloved by old rose enthusiasts and abhorred by modern hybrid tea rose fans. All the roses mentioned here are semi-double or double. However, to enjoy the second splendour of the rugosas—their large, tomato-like fruits—one should grow the single varieties whose blooms are unfortunately more fleeting but no less prodigally borne. *Rugosa* 'Rubra' is the same colour as 'Roseraie de l'Haÿ', but with single flowers, the rich cream stamens of which show off the colouring perfectly. *Rugosa* 'Scabrosa', in spite of its unattractive-sounding name, is pleasant with 12·5-cm (5-in) flowers of deep mauve-pink and enormous autumnal hips. 'Frau Dagmar Hästrup' is the connoisseur's darling with silky, single, cream-stamened flowers of clear rose.

Pruning should be restricted to the removal of old or dead wood from the base. Any attempt to follow the traditional hybrid tea system of cutting back to three buds from the base will only spoil the bush.

Not least among the rugosas' garden virtues is their immunity to black-spot. Their rugged, serrate foliage has so far resisted all infection. Nor do they need perfect rose-growing soil. Not only will they grow in a chalk cliff, but they will form a hedge atop a dry bank or grow even on a sand-dune. In fact the poorer the soil the more freely they seem to flower and the deeper is their autumn leaf-colour of rich ripe corn.

Making big, free-flowering bushes like the rugosas are some of the modern shrub roses. One of the loveliest of these is 'Nevada' which makes a shrub 1·8 m (6 ft) high and in time perhaps 3 m (10 ft) across with arching, red-brown branches thickly set with almost single, creamy-white blooms 10 cm (4 in) across. 'Nevada' blooms in May and June and again in August with a few later flowers to follow. Its soft green foliage is small and neat and, like 'Zéphirine Drouhin', its stems are blessedly sparse of prickles. Like the *rugosa* roses, 'Nevada' is an ideal shrub to set in grass or to occupy a prominent place in a mixed border. For dry gardens 'Poulsen's Park Rose' is particularly good, with clusters of shapely buds opening to almost double, silvery-pink blooms. It flowers in two main bursts.

Showy, with full-blown quartered flowers of salmon-orange, 'Oratam' blooms only at midsummer. It is ideal grouped with mock oranges such as *Philadelphus* 'Virginale' and associated with a yellow rose such as the once-blooming 'Gold Bush', or 'Maigold' or the more continuous-flowering 'Mermaid', pruned to bush-shape. Other good shrub roses are 'First Choice' with single, flame-coloured, butterfly-like flowers, the salmon-pink 'Kathleen Ferrier', 'Marguerite Hilling' a deep pink sport from 'Nevada' to which it makes a good companion and the lemon-white 'Morning Stars'. All these yield two or more bursts of bloom a season.

Also attractive when grown in grass, or given a prominent position among shrubs or other flowers is the May-blooming 'Frühlingsgold' mentioned earlier in this chapter while 'Scarlet Fire' is another rose of this type with heraldically shaped, velvety blooms of bright scarlet. 'Scarlet Fire' flowers at midsummer only.

Suitable to place in grass or to train as an informal hedge within the garden are the hybrid sweet briars with typical *rubiginosa* fragrance and single flowers in pink, copper, buff or crimson. 'Amy Robsart', 'Lady Penzance', 'Lord Penzance' and 'Meg Merrilees' are all good. A *must* to use in grassy places in larger gardens is *Rosa moyesii* with tall arching growth and perfect, blood-red Tudor roses followed by splendid, scarlet, bottle-shaped fruits. *R. m.* 'Sealing Wax' is similar but with cherry-pink flowers. The threepenny-bit rose, *R. farreri persetosa*, has a charm of its own and is valuable in early summer with its pale pink flowers that are the size of an old silver threepenny piece.

These vigorous shrub roses need little pruning—cutting out of really old or dead wood is sufficient. Many of the other roses mentioned in this chapter may be treated in the same way. Indeed on our former alkaline clay we found it best to treat even the hybrid teas and floribundas in this manner. Where roses are growing strongly I think it best to regard them as flowering shrubs, which in fact they are, and to prune them only lightly.

Weak-growing roses need to be stimulated by more severe pruning, but it is even more important that they should be fed. Mulches of manure or hop-manure should be applied in February or March, supplemented by a general rose fertilizer and a later moisture-conserving mulch of peat or lawn-mowings as recommended earlier in this chapter.

Where a formal effect is desired the hybrid musk, China, gallica and damask roses may be pruned back hard in January, February or March. In the milder part of the country, winter pruning pays undoubted dividends by resulting in earlier crops of bloom. In colder areas where early buds might be frosted, pruning should be delayed until March.

TWELVE

Hedges for Alkaline Soils and Clay

When thinking of hedges for alkaline soils, beech comes naturally to mind. It grows well on light chalky or limestone soils and if clipped once a year at the right time, in August, retains its warm brown leaves through the winter. So, although not an evergreen, it does indeed strike a cheerful note in the colder months. However, a warning should be given here because although beech grows well on light alkaline soils it will not tolerate solid clay.

For clays hornbeam is preferable. Hornbeam retains its dead leaves during the winter in the same way as beech although their yellow colouring is perhaps not quite so attractive.

My husband and I planted a hedge of beech over twenty years ago in our old garden in a part where a foot of good loam overlies the clay and there it did well. However, finding the unrelieved brown tedious we interplanted some well-grown bushes of *Escallonia macrantha* among the beech so that its glossy, evergreen leaves might relieve the brown and give living colour in winter. This was a particularly happy choice because the escallonia bears spikes of rosy-red flowers in June and again in mild spells in November and December. For some inland districts, however the escallonia might not be sufficiently hardy and one might substitute holly, yew, thuja—or even all three. Indeed the famous mixed hedges at Hidcote Manor in the Cotswolds are the finest I have ever seen and are built up of green beech, copper beech, holly and yew, giving a most striking and handsome effect of contrasting colour and texture. An effective mixture would be, in the order of planting, seven green beech, two copper beech, one dark green holly 'J. C. van Tol', one silver variegated holly such as 'Silver Queen' or *Ilex aquifolium* 'Argenteomarginata', one holly 'J. C. van Tol', two copper beech, seven green beech, three yews. Such a hedge would give colour, interest and shelter throughout the year.

It might be argued that the hollies and yews, being slower-growing than the beech, might at first give a ragged effect. This need not be the case if the beech is cut back each August to induce bushy growth while the leaders of the hollies and yews are not stopped until the hedge has reached its required height. The sides should be sheared well back in August and a wedge shape induced, wider at the base and tapering towards the top to prevent snow-damage. After their first year, the yews in such a mixed hedge may be fed in April with a handful of nitrate of soda mixed with sand. This will speed up their growth but care must be taken not to let the mixture touch the stems. It should be dusted over the soil above the roots and kept at least 10 cm (4 in) away from the trunks. Holly and copper beech in the proportion of three hollies to two beech make an effective mixture.

The success of all hedges depends upon the preparation of the ground before planting. Where possible the ground should be trenched to a width of at least 60 (2) or, preferably 90 cm (3 ft); rotted manure, seaweed, hop-manure or compost being incorporated in the second spit. No hedge plants should be set less than 30 cm (a foot) apart and hollies, yews and thujas should be spaced at a distance of 60 cm (2 ft).

A mixed hedge such as I have suggested is suitable for any alkaline soil other than clay. On clays, hornbeam should replace the beech and it would be wiser to omit the holly and to use extra yews in its place. Another plant that associates with beech to good effect, and does well on clay, is the handsome evergreen laurustinus—*Viburnum tinus*—which is so effective in winter and early spring with its clustered heads of reddish buds opening to white, sweetly-scented flowers.

Hedges for Alkaline Soils and Clay

Near the shore on the cliffs in seaside districts, spray-resistant shrubs should be used and subjects chosen to give effective shelter as well as to make attractive boundary hedges. One of the best of these is the fresh green *Griselinia littoralis* with its slightly fleshy leaves. This will make a tall hedge, up to 2·4 m (8 ft) if necessary, or it may be kept lower. *Senecio greyi* is evergrey rather than evergreen and bears attractive lemon-yellow daisies in early summer. It will make a hedge of 1·2 to 1·5 m (4 to 5 ft) in height and should be allowed a width of at least 90 cm (3 ft) at the base. Standing the full assault of the wind it is an invaluable defence against the gales which sweep in from the sea. In the south and west *Hebe salicifolia* is another good hedging subject which seeds itself freely in seaside districts. Seedlings may usually be begged from fellow gardening enthusiasts, and cuttings strike easily. A proportion of violet, lavender and blue-tipped-white varieties might be included to vary the white bottle-brushes of the type. In mild districts all three do well on clay.

The daisy-flowered olearias make good hedges for seaside areas although they do need plenty of room. *Olearii haastii* is the rather dull 'daisy bush' that grows almost anywhere in the British Isles and is often seen in towns where it is useful as it seems able to withstand a considerable degree of air pollution. More exciting for seaside shelter hedges are *O. macrodonta* 'Major' with broad, grey, holly-like leaves and heads of white daisies that smell deliciously of honey in the hot June sun.

Where there is not enough room for the wide-growing olearia, *Escallonia macrantha* might be chosen, although at least 75 cm (2½ ft) must be allowed for the base of this. This is a well-known seaside hedging shrub with glossy, aromatic, evergreen leaves and spikes of pretty, rose-red bells in June and autumn. Less often seen and suitable for use further inland in all but the bleakest districts is the more compact *E.* 'Edinensis' with rose-pink flowers, which takes up less room than *E. macrantha*. *E.* 'Langley-ensis' is another hardy variety with rather deeper-coloured flowers borne on distinctively arching branches. All will succeed remarkably in poor, shallow soil.

A delightful hedge, which will succeed inland as well as at the sea and which will stand a great deal of wind, may be planted of *Elaeagnus pungens* or of its even better hybrid with the tender *E. macrophylla—E.* × *ebbingei*. Both are useful for shallow chalk or limestone. *E. pungens* is dark green in the type but it may effectively be interplanted with *E. p.* 'Maculata', the leaves of which are brightly splashed with gold. A watch should be kept on the latter, however, so that any plain green shoots may be immediately removed, thus keeping in check any tendency to reversion. *E.* × *ebbingei* was recommended in Chapter Five as a handsome evergreen for the mixed border. It is a splendid plant, its young leaves being silvery in spring and summer. Their top surfaces become a lively, glossy green in autumn and winter, reflecting the light and seeming to ripple as they glint in the wind. Both *E. pungens* and *E.* × *ebbingei* may be readily increased by layering.

For heavy, cold clay, *Phillyrea angustifolia* makes a fine hedge. It will stand any amount of wind and is very hardy, and quite decorative with narrow, dark evergreen leaves.

In milder districts one might plant instead *Osmanthus decora* with large leathery leaves and masses of small, fragrant white flowers in spring. This succeeds better on chalk than its more popular and, indeed, excellent relative *O. delavayi* which seems to be short-lived on shallow soils, although in North Wales on heavier soil it succeeds well. With tiny, dark, holly-like leaves and fragrant white 'daphne' flowers in April this is an adorable shrub. It stands clipping well and should be trimmed immediately after flowering although like all flowering hedges it should not be cut back more than necessary as the cutting inevitably results in the loss of some flowers.

Chamaecyparis lawsoniana and its varieties are often used for hedging but such use is not really fair to the trees. Chamaecyparis of all kinds make valuable screens and are beautiful where they are allowed to attain their full height. They are not really suitable to be kept to hedge height. Nor are the thujas which, however, often prove more satisfactory than the chamaecyparis. The less vigorous common juniper—*Juniperus communis* makes a fine hedge for windy, downland areas while of the cupressus group *Chamaecyparis* 'Green Hedger' and *Cupressocyparis × leylandii* give the most satisfactory results.

Cupressus macrocarpa should never be planted as a hedge because its foliage becomes too dense when clipped and shuts out light and air from the stem with the result that the plants often fall a victim to aphis and the hedge dies in patches. Where this has happened to an established hedge one can either plant a second hedge within the dying cupressus, removing the cupressus when the inner hedge has grown, or one may plant ivy or euonymus to climb up the dead trees and fill in the gaps. My husband and I had this problem on our own hands because we planted *C. macrocarpa* round part of our old garden, hoping for quick shelter to enable us to grow choice shrubs. By pruning with the secateurs and admitting as much air and light as possible to the stems we managed to avoid aphis. We allowed the hedge to reach 42 m (14 ft), feeling that it was more likely to succeed if not kept too low, but the trees were subject to windrock. We anchored them with boulders over their roots yet after every gale had to firm in one or two and felt sure the time would come when some of them would die. We made some provision for this by planting an inner barrier of *Hebe salicifolia* down one side of our boundary, but on the other two sides there was little room. If the unhappy day came and any of our cupressus died we could have chosen the vigorous *Eunonymous fortunei* 'Silver Queen' to clothe any dead part of the hedge. This variety, with broad evergreen leaves brightly variegated with silver, will climb to a good height. However, though we left this garden some fourteen years ago, we frequently visited it when we returned to Wales after a brief stay in Cornwall and saw that, astonishingly the *C. macrocarpa* hedge survived in spite of heavy cutting back. But when we last saw it it was still rather bare and I would never again plant it in that climate.

All the eunonymus do well on lime and chalk and the shrubby evergreen *E. japonicus* is worth considering as a hedge plant, particularly in town or coastal gardens as it stands air-pollution and salt-bearing winds remarkably well. Where a lighter effect is needed, the silver-variegated *E. j.* 'Macrophyllus Albus' might be included in the ratio of 7:2. Care must be taken to write clearly when ordering or the slower-growing small-leaved *E. j.* 'Microphyllus' might be delivered instead!

Cotoneaster lacteus makes a fine evergreen hedge with handsome foliage and colourful berries. It should be pruned with secateurs rather than shears when time allows.

A prickly hedge, which though not evergreen is remarkably proof against boys, dogs and other garden invaders, is *Berberis thunbergii* which bears red berries and colours brilliantly in autumn. Its dark-leaved variety *B. t. atropurpurea* makes a very effective hedge that is still not often seen. Both may easily be kept to a compact shape. For a hedge within the garden *Chaenomeles × superba*, either in a single variety or mixed, makes a delightful informal hedge. It needs pruning with the secateurs rather than clipping and this job is best done in January when one can see the flower buds and so not remove more of them than necessary. A light shearing in July to remove the aggressively spiny shoots before the wood becomes hard will act in the same way as the summer pruning of fruit trees and help flower production. Chaenomeles may be interplanted with holly or with the spring-flowering *Berberis × stenophylla* where there is room for a wider hedge.

Another thorny subject which makes an excellent boundary hedge to shut out straying cattle and sheep is *Pyracantha rogersiana*. However, this should only be planted where there is room for it to be allowed to grow informally so that one may get the full benefit of both flowers and fruit.

An interesting plant for a dwarf hedge, perhaps to define a terrace or rose garden, is the crimson-leafed form of *Prunus* called 'Cistena', the purple-leaf sand cherry. The top six leaves of the growing shoots are an almost unbelievably bright crimson, giving an effect rather like that of *Pieris forrestii* on acid soils and making the hedge look as if it bore bright red flowers. Its actual flowers, too, are attractive—white with blush-pink centres—and very freely borne on both young and old wood in March and April. To be seen at its best this prunus should be planted in well-prepared ground. An annual dressing of nitrogen should be given every spring and it should be cut well back immediately after flowering. A mulch of damp peat after rain in May will be beneficial and in dry spells the hedge may need watering. It does well on improved clays.

Lavender is a favourite subject for hedges within the garden and is particularly suited to sunny, dry slopes. For a hedge of about 60 cm (2 ft) 'Twickel Purple' is the variety to choose and is effective in flower with good dark purple spikes. A variety known as 'Folgate' has greyer leaves and lighter flowers and is dwarfer and best sheared back to 45 cm (18 in) after flowering. The 'Hidcote' varieties are really too dwarf for hedges and best used on rock gardens or banks, planted at the forefront of other shrubs or used to edge a rose-bed. They should be sheared back to tight cushions of growth in September. The 'Old English' or 'Mitcham' lavender, 'Dutch Lavender' and the 'Seal' lavender have the finest scent and will make hedges of about 90 cm (3 ft) in height. They, too, must be sheared back severely after flowering otherwise they will become leggy and straggly and will break in the wind. Properly cared for, lavender hedges will go on for years. When they approach old age it is as well to have a reserve stock of young bushes grown from cuttings taken with a heel in June and dibbled in a shady, moist bed to grow.

Rosemary, too, makes a pleasant hedge. Taller-growing than lavender, it may be used to make a hedge up to 1·2 m (4 ft). It is said to be not quite as hardy as lavender but will succeed in most districts if planted in full sun and sharply-drained soil. We had a rosemary hedge in North Staffordshire at a height of 210 m (700 ft) above sea level which survived the worst of the war-time winters without ill-effect. Rosemary is best sheared in spring as soon as the flowers fade.

In conjunction with lavender and rosemary one thinks naturally of roses. Acceptance by the gardening public of some of the recent cheap offers of so-called 'hedging' roses (many of which

are none other than nurserymen's reject rose-budding stocks)
has led to so much disappointment and disgust that something
must be said about those roses which will satisfactorily form
decorative hedges within the garden itself. I say 'within the
garden' because no rose is to my mind suitable for boundary
hedging. For the boundary a tough, clippable, sturdy, and
preferably evergreen, subject is necessary. The function of the
rose hedge is attractively to divide the garden into its separate
sections—to enclose a rose garden, to screen the vegetable patch,
to shut off a lawn from the drive—for all these purposes a rose
hedge is admirable.

There are two types of rose hedge. In one the roses are trained
upon wires. In the other the bushes are clipped to become
sturdily self-supporting and to form a dense barrier of growth.
The second, naturally, is the least trouble and, I think, the most
effective.

Where a hedge up to 1·5 m (5 ft) is required, the fragrant,
hybrid-musk roses are excellent. The silvery-pink 'Felicia',
yellow 'Francesca', lemon-white 'Moonlight', ivory 'Prosperity',
'Pink Prosperity' and the newer, sweet-pea scented, coppery-
yellow 'Daybreak' are all good for this purpose. They give a long
season of bloom and from June until October are seldom without
flowers. The soil in which they are to be planted should be deeply
dug in autumn and enriched with hoof and horn and hop manure,
farmyard manure or matured garden compost before planting
the bushes 90 cm (3 ft) apart. Shortening of the shoots by a third
each spring will result in sturdy, compact growth and a long
succession of flowers. An equally floriferous and even sturdier
barrier may be made by planting the Japanese *rugosa* hybrid
'Sarah van Fleet' with her scented saucers of delicate pink.

The main effect of *Rosa rubrifolia* lies in the plum-like bloom
of its foliage rather than in its single, bright pink flowers. It makes
a quietly pleasing hedge—an ideal background to a bed of old-
fashioned roses and other flowers or to enclose a herb garden.
This is a rose that thrives on clipping. In fact, the harder you cut
it back in March, the finer its leaf-colour.

To train upon wires, roses of stronger growth must be chosen. Many of the ramblers are ideal, though I would again plead a trend away from 'Dorothy Perkins' and 'American Pillar' in favour of the subtler 'Goldfinch', 'Amethyste', the frilly pink 'Débutante', and that muskily fragrant white rose 'The Garland'. They should be planted 3 m (10 ft) apart. Some of the sweetly-scented Bourbon roses may be similarly trained. Of these the old favourite 'Zéphirine Drouhin' is one of the most successful, producing seemingly endless bursts of its loose, raspberry-pink blooms from late May until November. 'Zéphirine Drouhin' should be planted 1·5 m (5 ft) apart, though I would place its paler sport 'Katherine Harrop' at 90 cm (3 ft) 'Mme Ernst Calvat' is another Bourbon for close planting. This is a delightful rose with very large, many petalled, globular blooms of clear pink, quilted and quartered in the most enchanting way.

THIRTEEN

Shady Borders and Underplantings

Most gardens have a shady border, perhaps on the north side of the house or garage, or against a hedge or under large trees. All these places tend to be dry because the overhanging shade keeps off the rain to some extent. However, the dryness on the north side of a wall may be easily corrected by the incorporation of moisture-holding humus and when this has been done many interesting and beautiful plants will thrive, even in very limy soils. The dryness caused by the roots of a greedy hedge or by large trees is not easily overcome and for such areas plants must be chosen that will grow in poor, dry soil.

One of the best carpeters for such ground is *Symphytum grandiflorum,* a dwarf comfrey with dark, evergreen leaves and croziers of ivory bells, tipped with orange, which arise very early in the year. *S. grandiflorum* is a quiet plant but a charming one and it spreads vigorously, rooting as it goes and colonizing difficult areas with its tight-packed growth so closely that no weeds can penetrate. It is one of Nature's best gifts to the over-gardened gardener who has not enough time to cope with the weeds.

Another fine carpeting plant for either dry or moist soil is the dwarf periwinkle, *Vinca minor,* which is a delightful plant in its own right. Apart from the type there are forms with silver and golden variegated foliage that are ideal to brighten and lighten dark corners. There are also several forms with particularly fine flowers: I have a starry, deep blue form which the late Mr. A. T.

162

Johnson collected from the Italian lakes; there are also a double blue, the excellent powder-blue single 'La Grave', a white variety, *V. m.* 'Alba', a claret-purple known as *V. m.* 'Atropurpurea' and 'Multiplex', a double claret. More forms used to be in cultivation and may still be found in different gardens and nurseries. All are worth growing and would be pleasant to collect. To ensure close, dense, weed-smothering growth and plenty of flowers, the dwarf periwinkles should be sheared over as soon as flowering finishes in the spring. A second crop of blossom usually follows in the autumn, but like the autumn-flowering of primroses and violets this is rather dependent upon mild weather.

The various ivies may also be used to carpet difficult, dry and shady areas and so render them trouble-free. Some may prefer the plain green *Hedera colchica* with its great, glossy leaves, while those who enjoy variegated foliage may prefer its cream variegated variety 'Dentata Variegata' with more sharply cut leaves. In most sunny and sheltered places the slightly tender *H. canariensis* 'Variegata' may be used to carpet the ground under shrubs or trees. This ivy has especially beautiful leaves of pale grey-green, shading into darker green, irregularly marked and margined with white. Hardier and suitable for the roughest, darkest places are the varieties of common ivy—*H. helix* 'Marginata' has smaller but similarly-coloured leaves and *H. h.* 'Buttercup' has leaves marked with yellow, giving a particularly sunny effect. *Pachysandra terminalis* is another useful carpeting plant suitable for clothing dry and rooty places.

The ivies are rather slow starters but the other plants mentioned, together with *Lamium maculatum,* the variegated creeping dead-nettle with evergreen, silver-splashed leaves and pinky-purple flowers, will clothe the soil of a desired area in a very short space of time and will efficiently smother and prevent weed growth. Far from impoverishing an already dry area of poor soil they will, by blanketing the earth, help to conserve soil moisture and to protect the roots of the trees and shrubs from drought and frost alike. They help to prevent fungus diseases by covering the soil so that no spores may fall there to breed. A garden in which the soil is for the most part covered is a healthy garden.

Ajuga reptans 'Atropurpurea', the coppery-leaved bugle with spikes of blue flowers in summer will quickly cover vacant spaces, forming a dense carpet and keeping down weeds. *A. reptans* 'Multicolor' is even more attractive, with tortoiseshell variegated foliage.

So far we have been dealing with lowly carpeting plants for troublesome, dry, rooty places. There are one or two taller subjects which will also grow in such places and help to give a decorative effect. Chief among these is the hartstongue fern which enjoys a limy soil. This is found in the catalogues under *Phyllitis scolopendrium* or *Scolopendrium vulgare*. There is a very pretty variety of hartstongue with crinkly leaves, known as *crispa*, which is worth planting along with the type to give added interest. The evergreen polypody ferns are natives of the chalkland and will do well in shady, rooty places, the sturdy *Polypodium vulgare* 'Cristata' with crinkly, divided crests at the top of the fronds is an interesting variation. Not all ferns will grow on lime and chalk. The dryopteris, the buckler fern, the royal fern, *Osmunda regalis*, and the blechnums, will not succeed. The graceful lady fern, *Athyrium filix-femina*, does well on alkaline soils but is a subject for a moister shady border.

Another taller plant for dry or moist shade is a relative of the dead-nettle which has a pleasant old-world charm. This is *Lamium orvala* with short dense spikes of pink flowers. There is also a seldom-seen white variety of this dead-nettle and the two are particularly charming when allowed to naturalize together. Increasing well by seed they make effective ground cover for the spring and summer although being herbaceous they die down completely in the winter.

In poor, rooty soil, the beautiful epimediums will thrive. Members of the berberis family, the epimediums bear dainty sprays of flowers shaped like tiny columbines. Their handsome foliage is evergreen, tinged with red, heart-shaped and dense and they make a first-class underplanting for shrubs or to grow on the shady side of a hedge to prevent weeds entangling the base. *Epimedium* × *versicolor* 'Sulphureum' is especially vigorous and dense and one of the best for ground cover. As its specific name indicates its flower sprays are pale yellow. *E. versicolor* with parti-coloured flowers in red and yellow, *E.* 'Rose Glow' the coppery *E.* × *warleyense,* the crimson *E.* × *rubrum* and the creamy-white *E. grandiflorum* are all good but the charming white-flowered *E.* × *youngianum niveum* with its light green foliage is dwarfer and more compact and so less suitable for our purpose of weed-suppression and ground cover although it would be delightful to plant in a small group as an incident in a shady border.

For moister soil in shade or for the prepared soil of a shady border against the house there are many delightful plants from which to choose. As a background or against the wall any of the Alba roses such as 'Maiden's Blush' will thrive. So will the climbing 'Gloire de Dijon' and the beautiful single 'Mermaid'. The deutzias flower quite freely even in full shade and one might choose the soft pink large-flowered *D.* 'Magician' or the bridal *D. setchuenensis corymbiflora* with its foam of white lace. Other good shrubs for shade are *Spiraea vanhouttei* with late-spring flowers and rich autumn tints, *Choisya ternata* the Mexican orange blossom with sweetly-scented white flowers and handsome evergreen leaves, lace-cap and mop-headed hydrangeas, and hypericums such as 'Hidcote'.

Foxgloves will thrive in shade and here the white variety will look particularly lovely. Seed of the white may be bought and although all the plants may not come true it is easy to recognize and discard the purple-pinks by the reddish colour of the stem and leaf stalks. Of the mixed strains in shades of pink and cream with their distinctive and beautiful spotting the Shirley strain raised by the Reverend Wilks of Shirley poppy fame is the best. The modern Excelsior strain with flowers all round the stem and the rosette-topped strain, rightly named Monstrosa, are anathema to me. They are distortions of the grace and beauty of the true foxglove.

Lovely, too, are the members of the hellebore family, none of which objects to alkaline conditions and which in fact thrive even on chalk where the ground has been broken up and a bucketful of loam and compost incorporated with the rubble. The hybrids of *Helleborus orientalis* and its allied species known as the Lenten roses will grow under hedges or in dry, rooty places among shrubs but the Christmas rose, *Helleborus niger* needs slightly richer fare and will benefit from a mulch of rotted manure after flowering while the Lenten roses ask only a blanket of leaves.

The Christmas rose hates disturbance and to protect its chaste blooms and hasten them so as to ensure a supply for Christmas, a hand light or polythene cloche should be placed over the clump at the end of November. Christmas roses take two or three years to flower freely so it is as well to plant only fine varieties to make the waiting seem worth while. *H. macranthus*, *H. niger* 'St. Brigid', *H. n.* 'Potter's Wheel', and the variety often wrongly labelled as *H. n.* 'Altifolius' are all fine forms. The wine-purple *H. atrorubens*, sometimes erroneously called the red Christmas rose is valuable, too, because it usually flowers in late December. It is easier to grow than *H. niger*, belonging as it does to the *orientalis* section and like the Lenten roses will do well in rougher ground under shrubs and hedges.

Next in importance are the Lenten roses themselves. They are misnamed, because they do not wait until Lent to bloom, often starting to flower in the first week or two of the New Year. These are hybrids with *Helleborus orientalis*, *atrorubens*, *guttatus*, *abchasicus* and *olympicus* as parents. They offer pendent, graceful, bowl-shaped blooms in shades of greeny-white, apple-blossom, dull red and darkest bloomy maroon-purple, often with attractive shadings and pepperings of colour. On the north side of a hedge or among shrubs they form delightful and unexpected patches of quiet beauty in the depth of winter. Cut and brought indoors they could be the answer to a flower-arranger's prayer. I say 'could be' because so often their treatment is not understood and they wilt within the hour. Cut with long stems, the stems split for 7·5 or 10 cm (3 or 4 in) and plunged to the neck in hot water, they will last for at least a week. If, then, they show signs of flagging they may be revived by further hot-water treatment. The water should never be changed but topped up from day to day with a really hot supply.

A third kind of hellebore which enchants many discerning gardeners but which might be more widely grown is the species *H. lividus corsicus* with multi-flowered heads of chartreuse green. The leaves of this species are noble, toothed like holly, massive and leathery—an architectural feature in their own right. (In the island of Corsica, where we have seen it growing among the *maquis*, it seldom reaches the height it does in cultivation where it may sometimes need to be staked to avoid flopping.) A hybrid *H. × sternii* is a dwarfer plant, under 30 cm (1 ft) in height to the 60 cm (2 ft) stature of *H. l. corsicus*. The leaves are trifoliate but only slightly toothed, and are marbled in a pale green and flushed underneath with livid purple. The same purple suffuses the pedicels and flowers to a greater or lesser degree which darkens with age. This is a most attractive plant but not quite as hardy as *H. l. corsicus*. However, hybrids between the two are very hardy; some with flowers of chartreuse like those of *l. corsicus* but much larger—as much as 7·5 cm (3 in) across—and often with the marbling of the leaves formerly found only in *lividus pictus* and with the dove-grey-to-purple infusion of colour, tenderly beautiful as a pigeon's breast.

In addition to these, the true *H. orientalis* species is worth growing and has very beautiful, unspotted creamy-white flowers that are almost 7·5 cm (3 in) across and carried on 37-cm (15-in) stalks. *H. odorus* may sometimes be purchased under the name *H. kochii*. It has 5-cm (2-in) wide flowers of pale primrose and scents pleasantly of elder flowers.

Hostas (funkias) with their handsome foliage and spikes of cool bell flowers enjoy shade and lime although they may also be grown in full sun. Fine species are *Hosta sieboldiana* with large blue-green leaves, *H. fortunei* 'Aurea' with golden young foliage and *H. undulata* with much smaller leaves of apple green painted with white. Taller and very graceful is the Solomon's seal, *Poly-*

gonatum multiflorum, its tall arching stems strung with ivory bells. Lilies of the valley—*Convallaria majalis*—too, will succeed but they should be planted in really well-prepared ground with a generous helping of cow-manure or rotted chicken-manure incorporated. A section of the bed should be dug up and the crowns divided and replanted every second year, incorporating more manure. Lilies of the valley seldom flower well the year after division so by treating the bed in two sections one ensures a supply of flowers.

A late-summer subject that is both colourful and uncommon is *Platycodon mariesii,* the balloon flower with inflated bells of deep blue. Low-growing, it might be planted in front of the deep red *Polygonum amplexicaule* 'Speciosum' which grows to a height of 90 cm (3 ft). The spiky growth of the polygonum contrasts with the more sprawling habit of the balloon flower. The pink bergamot, *Monarda* 'Croftway Pink', with its unusual whorled flower heads might complete the group.

Other good plants for the shady border are the rudbeckias, solidagos, *Thalictrum adiantifolium,* often known as the hardy maidenhair, with sprays of ferny foliage, the tradescantias with their tricorne flowers of white or blue, *Rodgersia pinnata,* a fine foliage plant growing to 90 cm (3 ft) high, with horse-chestnut leaves and pink flower plumes, *Potentilla* 'Gibson's Scarlet', a sprawler with velvety scarlet, black-eyed strawberry flowers and strawberry leaves, *Physostegia virginiana* 'Vivid' with stiff spikes of showy rose-coloured flowers in late summer, the day lilies— hemerocallis—which will succeed in sun or shade, *Dicentra spectabilis,* the bleeding heart which, however, needs rich and fairly moist conditions, *Cynoglossum nervosum* growing to about 45 cm (18 in) high and bearing flowers of intense, bright blue from June to September, the feathery cimicifugas, the yellow scabious-like *Cephalaria gigantea,* the long-spurred columbines (Aquilegia), the Japanese anemones, the dark-blue helmeted monkshoods, which will be found in the lists as *Aconitum,* and the interesting *Acanthus mollis* with its massive sculptured foliage and tall pink and white flower spikes. In really moist shady borders

168

the astilbes will do well and bear quantities of their feathery plumes from June to August.

Specialities might be the hardy cyclamen, the leaves of which make delightful patches of foliage even when the flowers are over. These cyclamen like lime and chalk and will do well also under trees or hedges and will even grow among ivy or grass.

Scarcely anything in the garden gives greater delight than unexpected patches of these hardy cyclamen, with their petals like the shy ears of startled fawns. Most of the hardy cyclamen increase quite rapidly by self-sown seed, so it is rather surprising that the plants are not more widely known and grown. Some people have tried them, true enough, found the corms fail, and have given them up discouraged. It is from such unsuccessful attempts that the legend of the disappearing cyclamen corms has sprung. In fact, most of these disappearances can be traced to the cyclamen corms being planted too deep; the corms should be just pressed into the ground and barely covered with soil.

The species cyclamen are now expensive to buy but they will readily increase themselves by seed. I have bought corms from the chain stores which have established themselves readily. It is important, of course, to select such corms carefully, rejecting any that are not firm.

To cheer the early days of autumn there is *Cyclamen neapolitanum* (now *C. hederifolium*), perhaps the best-known of all hardy cyclamen, with its ivy-leaves and rose-pink shuttlecocks. There is a white form, 'Album'. To get the best effect, I think a drift of the pink should be planted near a smaller drift of the white, merging into each other. To make sure of establishing it readily one can usually buy growing plants from the nurserymen in August and September. These, planted out in the ground while in growth, will absolutely ensure success but as I said earlier I have never found even dried corms of this species at all difficult to start. Once growing strongly these cyclamen will go on for ever, the corms increasing in size until they are as large as a dinner plate and bearing literally hundreds of shuttlecock flowers.

C. coum, too, is easy even though it flowers in January. Plants listed as *C.* × *atkinsii,* and *C. hiemale* are very similar and it matters little which you plant. Rose-red and white forms are available and the leaves, though patterned only faintly with silver in *atkinsii* and *hiemale* and unmarked in *coum,* are not as sumptuous as those silver and green-shaded ivy leaves of *C. neapolitanum.* Nevertheless, they have a quiet appeal in their meek dark green and pleasantly-rounded shape. Flowering as they do in the midst of winter, this group needs a sheltered place. In our garden it did well on the north of a beech hedge and increased by seed.

C. repandum has leaves similar in shape to those of *C. neapolitanum* but more pointed and arrow-like. The flowers, too, have longer, slightly twisted petals and are of a bright rosy pink or red. *C. repandum* needs more sun than the others. We have lost it several times, from frost and slugs. For safety it should be tucked in between stones on a sunny rock garden pocket or wedged into a soil-filled crevice of a dry wall.

C. europaeum with us was a dead loss. We kept the corms which threw a few leaves from time to time, but they never flowered. I am told it does better in the south of the country and certainly it should have a sunny place. On the other hand *C. neapolitanum,* *C. coum* and *C. repandum* are all reliable and generous with their flowers even in quite dense shade. For the average garden they are the species to choose.

For ground cover in sun or shade some of the hardy geraniums are easy to grow and attractive in flower.

One of the prettiest of the hardy geraniums is a native wild flower of this country—*Geranium pratense*—and is often to be found at the roadsides in North Wales and in many other Welsh and English districts, especially along the Welsh border, in Herefordshire, and in Monmouth. In its best forms this geranium is a lovely blue with barely perceptible red veining. An especially good garden form is *G. pratense* 'Johnson's Blue', thought by some to be a hybrid. This is of an even better blue than the type and is more dwarf in stature, growing 30–45 cm (12–18 in) in height, to the 60–90 cm (2–3 ft) of the type. *G. pratense* may be grown from collected or bought seed, sown in the open in April. Still in commerce there are double forms in blue and white which are pleasant to plant with old roses and other old-fashioned flowers.

Another fairly common wild geranium is *G. sanguineum,* 'the bloody cranesbill', but some purists will frown at its magenta colouring. It is a plant more for sun than shade and its magenta is softened and made more attractive if the plant is grown in conjunction with a good pink-flowered form of *G. endressii.*

G. endressii is one of the best of all hardy geraniums, with open salvers of clear pink almost 2 cm (an inch) across and pleasing, neat foliage which persists through the winter and is dense and spreading enough to make an excellent weed smother. It grows and flowers as freely in shade as in sun. *G. endressii* grows to about 30 cm (a foot) in height and flowers from late June until October.

Another useful all-purpose geranium is the *G. grandiflorum* 'Alpinum', especially the form known as 'Gravetye Variety'. This gives on 30-cm (foot-) high stems large flowers, the prussian blue of which is accentuated by a white eye. It is hardy, very free-flowering, and easily raised from seed.

All the species so far mentioned thrive almost anywhere and will increase, without making a nuisance of themselves, by self-sown seed. *G. wallichianum* 'Buxton's Blue' is less easy. It needs stony, well-drained leaf soil in semi-shade, but the lovely, nemophila blue flowers on trailing stems are worth any amount of trouble. In some gardens this geranium is not too permanent and so a stock of cuttings should be kept to make good any losses.

G. psilostemon is tall-growing and brilliant with dark magenta flowers enlivened by a handsome black eye. It is useful for hot, dry places and is easy to raise from seed sown in the open or in pans under glass. However, the open-ground method gives such good results that it is hardly necessary to go to the extra trouble to sow under glass.

Another fine species is the beautiful *G. anemonifolium* with ruby-eyed, warm pink flowers like those of a single pelargonium, carried above massive ferny, evergreen anemone-like foliage. Extra special though this is, it is no 'miff' and can be raised just as easily as any of the other hardy geraniums from seed sown outdoors. It does, however, need a position sheltered from strong winds and shaded from the midday sun. Light, gritty loam is its ideal soil. I have read that this geranium is not fully hardy but with us it has survived –6° C (19° F) of frost and biting wind and in any case it ensures its own survival by self-sown seed.

G. anemonifolium is handsome on its own or grouped as a foliage plant. *G. macrorrhizum* is a true colonizer, sending out procumbent woody stems which root as they grow. Its deeply divided leaves make densely-packed mounds of foliage which effectively prevent weed growth. The flowers of *G. macrorrhizum* are small but striking—deep red, and borne in clusters. The leaves of this species and those of *G. endressii* are particularly aromatic, giving out a delightful oil-of-geranium scent. There is an attractive form of *G. macrorrhizum* known as 'Album' with white flowers nestling effectively in their pinky calyces. Other good geraniums for ground cover and flowers in sun or shade are the violet-blue *G. platypetalum,* and *G.* 'Russell Prichard' with silvery-grey foliage and bright magenta flowers.

Primroses are gems for the shady border. The old double-flowered primroses need rich, deep soil. I find they do best if cow-manure is incorporated in the soil beneath them at planting time. It does not seem to matter whether the cow-manure has had time to rot or not. I use it fresh with very good results. I remember reading Gertrude Jekyll's account of how she, too, used cow-manure, finding it cooling to put beneath her famous Munstead polyanthus primroses after their yearly division and replanting. The lilac 'Quaker's Bonnet', purple 'Our Pat', 'Bon Accord Gem' with rather muddled cerise flowers and the rosy-mauve, silver-edged 'Marie Crousse' are the easiest doubles to start with. The yellows are all difficult and I find the double-white temperamental as might be expected with such an old plant. 'Tyrian Purple', 'Bon Accord Lavender', 'Crathes Crimson', and the smaller-flowered 'Red Paddy', with its thin wire-edging of white, are all worth growing but it is as well at first to grow the easier and less-expensive varieties, feeling one's way as it were.

The Jack-in-the-green primroses, with their leafy calyces, setting off their flowers like green Toby-ruffs are comparatively easy while the hose-in-hose, duplex-blossomed primroses should have the same treatment as the doubles if they are to succeed. Miniature polyanthus are charming if grouped in drifts or patches of one variety. The pale pink 'Beamish Foam', yellow 'Lady Greer', brick-red 'Fair Maid' and candy-striped, bright pink-and-white 'Kinlough Beauty' are good. Like all primroses they need to be divided every second or third year.

FOURTEEN

Dry Banks

———

Chalk downs are more often built over than any other hill and most houses built on downlands and limestone uplands have steeply sloping gardens, sometimes with motor drives cut deeply into the strata and having high, steep banks on either side. These banks may be too steep for the gardener to be able safely to build his own dry wall. The only answer is to have retaining walls built high with cement by the builder. These walls present their own problem. Often one side at least is shady. The walls are cemented and so no plants can be grown directly in them without prising away the cement and loosening the structure. No garden owner wants to do this, so the question of how to clothe the walls becomes urgent. There are two ways of dealing with the matter. One may leave a bed at the base of the wall and there plant shade-bearers such as chaenomeles or *Garrya elliptica* or—and this, I think, is the more satisfactory method—one may plant at the top of the wall such plants as will trail down the wall, sheeting it with foliage and flower. Incidentally, the catkin-bearing garrya is never seen to better advantage than on the top of such a wall because then its branches assume an arching, gnarled appearance and one may look up and see the showers of silky, tasselled catkins above one's head.

The winter-flowering jasmine—*Jasminum nudiflorum*, is difficult to train up a wall, often becoming a mass of tangled shoots that have to be tied up into position. Grown on top of a retaining wall it will cascade down in a waterfall of golden stars. Its green shoots, following their natural inclination to grow downwards rather than up, will fall easily into position if it is desired to tie them in. *J. nudiflorum* will flower freely in either sun or shade and it is really as well to plant it on both sides of the drive as by planting in different aspects one gets a much longer period of bloom.

The spring-flowering *Clematis macropetala* will trail down, too, though it will, of course, be necessary to tie in its long growths to prevent wind-damage. The large-flowered clematises of summer may be grown in the same way and of these the deep-purple *C. × jackmanii* and the even finer *C. × j. 'Superba'* are particularly useful as they will flower in either sun or shade. All clematis need shade at the roots so it is helpful to place a slab of stone over their root area or to plant a low-growing lavender or even a clump of catmint to the south to shade the lower part of the stem. In some parts of the country wilt disease affects the large-flowered clematises, causing them suddenly to die off. This seldom happens when the plants have been set with the graft union 5 cm (2 in) below soil level thus enabling the grafted variety to send out its own roots. Clematis need a fair amount of moisture in the soil and for this reason the large-flowered hybrids sometimes fail in hot, chalky gardens. They are lime-lovers but they do need moisture so one should take out a generous hole when planting them and incorporate plenty of *moist* peat and compost or rotted manure with the soil. Care must be taken, however, to see that the roots are not actually in contact with the rotted manure or compost. A handful of bone meal scattered over the roots in spring is helpful, too.

If difficulty is experienced in providing a framework to which to tie the shoots, sheep-wire—a strong wire-netting with a regular mesh of about 10 cm (4 in) square—will be found to be effective. It should be firmly pegged at the top and bottom of the wall by wiring to screw-eyes in Rawlplugs set into the cement. The clematis will then ramble down, attaching itself by its twining leaf stalks as it goes. Netlon mesh is even better for the job:

some people think that during wet weather the drip from the galvanized sheep-wire is harmful.

Clematis are gross feeders and on poor, chalky soil, particularly, they need annual feeding in spring after growth has begun. Well-rotted manure, or compost fortified by bone meal and dried blood are excellent. Dry poultry-manure, mixed with old soot is also good.

All clematis should be pruned back in the first spring after planting to a pair of buds within a foot of the ground. Thereafter they may either be left unpruned or those of the *jackmanii* and *viticella* group may have their growth shortened in February to within 15 cm (6 in) of the base of the previous year's growth. Clematis of the *florida, patens* and *lanuginosa* groups should not be pruned until after flowering when the stems may be cut back to the first strong buds below the fallen flowers. This drastic pruning means that the plants are annually called upon to make very strong growth and so where it is carried out particular attention must be paid to feeding or results will be poor.

I restrict pruning to the cutting out of broken or straggly growths and train the clematis by guiding and tying-in the shoots to form as wide a framework as possible. It is by this means I think that in the end the best-furnished plants are built up and that the heaviest crops of flowers are regularly borne.

Apart from *C. × jackmanii* and *C. × j.* '*Superba*' there are many fine varieties from which to choose. Good plants of the same group are 'Comtesse de Bouchaud' with old rose flowers of an attractive rounded shape, 'Mme Edouard André' with starry, pointed flowers of deep red, 'Perle d'Azur' with light blue flowers borne on old and new wood and so best left unpruned at any rate until the second crop of flowers is over, 'Victoria' with semi-transparent flowers in soft heliotrope and 'Gipsy Queen' with very large and deep velvety-purple flowers.

The *patens* section bloom in early summer and so prolong the clematis season. All have large and very decorative flowers. Fine varieties are 'Barbara Dibley' with striped, starry blooms in pansy violet with deeper bars, the soft petunia 'Barbara Jackman',

'Daniel Deronda' which blooms in May and June with semi-double purple-blue flowers followed by a crop of single flowers in late summer, 'Edouard Desfosse' with enormous violet-mauve flowers with darker bars, the very fine 'Lasurstern' of deep purple-blue lit by yellow stamens, the twice-blooming, deep violet 'The President' and 'Mrs. George Jackman' with large satiny white flowers centred by brown anthers.

The *florida* group flowers with the *patens* in May and June and includes such doubles as the rosette-flowered pale mauve 'Belle of Woking', the white 'Duchess of Edinburgh' and the distinctive *florida* 'Sieboldii' (*bicolor*) which has white flowers with deep purple petaloid stamens.

The *lanuginosa* group has large flowers and like the *patens*, *jackmanii* and *viticella* sections will bloom on north-facing walls as well as those of other aspects. Some of the loveliest of all clematis are in this section. Among them are: 'Beauty of Worcester' with violet-blue blooms centred by showy white stamens, the dark-stemmed white *henryi*, 'Lady Northcliffe' with deep lavender flowers tinted bright blue and with white stamens, 'Prins Hendrik' with large, pointed blooms of soft sky-blue, 'Proteus' with pink flowers suffused with violet, and the exceptionally free-flowering lilac-coloured 'W. E. Gladstone'.

The *viticella* section contains some interesting and attractive varieties. This section seems to be wilt-resistant and its varieties are often very free-flowering and vigorous but have rather smaller blooms which are carried in late summer. They are useful either to grow on walls, or to scramble through old roses or over large evergreen shrubs. Of the *viticella* group I would recommend the soft purple 'Abundance', the larger-flowered petunia red 'Ernest Markham', 'Kermesina' with small, bright red flowers, 'Little Nell' with masses of small slaty-mauve blooms, 'Minuet' with cream-centred flowers ringed by an outer broad band of purple, the deep velvety-purple 'Royal Velours' and the pink *vedrariensis* 'Highdown'.

Other clematis worth growing are the early-summer flowering *C. armandii* species with its aptly named varieties 'Snowdrift' and 'Apple Blossom'. This species is evergreen and needs a warm, sheltered wall. *C. montana* in both white and pink forms is a vigorous, easy plant, useful to grow through an old tree, which it will not harm, or to ramble over a hedge. Even more attractive is the larger-flowered, pale pink *C. chrysocoma*. For a similar purpose one might use the uncommon pale hyacinth-blue *C. campaniflora* with small, nodding, bell-like flowers. The yellow-flowered *C. tangutica obtusiuscula* has thick-sepalled bells of lemon-yellow followed by shaggy Skye-terrier heads of seed. This is particularly effective trained over a low wall where *Wisteria floribunda* in its white form, 'Alba', and the pale rosy-lilac 'Rosea' would also look well. These wisterias are less vigorous than the more commonly seen *W. sinensis* and have longer flower racemes of greater substance. *W. venusta* is effective, too, with short but chubby white racemes against bronze-tinged foliage. All wisterias so grown should be spur-pruned, their long growths being constantly pinched back to two buds. This encourages the production of flower buds as well as helping to keep the plant within bounds. Unfortunately there are still some shy-blooming seedling wisterias in commerce and where spur-pruning has been persistently tried without result one must scrap the plant and replace it with one from a more reputable source.

Cotoneaster horizontalis and *C. microphyllus* may be planted on top of a retaining wall and allowed to grow down, or they will form an arching cradle of growth over an unsightly low boundary wall.

The various ivies will curtain a retaining wall effectively from the top downwards and the rambler roses may be used in the same way. Of the roses, 'Alberic Barbier' will make a fan of frothy cream. The crimson 'Excelsa' interplanted with the lovely yellow 'Emily Gray' is effective. More subtle and giving a lovely cool effect would be a combination of 'Goldfinch' and 'Amethyste', and the old 'Seven Sisters' rose may still be obtained and would give a delightful chintz effect rambling down over a retaining wall of mouse-grey or honey-brown stone. Needless to say all these roses should be given a good send-off in a well-prepared site, the soil being broken up to a depth of at least 60 cm (2 ft) and the planting hole filled with a mixture of good loam generously interlaced with rotted stable- or hop-manure.

Many gardens on the chalk downs or limestone hills need too much hard work to cultivate in the conventional manner. So little soil overlies the chalk or limestone that it is impossible to find sufficient depth to make a good flower border. The excavation of sites for single plants is all that can be achieved and it is hard work to wheel a barrow up and down. Shrubs planted in separate sites by taking off a square or ring of turf and breaking up the chalk or limestone with a pickaxe are the best solution. Tough, coarse-rooted shrubs must be chosen which will thrive as improvements on the hawthorn and dog-rose and blackberries that the birds bring. Shrubs should be chosen that will survive both wind and drought. In such a garden one flowering shrub must take the place of a whole group of plants. To earn its place it must become a bower of flowers, or a cauldron of berries, or by sheer character of foliage it must hold the eye and steal the scene.

For flower-power in early spring the forsythias are hard to beat and a group consisting of *Forsythia × intermedia* 'Spectabilis' planted behind *Chaenomeles* 'Rowallane' and 'Nivalis', both of which may be grown as low, mounded bushes without too much pruning being necessary, would give a long-lasting display of gold and scarlet pleasantly cooled by white. In some districts the bullfinches take all the forsythia buds year after year, and there one might plant *Stachyurus praecox* instead. This stachyurus is hardy and accommodating and although it does not give such a mass of colour as the forsythia its stiff ropes of yellow bells are pleasing and spring-like. As the forsythia and stachyurus go over in April another good yellow shrub *Kerria japonica* might take up the tale, keeping company with the chaenomeles which often carry a second flush of flowers, sometimes blooming over a period of six or eight weeks. This is the single form of the old cottage-garden kerria, well known for its golden pom-poms of very double flowers, and is a much better garden shrub than the double kerria. It flowers very freely and makes a large bush with attractively arching growth pleasantly studded with shapely yellow flowers. A good colour picture may be achieved if the deep blue, very hardy *Ceanothus impressus* is planted in association.

In May, the first of the shrub roses come into bloom. As explained in Chapter Eleven they make fine specimens when grown in grass. A May-blooming rose not already mentioned is *Rosa* × *cantabrigiensis* which makes a large bush with very attractive double sulphur-yellow flowers.

Notable for their effect in bloom are the cistuses, the butterfly flowers of which last only a day, often dropping at tea-time to be replaced on the morrow by a freshly-opening crop. So prolific are these shrubs that a three-year-old plant will be a mound of colour for two or three weeks at a time. Some, like *Cistus* × *skanbergii* with its small, wild-rose pink flowers and soft grey leaves carry a second and a third crop of bloom. One of the hardiest and longest lived is *C.* × *cyprius* which bears, on a bush which will reach 1·8 m (6 ft) when fully grown, large white flowers with a bold central blotch of maroon. *C.* × *purpureus* is not quite so hardy but like *C.* × *skanbergii* should survive most winters on the sharply-drained, sunny chalk banks of the downs. The flowers of *C.* × *purpureus* are a warm magenta-pink, centrally blotched with maroon. *C.* 'Silver Pink' has similarly large flowers, of *C.* × *skanbergii*'s wild-rose pink, and greyish leaves. All these cistuses have evergreen foliage to add to the year-round garden scene and a delightful smell—the scent of the maquis, redolent of hot sun on aromatic foliage. Above them one might grow *Genista cinerea*, a tall-growing broom reaching to 2·4 or 3 m (8 or 10 ft) and bearing an elegantly drooping mass of fragrant, golden yellow, small pea flowers in June and July. Another Madeiran broom, *G. tenera* (syn. *G. virgata*) is even lovelier, having silky grey foliage to set off its flowers. Both these brooms need secure staking or guying against the wind. A rubber collar cut from an old hose-pipe or bicycle tyre is most effective, secured round the main stem at a height of 1·2 m (4 ft) and guyed to tent-pegs.

The weigelas and deutzias often find the chalk banks too dry, and fail to give of their best, but the mock oranges never let one down. Two that are full of flower quality and very floriferous are the spreading *Philadelphus* 'Beauclerk' with large, milk-white flowers flushed at the heart with cerise and the more upright *P.* 'Burfordensis' with large, cup-shaped flowers of pure white, centred by prominent golden stamens.

Two showy, yellow-flowered, grey foliage shrubs for summer, both of which retain their leaves in winter, are *Senecio greyi* (now *S.* 'Sunshine'), which will stand full wind exposure, and *Phlomis fruticosa*, the Jerusalem sage, which with its whorled heads of large, helmeted, golden sage flowers, is more distinctive than the senecio with its yellow daisies. I think, however, that the senecio stands the wind better.

In summer, shrub roses are useful and make a fine show of bloom, among them the copper-flowered sweet briar 'Lady Penzance', the useful 'Stanwell Perpetual', a *spinosissima* hybrid growing to 1·8 m (6 ft) with arching, grey-foliaged stems and soft, pale pink quilled double flowers, the brilliant single 'Scarlet Fire' and all the modern shrub roses, the hybrid musks and Chinas and rugosas.

Colouring well on chalk, *Cotinus coggygria* 'Notcutt's Variety' has striking deep purple foliage and feathery flower panicles of smoky lavender in July. When fully grown it may measure 2·4 m (8 ft) tall by 3·6 m (12 ft) in diameter and so make a striking focal point in an upland garden. This shrub tends to get leggy in time and so should be pruned to keep an attractive mounded shape. Pyracanthus, mountain ash, cotoneaster and berberis all do well on chalk and limestone uplands. It is wise to choose the later-fruiting types and those with yellow or white berries if the display is not to be ruined by birds. The spindles, too, are good and for winter colour one might plant the spreading, white-flowered *Erica carnea* (now *E. herbacea*) 'Springwood' and its variety 'Springwood Pink' with the taller *E.* × *darleyensis*, while *Cornus mas* may be relied on to make a bush of up to 6 m (20 ft) and to envelop itself each February in a cloud of tiny golden stars.

Dry banks of cultivated soil are a problem in all gardens

whether limy or otherwise. They may be carpeted with peri-winkles, *Hypericum calycinum* or any of the other dry-shade, weed-suppressors advised in Chapter Thirteen. Another interesting method of treatment is to plant a community of maquis shrubs such as might be found in Corsica or the south of France and which will grow together in a flowery, aromatic evergreen mass so thick as to keep down all weeds. Shrubs to use for such a planting are *Erica* × *darleyensis*, *E. mediterranea* and its varieties, cistuses, rosemary, *stoechas* lavender—a 30-cm- (1-ft-) high bush with square-cut flower spikes topped by showy purple bracts, the low-growing × *Halimiocistus sahucii* with pretty white, gold-bossed sun-roses about 2 cm (1 in) wide which although only about 25 cm (10 in) high will form a mat of growth. *Halimium lasianthum* is taller-growing with glistening-yellow, little roses blotched with chocolate. Also suitable are the late-summer flowering, hardy hibiscuses with their gay mallow flowers in blue, red, lavender or showily-blotched white, and the autumn-flowering *Erica terminalis*—the dense-foliaged Corsican heath—with its dark green foliage and terminal heads of pink urn-like flowers.

Chalk banks may also effectively be clothed with dwarf conifers. A colourful tapestry may be built up by the use of junipers such as the creeping *Juniperus horizontalis* 'Douglasii' with glaucous foliage which becomes violet-purple in autumn, the colour lasting throughout the winter, the bright green, widely-spreading *J. sabina tamariscifolia*, the more prostrate, bright green *J. conferta*, the yellow fans of *J.* × *media* 'Pfitzerana Aurea', and *J. squamata* 'Meyeri' which becomes perhaps 90 cm (3 ft) high in time with widely-arching growth and dense blue-grey foliage. Add the dark green pyramid of *Picea glauca albertiana* 'Conica', a baby fir of 90 or 120 cm (3 or 4 ft) and the tawny gold of *Thuja occidentalis* 'Rheingold' with the colourful mounds of some of the euphorbias (spurges) such as the evergreen *E. wulfenii* with its curious yellow flower heads in early spring, *E. griffithii* with its orange-flame bracts and the glinting yellow of *E. polychroma* (syn. *E. epithymoides*). When established the conifers will give a neat, clothed appearance to the bank and be entirely trouble-free. Space must be left, however, for their ultimate spread, so until they have grown enough to do their own weed-suppressing one must do it for them by mulching in autumn with a 10 cm (4 in) layer of leaves. This will do a twofold job by retaining soil moisture and so helping the growth of the shrubs. Soil should be scattered over the leaves to hold them in place and prevent their being blown about by the wind. If leaves are unobtainable, bracken or moist peat may be used instead.

FIFTEEN

Widening the Plant Range
to Include Forbidden Joys

Commonsense it may be to content oneself with growing the plants which do well and grow easily in one's own particular soil, but there comes a time when most gardeners on lime want to become more adventurous and to extend their range of plants. This may be done in two ways, by discovering whether there are any lime-tolerators among the general run of calcifuge species in a genus, or by using every means one has available to overcome the physical deficiencies inherent in the soil of one's garden so as to be able to grow genuine lime-haters there.

One must recognize, too, the fact that many sweeping statements have been made about lime-haters in the past and that a number of plants have been labelled calcifuge which are not in fact in the least affected by the presence of lime. Some, like the schizostylis and the tricuspidaria, may be grown in limy soils provided their humus needs are adequately met.

Eucryphias are often labelled as lime-haters yet the only true lime-hater in the genus is *Eucryphia glutinosa*. The vigorous, columnar evergreen *E. × nymansensis* will grow well enough on lime provided it has adequate humus and moisture. *E. × intermedia* is smaller and so more suited to the average garden. It, too, is lime-tolerant. For years I regarded *Crinodendron hookeranum*—the very desirable, tall, evergreen, lantern bush, with dangling crimson bells like some gigantic fuchsia—as a lime-hater because I had always been told that it was one. Then I noticed crinodendrons growing well on the limestone in our district. I obtained a plant by rooting a layer of one of these and five years later I had a thriving bush of 1·8 m (6 ft) high growing in untreated heavy alkaline loam above limy clay. The *p*H of its site is 7·5. Like most Chilean plants the crinodendron needs humus and moisture. I do not think it objects at all to lime—many Chilean plants do not. It does, however, appreciate semi-shade as do many of its compatriots and in hot, dry southern gardens may succeed best in the shade of a north-facing wall. In my experience, the same applies to the holly-like *Desfontainea spinosa* with showy trumpet-flowers of scarlet and yellow. I successfully struck our two plants as open-ground cuttings in an untreated soil of *p*H 7·5 in the shade of a wattle fence. The desfontainea definitely needs shade and moisture and so does best in the moister western districts of the British Isles.

We experimented with *Embothrium coccineum,* knowing that this needs a drought-proof and sheltered position with shade for the lower half of its stem. The rarer Chilean shrubs in our garden were planted at normal soil level in bracken peat and mulched with rotted bracken every winter. No chemical aid was ever given them. We moved the embothrium to our new garden where it grew well on a neutral soil. I feel it might have succeeded in the former garden, given constant bracken mulching.

We grew camellias and rhododendrons also in bracken peat and mulched them with bracken, cut green, in June and again with rotted bracken in winter. This gives the rooting conditions that they need. Care must be taken to plant both genera at the same level at which they were growing in the nursery. This can be judged by the soil marks on the stem. Camellias and rhododendrons must never be stamped in. The fibrous roots are very sensitive and the root ball must be kept intact. Only bracken peat or rhododendron peat should cover the root-ball and care must be taken to keep the mulch away from the stem, otherwise it may clog, so suffocating the roots which must be able to breathe.

Even in a chalk pit, camellias may be grown in excavated holes 60 cm (2 ft) deep and square filled with acid material. They should be watered, preferably with rain-water, and, if they show chlorosis, should be treated with a sequestered form of iron. It is essential however, that the planting hole should be lined with heavy black polythene punctured with drainage holes at the bottom. Without this barrier the camellias will eventually die out, as they have done in the late Sir Frederick Stern's chalk-pit garden at Highdown.

Like camellias, rhododendrons need a spongy, moisture-retaining rooting medium. Both genera must have a well-drained site.

Some species of rhododendrons need less iron than others, notably the small-leaved rhododendrons from the moorlands and mountains of Asia and also many of the deciduous species, including azaleas and, to a lesser extent, the evergreen group of Japanese azaleas. In our district all these types could be grown quite satisfactorily in a mixture of peat and acid leaf-mould or rotted bracken and even in chalky districts in the drier south they may be grown in a 20-cm (8-in) layer of bracken peat above the surface soil. We grew the winter-flowering, leaf-losing *Rhododendron mucronulatum* and *dauricum* in bracken peat mixed with the soil, also the mollis, Ghent and Knap Hill types of azalea hybrids, the Kurumé group, and a number of small-leafed evergreen rhododendrons, 'Blue Tit' 'Blue Bird', 'Blue Diamond', 'Sapphire', the yellow *R. chryseum, tapetiforme,* 'Yellow Hammer', *lepidostylum,* and *moupinense.* Larger-leafed hybrids—'Roman Pottery' (a form of the 'Fabia' cross), 'Goblin', 'Avocet', 'Nobleanum Venustum', 'Britannia', 'Fastuosum Flore Pleno' and 'Carita' showed some chlorosis and needed help. All these were given quite heavy doses of *Sequestrene 138 Fe* as it was then called—over 14 g ($\frac{1}{2}$ oz) in three doses—in fact 'Fabia' and 'Humming Bird' showed a scorching at the leaf-edges which we took to be a danger sign of toxicity. Some of the leaves became a very dark green but in 'Humming Bird' (a small-leaved hybrid of *williamsianum*) the younger leaves were still yellow, and in 'Roman Pottery', 'Avocet' and 'Goblin' a yellow mottling showed in the dark green. The hardy-hybrid types—'Britannia', 'Nobleanum Venustum', 'Fastuosum Flore Pleno', 'Lady Eleanor Cathcart', 'Susan' and 'Carita' and 'Goldfinch' (both of *campylocarpum* parentage) improved steadily but slowly. 'Lady Chamberlain' and 'Remo'—both rather small-leaved hybrids—had no treatment and showed no symptoms. Spraying the foliage of 'Humming Bird', 'Roman Pottery', 'Goblin' and 'Avocet' with a solution of manganese sulphate (14 g to 9 l ($\frac{1}{2}$ oz to 2 gal) applied in the evening of a dull day) restored the leaves to full green. However, after flowering and making new growth the same mottling became apparent in 'Roman Pottery' in August 1961. The soil was watered with *Sequestrene 138 Fe* at a dilute strength of 1 g to 9 l ($\frac{1}{32}$ oz to 2 gal) of water and a fortnight later the foliage was again sprayed with manganese sulphate. Both 'Goblin' and 'Avocet' which had been treated with magnesium sulphate (Epsom salts watered into the soil in solution) showed no recurrence of the trouble. A soil test from the root area of 'Goblin' three months after treatment (in all, this plant received three waterings at fortnightly intervals with 1 tablespoon Epsom salts to 9 l (2 gal) of water) revealed a pH of 6·5—a definite acid reaction.

It seems to me, therefore, that rhododendrons and azaleas showing chlorotic symptoms in alkaline soils need magnesium and manganese in addition to iron. (My *Note* on p. 37 points out that *Murphy Sequestrene* contains manganese and magnesium sulphate in addition to the sequestered iron. However, further applications of manganese and magnesium sulphate may still be necessary.]

In America the standard treatment differs. There, growers of rhododendrons, azaleas and camellias on alkaline soils incorporate flowers of sulphur, 68–136 g per sq m (2–4 oz per sq yd) and aluminium sulphate, 136–272 g per sq m ($\frac{1}{4}$–$\frac{1}{2}$ lb per sq yd) with the soil before planting. The disadvantage of this is that aluminium sulphate leaves behind an aluminium salt. Epsom salts (magnesium sulphate) on the other hand leaves only magnesium carbonate which is rather like a finely divided magnesium limestone —the type of limestone upon which rhododendrons are sometimes found growing wild in Asia and to which they do not in the least object. Nevertheless, the aluminium sulphate method succeeds well with rhododendrons in America. We used it with hydrangeas in our old garden for nine years with no harm ensuing. Moreover, an application of aluminium sulphate at the given rate will cure severe chlorosis within two weeks. For the rhododendron-lover who finds himself gardening upon lime I would say it is well worth a trial. Flowers of sulphur, in any case, seem completely harmless. We always mixed 14 g ($\frac{1}{2}$ oz) with the soil before planting any rhododendrons or azaleas in this garden as a routine measure and also used flowers of sulphur to line the planting holes.

I can well believe that it is impossible to grow rhododendrons and azaleas in a chalk pit or at the bottom of a chalky hollow, but fifteen hybrid rhododendrons, twelve dwarfs, two deciduous rhododendrons, sixteen Japanese azaleas and eleven Knap Hill and Ghent azaleas flowering freely and growing well in our garden proved that it is perfectly practicable, with the help of chemistry and due care, to grow such extreme calcifuges in an obstinate alkaline clay.

Growing dwarf rhododendrons and azaleas, at least, on the limestone uplands in the west and north provides no real problem so long as the drainage is good, the rainfall is heavy enough to leach away the lime, and there are a few inches of fine organic soil from decayed vegetation above the rock.

When attempting to grow rhododendrons and other expensive calcifuges in alkaline soil it is best to feel one's way, growing only one or two plants at first and then if all goes well increasing one's range.

Nor are alkaline soils alone in their deficiencies. Tests of the soil in which acutely chlorotic rhododendrons were growing in the garden of the late Mr. A. T. Johnson at Bulkeley Mill in the Conway Valley showed a pH of 4·5—generally considered to be the optimum acid reaction for rhododendrons. An analysis of rhododendron leaves by Dr. Henry Tod of the Edinburgh College of Agriculture suggests that magnesium deficiency is to blame.

Apart from separating the true lime-haters from those whose real need is for more humus, and apart from using chemicals to widen the range of plants that can be grown on alkaline soils, the gardener may also defeat the lime-imposed ban by growing lime-haters in various containers. These containers may be either sunk in the soil, if they are of purely utilitarian character, or used decoratively if they are in themselves aesthetically satisfying.

The Japanese *Iris kaempferi* is a very desirable and beautiful plant that may be grown in this way although in this case the container needs to be sunk in the ground so that the irises may get as much moisture as possible during the growing season. An old sink with the outlet crocked but not blocked, or a plastic wash-bowl with drainage holes punched in the bottom, is ideal for the purpose. These irises like a rich, moist compost and do very well in coarse peat mixed with rotted cow-manure. They should be kept well watered after growth begins in spring but kept drier from autumn on.

Flowering in late June and into July, they carry on 60–90 cm (2–3 ft) stems large and lovely flowers in shades of blue, purple and claret. There are also white forms and whites veined and stippled with blue or purple. Single and doubles exist. I think the singles are the most beautiful but the doubles are lovely, too. In the singles the falls are horizontal while the standards are very short, forming a mere lip to the flower. The doubles have six flat, horizontal petals instead of three, giving a clematis-like effect. Of the older varieties 'Purple East' is a magnificent single with velvety purple petals without markings or veinings. The single white, 'Morning Mist' was lightly veined with blue and made a good companion for 'Purple East' but I do not know whether it is still available in commerce. However, the double-flowered 'Moonlight Waves' is a fine white which may be used in its place with good effect.

Some nurserymen have imported *Iris kaempferi* from Japan, and the Knap Hill Nurseries offer named varieties of these irises. *Iris kaempferi* look well near water or in the border. They enjoy a fair amount of sun.

A charming moisture-and-sun-loving ericaceous shrub that may be grown under similar conditions is *Kalmia angustifolia* 'Rubra' the calico bush of the Southern States, with narrow evergreen leaves rather like those of some species of rhododendron and pretty cupped flowers of rich rosy-red. The stamens are attached to the petal edges until the pollen is ripe and this gives the flowers the effect of tiny half-opened parachutes. The name of calico bush is obviously derived from the chintzy pattern of the open flowers

It is usual when growing calcifuge plants to water only with rain-water or with soft tap water. It has been suggested that water from a water softener might meet the case but, living in an area where the tap water came from a peaty mountain lake, I was unable to put this to the test. When living in North Staffordshire, where the soil is acid and the water hard and limy, we often used without ill-effect water which had passed through a water softener. Our rhododendrons and azaleas thrived so it does seem to be a practicable possibility. I must add though that many of them were also watered from time to time with unsoftened tap water and suffered no harm. So it also seems as though the danger of hard tap water may not be so great after all.

Lime-hating autumn-flowering gentians such as the sapphire trumpeted *Gentiana sino-ornata* will grow well and easily in a stone trough above ground or in a sink sunk to ground level. In very chalky gardens, however, the sink edge should be just above the ground to prevent seepage of limy surface water. This gentian is very sensitive to lime—bone meal is death to it and so is wood ash. A good compost would consist of one part peat to one leaf-mould from a wood on acid soil and one lime-free loam (parts by bulk), or it would grow in a compost of peat and leaf-mould. Care must be taken not to let the gentian dry out. It needs moisture and even semi-shade. Rhododendrons of moderate size and most camellias can be grown successfully in old earthenware bread-crocks which are often of very attractive appearance. Olive-oil jars, too, are suitable and so are scrubbed vinegar barrels or wine casks. Concrete containers are to be avoided on account of the lime content of the cement which may affect the plants. It is possible, however, to paint the inside of the container with a bitumen paint to seal in the cement. A suitable compost for rhododendrons and camellias is one-third (by bulk) peat, one-third lime-free loam and one-third sand with a 10-cm (4-in) potful of hoof and horn meal, which unlike bone meal is not alkaline, to each barrowload of compost. Drainage holes are necessary and the container must be well crocked. The layer of crocks should be covered with a layer of coarse peat. Then one puts some of the compost over the peat and firms it, planting the rhododendron or camellia so as to bring the top of the root ball to within 5 cm or so (a couple of inches) of the top of the container. Care must be taken to work the compost well around the root ball and lightly to cover the top to the soil-mark on the stem. The compost must be well rammed down so as not to leave air pockets. There should be 2·5 cm (an inch) clear between the soil surface and the top of the container to leave room for watering.

The late Mrs. Margery Fish of East Lambrook Manor, Somerset, author of the delightful *Cottage Garden Flowers* and other very helpful books about her own garden, imported greensand from Dorset to make a raised bed in which to grow plants which did not do well in her alkaline soil. Greensand is heavy to transport but it is an idea worth the attention of those gardeners with friends in the greensand areas who will let them remove a few bucketfuls of soil at a time. Mrs. Fish told me that the greensand had the advantage of keeping more moss-free and weed-free than peat, and that her calcifuge plants did well in it. She also used it to fill a large trough. Incidentally, Mrs. Fish occasionally watered her lime-haters, both in the greensand and in peat beds, with limy tap water and found that it did her plants no harm. Certainly it is better to use hard tap water than to let plants die of drought. The garden at East Lambrook Manor is still open to the public and Mrs. Fish's nephew, who inherited the property, operates a small nursery there from which many of her specialities can still be purchased. Many of her books are still in print.

We grew *Grevillea sulphurea* directly in our untreated soil with only a bracken mulch to offset alkalinity. Occasionally it showed a yellowish tinge in its foliage but we found that watering the root area with the old *Sequestrene 138 Fe*, a saltspoonful to 9 l (2 gal) of water—quickly restored the green. This is a plant for which sequestrene seems particularly helpful. *Pieris floribunda* is another which benefits in the same way. This pieris was planted in bracken peat and received an annual bracken mulch. Towards the end of the summer the foliage yellowed. We watered the root area with *Sequestrene 138 Fe* and the leaves quickly greened again.

Meconopses do not actually pine and fade away if lime is present in the soil, but the pure sky-blue of *Meconopsis betonicifolia* and the kingfisher of the best forms of *M. grandis* become a muddy purple if much lime is present. They are safer grown in beds of greensand or in specially constructed peateries as described in the next chapter. *M. betonicifolia*, of course, should not be allowed to flower until more than one crown has formed—otherwise it may die.

Most of the Asiatic primulas are reputed to dislike lime. In our garden we had no trouble at all with any of the ones we grew. Their rosettes of leaves became as fat as cabbages and they increased like weeds by self-sown seeds. They certainly need humus and moisture and I think it probable that limy gardens vary a great deal as to what plants will or will not grow in each. When in doubt, experiment was always our motto and we were lucky. Where expensive plants are concerned, however, it is worth while meeting each plant's particular requirements as far as possible. For the Asiatic primulas this means humus—peat being the most appreciated—and a reasonably moist site. In hot, southern gardens part shade is desirable. Many of the Asiatic primulas will thrive in a north-facing bed. Some of our *Primula japonica* plants were in a shaded rectangle between house, garden hut, and garage. They got sun for only an hour or so in the morning, yet they flowered particularly freely.

Sir Frederick Stern found at Highdown that few Asiatic primulas were really happy in his hot, chalky soil. In *A Chalk Garden*, he describes how some of them will thrive in damp ground near a pond. There he grew the brilliant pink, April-flowering *P. rosea*, *P. heladoxa* with its tiers of golden flowers and the lighter yellow *P. prolifera*. He also grew *P. florindae*, with drooping flowers like a giant cowslip, and its red-flowered hybrids. The magenta-red *P. lichiangensis* did well in drier places in the shade and the little, delicate pink *P. clarkei* grew under similar conditions. It would seem therefore, that soil texture, moisture and humus content are the governing factors in deciding whether many Asiatic primulas will grow or not, rather than the alkalinity or otherwise of the soil. They thrive in clay.

In our garden *P. japonica,* in brick red, magenta and pink grew equally strongly in the soil of the one-time vegetable garden (which had received dressings of hydrated lime in addition to its own alkaline content) and in the peat mulch surrounding our rhododendrons. The apricot *P. bulleyana* with its whorled heads, the mealy-stemmed, magenta P. *pulverulenta* and its delicate pink 'Bartley' strain, the cowslip-flowered *P. sikkimensis* and the little bright orange *P. chungensis* also thrived and increased by self-sown seed—the surest sign that any plant is happy and at home. *P. denticulata,* the Himalayan drum-stick primula did particularly well with its deep violet, lavender, white and claret flower-heads.

Many of these primulas are still there. Oddly enough they did not do nearly so well and tended to die out in the neutral soil of our next garden which was less clayey but which in spite of our efforts, remained in part badly drained due to an underground stream only apparent in winter. This may show that while the primulas enjoy a heavy soil they cannot stand winter waterlogging or stagnant moisture.

When growing plants and particularly shrubs and trees that are alleged lime-haters it is as well to remember that many plants from Japan really do fail where the soil is alkaline. Many, but by no means all, of the shrubs that come from North America, too, are true lime-haters. There are few real lime-haters among the great wealth of plant material that comes from Chile and those Chileans that are said to dislike lime are worth trying if planted in peat or rotted bracken. Pernettyas are reputed to be lime-haters, yet they grow and berry in several limy gardens known to me in different parts of the country. Most European plants, particularly those from the Mediterranean area, are lime-tolerant. The only recognized lime-tolerant rhododendron, *Rhododendron hirsutum* comes from the Alps, and *Erica australis,* a tree-heath from Spain, though supposed to be calcifuge has with us shown no objection to quite a high concentration of alkalinity.

Most Chinese plants are lime-tolerant. This explains in part the apparent contradiction that so many lime-tolerant plants come with the undeniable calcifuges from the completely acid soil of Japan. The so-called 'Japanese' cherries and 'Japanese' tree-peonies are probably garden varieties bred by the garden-minded Japanese from species imported from China. Exceptions are to be found among the dogwoods. The striking *Cornus kousa* with its showy white bracts is a Japanese that does not mind chalk. The even lovelier *Cornus nuttallii* with its fresh green leaves and appealing symmetrical, creamy bract 'flowers' centred by a cluster of true flowers comes from the west of North America and is not really a lime-hater. Given a barrier of peat and humus to retain moisture it will grow in many limy gardens that are not too dry.

Shrubs from the west of North America are more likely to be lime-tolerant than those from the east. The genus of ceanothus from California is a good example of this lime-tolerance. On the other hand *Chionanthus virginicus*—the North American fringe tree from the east will not grow where the soil is alkaline. The Chinese fringe tree *C. retusus,* however, does not suffer when lime is present and grew successfully even in Sir Frederick Stern's chalkpit garden.

By using this knowledge and seeking out the lime-tolerant members of mainly calcifuge genera the gardener on lime may considerably widen the range of plants that he can grow.

It is important for individual gardeners to experiment with their own land. Gradually they can then determine what they can or cannot grow. I feel I should point out that our North Wales garden was a somewhat borderline case. The limestone beneath the clay was porous, the clay had been improved by treatment until it had broken down into a fertile heavy loam, and all plants that were suspected not to tolerate lime were carefully watched, treated with manganese, magnesium and sequestered iron. In addition, they were constantly supplied with acid peat, rotted bracken from acid ground and acid-reacting leaf-mould. For the average gardener it may be easier and certainly wiser to grow all suspects either in containers, or in raised beds shut off from the possibility of lime seepage by a barrier of heavy-duty black polythene containing only such drainage holes as are strictly necessary.

The majority, quite rightly, will decide to stick to those plants which are known to thrive in their areas and on their type of soil. If they want to grow a camellia, for instance, one or two evergreen azaleas or a clump of the glorious *Lilium auratum* hybrids, which are known to be sensitive to lime, they will grow them in tubs or other containers so as not to take the risk of losing valuable plants.

When growing calcifuge plants in containers, one cannot do better than to use the Royal Horticultural Society's recommended compost for camellias. This consists of 7 parts by bulk of turfy lime-free loam, 3 parts granulated sedge peat and 2 parts gritty, lime-free sand. To 36 l (8 gal) should be added 45 g (1½ oz) of hoof and horn and 45 g (1½ oz) of bonemeal. This will accommodate any of the Chilean shrubs such as crinodendron, desfontainea, the vivid embothrium, or climbing mutisia. It is ideal for camellias, though, if you want to do them really well you should add half-a-shovelful of well rotted cow manure to each tub. Dried blood, and urea, can also be fed from time to time.

When growing rhododendrons (as distinct from the more accommodating azalea series) in containers, I would always omit the bonemeal as I have found certain species and hybrids to be so sensitive to lime as to show chlorosis after being fed with bonemeal.

Watering is always of the utmost importance when growing plants in tubs. With camellias in particular, attention must be paid to watering when the buds are enlarging during the winter months as drying-out is a frequent cause of bud-drop. On the other hand, too much water will cause yellowing and falling. It is essential to find a happy medium.

Particularly good for container cultivation are camellias 'Adolphe Audusson' (scarlet with showy golden stamens),

'Donation' (shell pink) and the pale pink 'J. C. Williams'. In Scotland and the far north of England only the latter two can be relied on to flower freely.

Small and medium rhododendrons which will do well in pots are 'Humming Bird' (cherry), 'Bow Bells' (pink), 'Yellow Hammer' (small-leaved and upright), 'Blue Tit', 'Blue Diamond' and the hardy evergreens of the azalea series.

When growing shrubs out of doors in containers it is important to protect the containers and roots from frost. I always do this by using the pot-within-a-pot system, sinking the original pot inside a decorative container and packing peat into the space between the two.

Those interested in the growing of lime-haters and other plants in containers might care to consult my *Window Box and Container Gardening*. They will also find particular information about the cultivation of rhodendrons and azaleas in my book of this title.

On chalk and limestone it is possible to grow camellias in excavated cubes, 90 cm (3 ft) in dimension for each plant, lined with heavy-duty black polythene and supplied with drainage holes. The bottom 10 cm (4 in) should contain washed gravel for drainage. The excavations should then be filled with the R.H.S. camellia compost already recommended. On clay, however, such planting holes would tend to fill with water and the plants would drown from waterlogging.

On any soil it is possible to make raised beds, supported by walls of sandstone, or other non-alkaline rock, filled with lime-free compost and standing on heavy-duty polythene at the base. In this case, the retaining walls should be supplied with drainage channels, otherwise waterlogging might result with consequent bursting of the walls. In raised beds of this type, filled with acid-reacting compost, it is possible to grow most small-to-medium leafed subjects. Large-leafed rhododendrons would probably suffer from drought under such conditions.

SIXTEEN

Peat Gardens

Perhaps a peat garden may sound rather an elaborate project to contemplate, but even a small raised peat bed will enable the gardener on lime or chalk to grow a number of small and choice plants that would not grow elsewhere in the garden.

To be effective the beds must be raised above the level of the surrounding alkaline soil in order to prevent the seepage of lime-contaminated water. When peat gardening first became popular the beds were generally built up as a series of terraces with blocks of peat used to build low retaining walls. Sometimes fuel peat blocks were used and often these subsequently disintegrated. Care should be taken to obtain blocks of top spit peat containing either heather or sedge roots to help bind the whole. Such peat is often looked upon as waste material by the peat diggers and if one can contact a reasonably local source of supply it is possible to obtain blocks of this sort for little more than the cost of taking them away.

Peat blocks should always be as big as is practicable and should not be less than 30 cm (a foot) long by 20 cm (8 in) wide and 20 cm (8 in) deep. Low walls of 75 cm ($2\frac{1}{2}$ ft) or less are best and should be protected against collapse by driving stakes vertically through them and into the ground at regular intervals.

All peat blocks, and indeed all peat, should be thoroughly soaked by immersion in a tub or tank before use. It is impossible to get dry peat blocks into a moist condition by watering after building. Peat is apt to dry out in full sun and if this happens the plants in it die. Peat beds should, therefore, always be sited in at least part shade. Fortunately, most peat-loving plants do best in shady places in moist soil.

Peat beds may be built up as a series of terraces on sloping ground or they may be built as table beds in the way described in Chapter Seven, only instead of using inverted turves, peat blocks are used for the central core of the bed. Walling blocks, either when surrounding table beds or supporting terraces, should slope slightly backwards and loose peat-debris from the blocks may be used as mortar. Further experience has shown that on pure chalk soils it is important to lay a barrier of heavy black polythene, provided with drainage holes, between the peat and the existing soil. On clays this is not strictly necessary but it may help to avoid the peat drying out. When drying-out occurs the blocks tend to crumble and slip. This can be prevented by proper attention to watering but as a precaution it is wise to reinforce the peat walls by 'stapling' with wire hoops at regular intervals.

Peat does not contain much nourishment for the plants so it is as well to use a mixture of peat and leaf-mould from an area of known acid soil to fill in the terraces or to cover the top of table beds. It may also be used as mortar or to fill in pockets in the peat wall where it is intended to plant shade-loving crevice plants. A warning must be given here that plants actually set into the peat walls are especially vulnerable to drought and particular care must be paid to regular watering. It is really safer to let the blocks moss over naturally and to restrict one's planting to the peat pockets which should always slope backwards to trap all available moisture and so to prevent the peat from drying out. It will be realized that peat is very thirsty stuff! A few dwarf ferns, however, might be risked in the wall crevices and would look effective while their roots would be useful in helping to bind the wall. The little maidenhair spleenwort—*Asplenium tricho-manes*, and evergreen *Cystopteris fragilis*—the brittle bladder fern which looks rather like a small lady fern, and *Gymnocarpium dryopteris* the native oak fern, would be ideal.

Peat Gardens

Another method of peat gardening and one which I use myself is to build up sloping beds of peat and acid-reacting leaf-mould, 25–30 cm (10–12 in) above the surface of the soil, retaining the peat with granite or sandstone rocks, and using larger rocks to form pockets. Care must be taken to use only moist peat and attention must still be paid to regular watering. This method overcomes the objection that many gardeners have to moss and weeds appearing in the peat wall and lessens the risk of drying out. The larger rocks help to retain moisture in their immediate vicinity and offer a cool root run that many plants love.

So much for peat garden construction. Now for the delightful task of deciding what to grow in one's peat garden.

Many of the dwarf rhododendrons will do well in raised peat beds however limy the garden may be, but the species must be selected with care. Hybrids of the 'Yellow Hammer', 'Blue Diamond' and 'Humming Bird' class grow far too big over the years for a small peat garden. Ideal plants are the smaller of the April-flowering lapponicums such as the charming lavender, starry-flowered *Rhododendron intricatum*, the slightly deeper blue *R. impeditum* and the yellow *R. chryseum*. Later-flowering, to prolong the season, is the low-growing *R. prostratum* with wide-open blooms of purple-rose, the creeping *R. radicans* rooting as it spreads and bearing flat purple saucers, the grey-foliaged *R. calostrotum* with rosy-purple flowers of similar shape and the pretty, daphne-like *R. cephalanthum crebreflorum* with sweet-scented rosy tubes. In sheltered gardens, particularly if backed by a north wall or fence or evergreen shrub or even a large boulder, it is worth trying *R. leucaspis* with its milk-white salvers endeared by chocolate anthers, while Farrer's dwarf form of *R. racemosum* in apple-blossom pink is slightly later-flowering.

A quaint rhododendron that is full of character is *R. campylogynum myrtilloides* with rose-pink thimble-bells above a flat mat of small dark green leaves.

Rather similar in character to the rhododendrons is *Kalmia polifolia* with long narrow leaves that are bright green above and glaucous beneath. It blooms in April and its typical calico bush flowers are a pleasing lilac-rose. Also suitable for the raised peat bed is the more compact, rich rose-red *K. angustifolia* 'Rubra' which flowers from June to September.

The bilberry family, vaccinium, and the closely allied gaultherias are often linked in the minds of gardeners. Personally, I think the gaultherias offer much the finer garden plants and it is from this genus that I would make my selection for the peat garden. All the gaultherias have neat evergreen foliage and pretty, heather-like, urn flowers in white or pink followed by blue, white or red berries.

Of the blue-berried species the best for the peat garden is the little *Gaultheria trichophylla* which forms a low mat about 10 cm (4 in) high of shiny, dark green, hairy foliage. Its pale pink flowers are set off by red sepals and followed by large fruits.

The 10-cm (4-in) high *G. procumbens* from eastern North America has glossy dark green leaves, some of which colour in autumn to red. Its flowers are pink-tinged and followed by bright red fruits. Although a carpeter it should not cover more than 60 or 90 cm (2 or 3 ft) of space over a number of years.

Attractive white-berried species are the 17·5-cm (7-in) Japanese *G. miqueliana* with bright apple-green leaves and *G. cuneata* which comes from China.

A fine red-berried shrublet for peat is the dwarf *Pernettya tasmanica* with neat small leaves and a prostrate habit. The foliage becomes bronzy in autumn and with the large scarlet berries makes an effective contrast for the autumn-flowering *Gentiana sino-ornata* which also does well in the peat garden. To complete the association one might plant *Polygonum vacciniifolium* with its reddish foliage and heath-like spikes of pink flowers.

Cassiope is a genus of beautiful shrubs which are often classed as difficult. In the peat garden, however, one or two species may be grown without much risk of failure. The cassiopes are evergreen, little, heath-like shrubs with frilly-edged white bells and tiny imbricated leaves which are pressed close against the stems, giving the effect of whipcord. The easiest to grow is probably *Cassiope lycopodioides*, a prostrate shrub with slender, spreading branches which in time form a cushion of dark green. The delightful little bells are freely carried above the foliage on 2-cm- (inch-) high stems. *C. tetragona* also is reasonably easy to grow in a shady peat bed. It is taller than *C. lycopodioides*, with 30-cm- (foot-) high stems and nodding white flowers that are sometimes flushed with pink at the base.

Another delightful little shrublet for the peat garden in milder districts is *Myrtus nummularia*, a creeping myrtle with interlaced wiry stems which make a dense mat about 7·5 cm (3 in) high. It has small, round, glossy, evergreen leaves and tiny, fluffy white myrtle flowers followed by pink berries.

However delightful and charming these shrublets may be, care must be taken not to overweight the peat bed with shrubby subjects. Room should be found for peat-loving bulbs and herbaceous plants. Where the candelabra primulas will not grow in the open garden they may be relied on to succeed in peat. They flower just as well in shade as in sunlight. A tiny, fairy primrose which I raised from seed and which gave us much pleasure every spring is *Primula frondosa* with silvery rosettes of leaves from which rise, on mealy stems, perfect scapes of miniature lavender-lilac flowers. The much larger petiolaris primulas are reckoned as difficult plants to grow. Yet on the lower slopes of a north-facing peat bed, nestling back against a rock or the retaining wall of a higher terrace so that their crowns are protected from winter wet they should not prove too obstinate. Some of the easier primulas in the petiolaris section are the incomparable soft lavender, very early-flowering *P. edgworthii*, the bluer *P. bhutanica* with squarer flowers and more crinkly, bristly leaves and the really easy lilac-pink *P. gracilipes*.

All the meconopses do well in peat but one of the most pleasing, the dwarf *Meconopsis quintuplinervia*, Farrer's harebell poppy, with its mass of lavender bells is seldom seen.

The North American wake robin or trinity flower—*Trillium grandiflorum*—is another beautiful peat-lover with its three-petalled, three-cornered flowers of milky white which appear in spring. From the same part of the world comes *Cypripedium reginae*, a hardy slipper orchid that has large baggy moccasins with a pink-lipped pure white pouch. Sphagnum moss established on the peat around this plant will help to make it feel at home.

Fom North America, too, come the dodecatheons or shooting stars with slender stems and airy flights of rosy or purple shuttle-cocks that have reflexed petals and pointed mouths like tiny winged darts. We grow these from seed sown in pans in January and put out to withstand the frost and snow, after which they germinate readily when brought indoors in April. Peat, sand and a little lime-free loam make an ideal seed-compost for them and the mixture should be topped with chippings so that it will not be too flattened by rain.

Epigaea repens is a North American shrublet of carpeting habit. In early summer its neat dark green foliage becomes starred with sweetly scented white may-flowers that are prettily tinged with red. This is a much-loved plant that often proves reluctant to become established even on acid soils. In peat it should offer little difficulty provided that the peat is not allowed to dry out. *E. asiatica* sometimes proves easier.

Equally esteemed, the shortias are sometimes difficult to please. However, *Shortia uniflora* with its nodding white bells and handsome leaves will usually do well in peat and half shade. The North American *Shortia galacifolia* is more temperamental and seems to need altitude as well as peat to be really happy. A fine drift—so fine as to be almost legendary—existed in a garden at Bettws-y-Coed in North Wales before I was born and was said to be fed upon a diet of pine needles. Certainly *S. galacifolia* likes pine needles—and so do many other acid-soil plants. Some-times one hears it said that pine needles are poisonous to plants but this is not the case. I have used them for camellias, azaleas and dwarf rhododendrons for a number of years without any harm resulting.

Sanguinaria canadensis, the Canadian blood-root is a wood-land dweller that readily establishes itself in the peat garden. Its foliage is lovely, glaucous grey and scroll like, and its flowers are like snow-white anemones. Unfortunately, they are rather fleeting but those of the double form, *S. c.* 'Plena' can be relied upon to last well.

Some of the daintier iris species make attractive peat-bed plants. The western American *Iris douglasiana* bears prettily-marked, graceful flowers on 25-cm (10-in) stems and is easily raised from seed sown in autumn and left to over-winter out of doors to germinate the following spring. Seed may even be sown where the irises are to flower with good results and a patch of seed should result in varied colour forms. Burgundy, violet, lavender, buff, white, yellow and apricot all regularly occur and make gay and delightful groups in the peat garden.

I. innominata is another plant for peat. The colour of this species varies from lavender to yellow and apricot, all with their falls marked as prettily as the petals of a pansy. It is just as easy to raise as *I. douglasiana* and all the seedlings are pretty—I have never seen a poor one yet.

Suitable for the top peat bed where they will be nearer the eye are the tiny *I. cristata* and *I. lacustris*. To grow them well the peat should be mixed with sharp sand and fine gravel as they demand good drainage and like the feel of grit around their roots. A mulch of chippings over the surface will encourage them to spread. Care must be taken, however, not to let them dry out. They like moisture as well as drainage, so the peat pocket in which they are planted should slope backwards to help retain some moisture. *I. cristata* is only 7·5 cm (3 in) high with orange-crested, lilac-blue flowers. *I. lacustris* is very like *I. cristata* but its flowers are slightly smaller.

The North American dog's-tooth violets are delightful with reflexed turkscap flowers above leaves that are often speckled like a trout—in fact trout lily is a popular American name for some of their native erythroniums. *Erythronium californicum* is a solid creamy-white with yellow-centred flowers and *E. revolutum* is a pink, delicate and graceful with a truly airy charm. The hybrid 'White Beauty' is well known and there is also a form known as 'Rose Beauty'. All these forms appreciate moist and shady conditions and so the peat garden is their natural home.

SEVENTEEN

Fruit and Vegetables
on Alkaline Soils and Clay

Fruit trees have hungry roots and need a reasonable depth of soil if they are to succeed. They cannot be expected to fruit where solid limestone or chalk lies directly below the soil. On the other hand, where the chalk or limestone is rubbly or where the rock can be broken up with a pickaxe many of the stone fruits will do well provided that holes equal to twice the spread of the head are prepared for them, filling in with loamy, humus-containing soil.

Cherries, plums, gages, damsons, peaches, apricots and nectarines need a certain amount of lime if they are to yield the best-flavoured fruits. Cherries, however, need rather better soil than plums and damsons and a little less lime. It is useless to attempt to grow cherries in a really dry, chalky garden. Such a site, however, has the efficient drainage that plums need and plums, damsons and gages are the fruits to choose.

Apples and pears do best in a rich, heavy, neutral loam although they will grow where lime or chalk is present provided steps are taken to meet any mineral deficiencies that may show themselves in chlorosis of the leaves. Magnesium is the element which apples and pears often lack in alkaline soils. The shortage may be made good by watering the root area with 27 l (6 gal) of water in which has been dissolved 3 tablespoons of Epsom salts. This dose should be repeated at fortnightly intervals throughout the growing season. Iron deficiency also may occur and may be remedied by watering-in sequestered iron.

Fruit and Vegetables on Alkaline Soils and Clay

Although most apples prefer a heavy soil some varieties succeed better on light chalky land than others. 'Beauty of Bath', 'Charles Ross', 'James Grieve', 'Blenheim Orange', 'Laxton's Superb', 'Ellison's Orange' and 'Worcester Pearmain' are the eating apples to choose, while to provide cooking apples, 'Bramley's Seedling', 'Newton Wonder', 'Annie Elizabeth' and 'Crawley Beauty' should succeed.

'Cox's Orange Pippin', 'Egremont Russet', 'Lord Lambourne', 'Laxton's Fortune', 'King of the Pippins', 'Monarch', and 'Grenadier' need a heavier soil as indeed do most varieties not already mentioned.

Pears, on the other hand, prefer a light soil but of a reasonable depth. They will succeed on both chalk and lime provided any deficiencies are remedied as described earlier in this chapter. In our own rather heavy alkaline clay we found that 'William's Bon Chrétien' and 'Conference' fruited well. We were careful, however, to give them a place sheltered from the wind in the drier part of the garden where the roots of a cupressus hedge prevented the land lying wet and cold in the winter. Many pears nowadays are grown on quince stocks which like moisture and need added humus on light land if the pears are to fruit well.

For medium and heavy alkaline soils, the superb 'Doyenne du Comice', 'Glou Morceau', 'Louis Bonne of Jersey', and 'Winter Nelis' also do well. For lighter soils 'Beurre Hardy', 'Josephine de Malines', 'Marguerite Marillat' and 'Pitmaston Duchess' are likely to fruit best. As stated earlier, however, it is useless to plant either apples or pears unless a reasonable depth of soil overlies the rock.

Generally speaking, raspberries and strawberries do best on acid soil although it is perfectly possible to produce good crops on chalk or loam provided their moisture requirements are met. Ground intended for the raspberry rows should be trenched and should have generous quantities of peat and moisture-holding humus incorporated into the soil. Lining the trench with old newspapers is a method I have in the past found to be especially effective in retaining necessary moisture on light soil.

Newspapers provide a fine source of humus that too often remains untapped. Potato peelings, religiously added to the compost heap, are mainly starch and water and like much other domestic waste contain relatively little humus to add to the soil. Bulk for bulk, newsprint, which is made from wood-pulp and consists of dry cellulose and hemicellulose is pure humus and is worth far more. Unforunately, nobody has yet found the means of composting newspapers. Like horsehair sofa-stuffing they remained unchanged in the compost heap for years. Used in two or three sheet thicknesses, however, either crumpled or spread flat, laid at the bottom of the garden trench and soaked with water from the hose before the soil is replaced they hold valuable moisture and eventually rot, forming a black, crumbly mould that permanently improves the structure of the soil.

Before planting our raspberries we lined each trench with five-page thicknesses of newspapers. Five years later, when in the course of extending our shrub belts we grubbed up the raspberries to replant with rhododendrons, no trace of the newspapers remained—but the soil which had been sticky, limy clay over limestone was a rich, dark, friable mould—a humus-full, woodland soil in fact.

Not only are newspapers valuable to retain moisture and supply humus for soft fruit, they are tremendously beneficial to the vegetable rows themselves. Staffordshire cottagers and allotment-holders have for years lined their pea and bean trenches with newspapers in the manner described, soaking well with water before replacing the soil. On chalky soil, particularly, where mid-season and late peas present great difficulties from lack of water, causing the pods to shrivel and the rows to wither prematurely, linings of wet newspaper in the planting trenches make all the difference. All vegetables and fruit—even apple trees—benefit from the moisture retained by a layer of wet newspapers beneath their roots and from the humus added as the newsprint rots.

Two-page thicknesses are sufficient for the pea and bean rows and are crumpled in the bottom of the trench before soaking with the hose. By the time the peas or beans are over and the ground is dug for the next crop, little will remain of the newsprint and the ground will indeed be ready for a further supply of newspaper-humus the following season.

Unlike straw and sawdust, which when dug in rob the soil of nitrogen, newspapers create no unbalance in the soil. Newsprint only, however, should be used—the pulp pages of the daily papers which are in abundant supply in every household in the land. The 'glossies' of the magazine world, and the Sunday colour supplements are not fit for roots to read!

Strawberries are more shallow-rooted than raspberries and do not need such deep cultivation. Top spit digging-in of quantities of slightly acid peat and hop-manure is the way to achieve success. Even so on light chalky soil the cultivation of soft fruits holds the ever-present danger of the soil drying out with conse-quent fruit-drop or a yield of miserably small fruit—all seed and no flesh. To avoid this it is necessary constantly to water, and to mulch after watering with all and any available material—peat, pig- or cow-manure, seaweed, compost, spent hops, straw and even green bracken which to avoid spreading and retain its nutriment has been cut in June before the spores are ripe. The well-known 'Royal Sovereign' variety has been found to succeed well on lime while 'Talisman' is worth planting as a slightly later crop. The 'Royal Sovereign' plants however should be set well away from the other variety in order to prevent them con-tracting any virus disease. The autumn-fruiting 'St. Claude' and 'Sans Rivale' should be dug up, divided and replanted each March, the opportunity being taken at the same time to dig in more humus of a slightly acid nature. With all strawberries on alkaline soil it is a good plan to use peat instead of straw to keep the berries clean. It should be of a slightly acid grade. Coarse rhododendron peat is ideal. A dressing spread over the bed 2·5 cm (1 in) deep will not only achieve its purpose in protecting the berries from mud splash but will also ward off slugs, keep down weeds and, even more important, will help root action by pro-viding a slightly acid medium for the shallow roots to seek.

Some chalk soils are so shallow, droughty and wind-swept that to attempt to grow vegetables is purely a waste of time. Where, however, a few centimetres (inches) of soil does exist it is worth while cultivating as deeply as possible and adding all possible humus.

Compost and farmyard-manure are invaluable. These days, this last may be practically unobtainable but a rich substitute lies in the poultry-manure readily available from the many broiler houses, batteries and chick-breeding stations that throng the land. Poultry droppings, however, while safe to incorporate neat in the compost heap, need special treatment before applying direct to the soil. In their plain state they are too fierce for use. To render poultry-manure safe, scatter superphosphate on the droppings at the rate of one part to eight and store in a dry shed for three months. Then add 112 g (4 oz) of wood ash or 28 g (1 oz) of sulphate of potash to the square metre (yard) to every 112 g (4 oz) of the manure spread on the ground as a fertilizer. For humus, deep litter may be bought in autumn from a battery house and dug-in during spring when the ground is being prepared for crops.

Pig-manure, too, is good if you can get it. On very poor, chalky land it is well worth while buying a load or two of clay to dig-in before the manure or compost is added. This will help to give the soil 'heart' or body—an essential to successful vegetable growing.

Luckily, one of the main vegetable groups, the brassicas, are lime-lovers and so do especially well on chalky or limy ground. Cabbage, cauliflower, broccoli, brussels sprouts, radishes, kale, swedes and turnips all belong to this important group and will not suffer from the dread club-root disease where the calcium content is high.

Peas and beans grow well on limy ground, but on chalk plenty of moisture-holding material must be incorporated if they are to pod well. Old newspaper used as described earlier is a useful aid. On all alkaline soils, however, peas and beans may suffer from shortage of phosphate. To counteract this, steamed bone flour should be added at the rate of 56 g (2 oz) to the square metre (yard) and sulphate of potash at the rate of 28 g (1 oz). Early peas are best on chalky land while maincrop and late varieties do better on heavier limestone and clay. Runner beans may drop their buds in hot, chalky gardens and here the Blue Coco bean which is both prolific and delicious, may be used as a substitute.

Onions need an extra-liberal supply of manure on chalky ground while on very heavy clay a dressing of salt should be added.

Potatoes are apt to suffer from scab when much lime is present. This can best be prevented by adding extra humus to act as a buffer, rendering the plants tolerant to a wider pH range. Humus helps strawberries in the same way as they, too, prefer slightly acid conditions.

For potatoes, newspapers, pig-manure and seaweed are satis-factory buffers. Pig-manure or seaweed should be laid above the wet newspapers in the bottom of the trench (20 cm (8 in) deep if the depth of soil allows) and covered with a thin layer of soil on which the potatoes are set. Add a dressing of sulphate of potash 34 g (1 oz) to the square metre (yard) or bonfire ash 136 g (4 oz) to the square metre (yard) when growth is through and earth up when they are 15 cm (6 in) high and again when the shoots are a further 15 cm (6 in) above the first earthing level.

Carrots as a rule do not do well on chalky soils and even where there is an adequate depth of soil do not produce prize-winning roots. It does not pay to sow long-rooted carrots on either chalk or lime but the early shorthorn types are a gamble that is worth trying. On alkaline soils of all kinds, carrots need extra potash. Sulphate of potash should be added at the rate of 34 g (1 oz) to the square metre (yard).

Beetroot will grow on both chalk and lime but like carrots it needs additional potash. As with carrots, too, the long-rooted beet will seldom do well under alkaline conditions. The globe and turnip-rooted varieties are the ones to sow. All beetroot, however, will sometimes produce wart-like growths on very alkaline soils.

With salad crops, humus is particularly important. Radishes belong to the broccoli family and so do well on chalk and lime. Celery, however, seldom succeeds on chalk or lime—not because it objects to the calcium content, but because it needs a rich, deep soil. Alkaline clays, however, if properly drained so that they do not lie cold and wet in the winter will often produce a good crop of the early-maturing variety. Provided sufficient depth of soil is available on chalky ground and it is well enriched with manure and compost, really good celery may be grown.

On light, chalky ground, lettuces are apt to bolt. The remedy is to dig plenty of humus into the top spit. Care must be taken to water regularly so that the plants do not suffer from lack of moisture at the roots. On dry, shallow soils avoid the cos lettuces. Choose rather the cabbage lettuce which is less demanding in its moisture requirements.

Humus is so all-important on alkaline soils—both to give body as well as to enrich shallow, hungry chalk and limestone land and to lighten and add humus content to the colder clays—that it is worth growing Russian comfrey to help supply it. Comfrey may be cut to dig-in as green manure or added to the compost heap as an activator.

Comfrey is a long-lived perennial and should be planted in a sunny place where it can stay undisturbed. The slender-stemmed Bocking No. 14 is the best variety to choose. Purchased offsets should be set 60 cm (2 ft) apart in autumn or spring. They should be left uncut until the July after planting so as to get established. Thereafter they can be cut down to 5 cm (2 in) at six-weekly intervals.

Comfrey is particularly rich in potash. It may be used to line the potato, or pea, or bean, trench or in place of sulphate of potash to balance the potash deficiency in poultry-manure. It can be spread along the raspberries as a mulch and is useful to supply necessary potash to carrots and beet. Used as a 5-cm (2-in) layer on the compost heap it will be as good an activator as any manure. It does, however, itself need manure (poultry-manure, pig-manure, or sewage sludge will do), spread on the surface in spring. On acid, sandy, and some neutral, soils comfrey needs added lime in autumn but on alkaline soils this is unnecessary. Fed well, two dozen plants will yield from April to November well over 152 kg (3 cwt) of mineral-rich foliage. I do not think any gardener on lime or chalk should be without it if he wishes to grow vegetables well.

However, even comfrey, sturdy doer that it is, will not yield its benefits from just any odd corner of the garden that is not wanted for more exciting things. It needs sun just as much as do the strawberry rows. Unlike raspberries it will not grow under trees. Nor can it be grown from seed. The Henry Doubleday Research Association supplies plants and their address is given in the address list that follows the end of this chapter.

Those who would like to know more about comfrey and, indeed, all keen fruit and vegetable growers, would do well to study *Comfrey* and *Down to Earth Fruit and Vegetable Growing* both by Lawrence Hills, Director-Secretary of the H.D.R.A., published by Faber.

Sawdust may be used as a surface mulch under shrubs or soft fruit bushes where it is unlikely to be turned into the soil. It should *never* be dug into the garden nor should unrotted bracken or leaf-mould. To do so would result in nitrogen-deficiency caused by bacterial activity as the material rots down. Wood-shavings litter from poultry houses, or pure wood-shavings from Forestry Commission plantations makes a good mulch for shrubs, or for blackcurrants or raspberries, provided that it is never dug in. Spread over light sandy or chalky soils during the winter it will prevent the rains leaching away plant foods and will partly decompose, its own nutriments washing into the ground. In the spring the unrotted ends should be cleared away and added to the bonfire while the black, rotted-down goodness is dug into the soil.

Pine and spruce needles, too, have their uses and may be mixed with ground limestone and spread as a 10-cm (4-in) layer above a bed of ashes, either raised or set in a trench, mixed with limestone grit, topped with 2 cm (an inch) of sifted beech-mould and used to form a slug-proof, seed-bed in which brassica and perennial seeds will germinate easily and grow as strongly as do the conifer seedlings in the similarly constructed Dunneman seed-beds used by the Forestry Commission.

In order to grow good vegetables, clay soils need only to have their crumb structure improved as described in Chapter One. Their great drawback, however, is impaction due to being walked-on in wet weather. To offset this in the vegetable garden, one can divide the ground into 1·5-cm (5-ft) strips, separated by 25-cm-(10-in-) wide paths, from which to work. At the same time the level of the intervening strips can be gradually raised with compost and manure, thus enabling the soil to warm up more quickly in the spring.

Some Useful Addresses

Bulbs
Walter Blom & Son, Coombelands Nurseries, Leavesden
Watford, Herts.
Broadleigh Gardens, Barr House, Bishops Hull, Taunton,
Somerset (small bulbs and treasures)

Clematis
Fisks Clematis Nursery, Westleton, Saxmundham, Suffolk

Comfrey plants
Henry Doubleday Research Association, Bocking, Braintree,
Essex

Herbaceous plants and bulbs
Wallace & Barr Ltd., The Nurseries, Mardon, Kent

Herbaceous plants and Underplantings
W. E. Th. Ingwersen Ltd., Birch Farm Nursery, Gravetye, East
Grinstead, Sussex (also rock plants and rock garden bulbs)
Perry's Hardy Plant Farm, Theobalds Park Road, Enfield,
Middlesex (also water plants and streamside plantings)

Manures
Organic Concentrates Ltd., Loudham's Wood Lane, Chalfont
St. Giles, Bucks.

Some Useful Addresses

Murphy Sequestrene
Obtainable from Boots Chemists and all good ironmongers and garden suppliers. Advice only can be obtained from the Murphy Chemical Company, Wheathampstead, St. Albans, Herts.

Peat
Alexander Products Ltd., Seaview Road, Burnham-on-Sea, Somerset

Rare and interesting plants, old primroses, and dwarf polyanthus
The Margery Fish Nursery, East Lambrook Manor, South Petherton, Somerset

Royal Horticultural Society
Vincent Square, London, SW1P 2PE
(Minimum subscription £7.50. Shows, monthly journal (*The Garden*), free seed distribution, advice, library, lectures and meetings)

Shrubs and trees
Hillier & Sons Ltd., Winchester, Hants
Oldfield Nurseries, Trowbridge Road, Norton St. Philip, nr. Bath (specialists in lime-tolerant subjects)

Shrubs for milder areas, and more uncommon shrubs
Treseders' Nurseries (Truro) Ltd., Moresk Road, Truro, Cornwall

Shrub roses and rose species
John Mattock Ltd., Nuneham Courtenay, Oxford
Murrells of Shrewsbury, Shrewsbury, Salop

Seeds
Alexander & Brown, The Scottish Seed House, South Methuen Street, Perth, Scotland
Samuel Dobie & Sons Ltd., Upper Dee Mills, Llangollen, Clwyd

General Index

abelia, 60
abies, 121
acer, 16
acid soil, 17–18, 19, 20
aconite, winter, 98–9, 100
Acta-Bacta, 27
agapanthus, 50, 93; Headbourne
    Hybrids, 94
Alginure, 31, 33
alkaline soils, 20, 44; distribution
    of, 18–19; fruits and vegetables
    on, 204–12; hedges for, 153–61;
    mineral deficiencies of, 37–43;
    testing for, 20; types of, 18
allium, 45, 100, 103–4
almond, 46, 111–12; dwarf, 128;
    Russian, 46
alpine, 27, 35, 45, 80, 90–1
aluminium, 40–1; sulphate of, 40,
    187–8
alyssum, 35, 50, 81, 90, 91;
    yellow, 35
amaryllis, 93
ammonia, sulphate of, 38, 42
anchusa, 48, 73
androsace, 87
anemone, 45; Japanese, 168
angelica, 77
anthemis, 62
Anti-Clay, 27
apple, 37, 204–5, 206
apricot, 204; Japanese, 111

aquilegia, 168
arabis, 90
arbutus, 49, 110
aster, 74
astilbe, 50, 64, 169
aubrieta, 35, 50, 81, 91
azalea, 19, 22, 42, 135, 186–8;
    Ghent, 186, 188; in containers,
    195, 196; Japanese, 186, 188;
    Knap Hill, 186, 188; on limy
    clay, 52; planting of, 190–1

balm, 77
balloon flower, 168
basil, 77
bean, 38, 206, 208–9, 210; Blue
    Coco, 209; French, 34; runner,
    209
beauty bush, 48, 60
beech, 153–4
beetroot, 209
berberis, 18, 125–6, 137, 164, 181;
    on chalk, 47, 49
bergamot, 77–8, 168
bergenia (megasea), 50, 53, 55, 57
birch, 19, 118–19; Chinese, 119;
    Swedish, 118
bladder sennas, 141
bleeding heart, 44, 168
blood root, Canadian, 202–3
borage, 76, 77
botrytis, 68–9, 106

215

Index of Botanical Names

Index of Botanical Names

225

Index of Botanical Names

Narcissus—cont.
Spur', 99; 'John Evelyn', 99;
'Mount Hood', 99; *obvallaris*,
99, 102; 'Pheasant's Eye', 99;
pseudo-narcissus, 102; *triandus
albus*, 82, 102, *t. a.* 'April Tears',
102, *t. a.* 'Raindrops', 102;
'Winter gold', 99
Nerine bowdenii, 93

Olearii: hastii, 155; *macrodonta*
'Major', 155
Onosma tauricum, 81
Osmanthus: decora, 156; *delavayi*,
46, 126, 156
× *Osmarea* 'Burkwoodii', 46, 126,
141
Osmaronia cerasiformis, 140
Osmunda regalis, 164
Osteospermum jucundum (*Dimorpho-
theca barberae* of gardens), 62–3

Pachysandra terminalis, 163
Paeonia: 'Bijou de Chusan', 68;
'Bowl of Beauty', 66; *cambes-
sedesii*, 67; 'Comtesse de Tudor',
68; 'Duchesse de Nemours', 66;
emodii, 67; 'Festiva Maxima',
66; 'Globe of Light', 66;
'Kelway's Glorious', 66; 'La
Reine Elizabeth', 68; *lobata*
'Sunbeam', 67; *lutea* hybrids—
'L'Esperance', 68, 'Souvenir de
Maxime Cornu', 68; *mascula*
(syn. *P. corallina*), 67; *mlokose-
witschii*, 66, 67; *officinalis*, 66;
'Red Flag', 66; 'Sarah Bern-
hardt', 66; 'Solange', 66; 'Yano
Okima', 68
Pentstemon: × *newberryi*, 81;
roezli, 81
Pernettya tasmanica, 200
Philadelphus: 'Albâtre', 59;
'Beauclerk', 181; 'Belle Etoile',
59; *brachybotrys*, 129; 'Burfor-
densis', 59, 181; 'Manteau
d'Hermine', 59; *microphyllus*, 59;
'Virginal', 59, 151

Phillyrea angustifolia, 156
Phlomis fruticosa, 181
Phlox: adsurgens, 88; *douglasii*, 88,
d. 'Boothman's Variety', 88,
d. 'Eva', 88, *d.* 'Rosea', 88;
stolonifera 'Blue Ridge', 88;
subulata, 81, 87, *s.* 'Betty', 87,
s. 'G. F. Wilson', 88, *s.* 'Temis-
kaming', 87
Phyllitis: crispa, 164; *scolopendrium*
(or *Scolopendrium vulgare*), 164
Physostegia virginiana 'Vivid', 168
Picea: family, 121; *glauca
albertiana* 'Conica', 49, 182
Pieris: floribunda, 41, 192; *forrestii*,
158; *japonica*, 41
Platycodon mariesii, 168
Polygonatum multiflorum, 167–8
Polygonum: amplexicaule 'Specio-
sum', 168; *vacciniifolium*, 200
Polypodium vulgare 'Cristata', 164
Potentilla: arbuscula rigida, 134;
'Day Dawn', 135; *fruticosa
purdomii*, 134; 'Gibson's
Scarlet', 63, 168; 'Katherine
Dykes', 134; *mandschurica*, 135;
'Maanelys' ('Moonlight'), 134;
recta 'Warrenii', 63; 'Red Ace',
135; 'Sunset', 135; 'Tangerine',
135; 'Vilmoriniana', 134
Primula: 'Beamish Foam', 173;
bhutanica, 201; 'Bon Accord
Gem', 172; 'Bon Accord
Lavender', 172; *bulleyana*, 193;
chungensis, 193; *clarkei*, 193;
'Crathes Crimson', 172;
denticulata, 193; *edgworthii*, 201;
'Fair Maid', 173; 'Faldonside',
82; *florindae*, 192; *frondosa*, 201;
gracilipes, 201; *heladoxa*, 192;
japonica, 192, 193; 'Kinlough
Beauty', 173; 'Lady Greer', 173;
lichiangensis, 193; *marginata*, 82,
m. 'Linda Pope', 82, *m.* 'Marven',
82, *m.* 'Pritchard's Variety', 82;
'Marie Crousse', 172; 'Mrs J. H.
Wilson', 82; 'Our Pat', 172;
prolifera, 192; *pulverulenta*, 193,

228

Index of Botanical Names